RETAILING IN EMERGING MARKETS

fb

RETAILING IN EMERGING MARKETS

EDITED BY
JAYA HALEPETE

FAIRCHILD BOOKS
NEW YORK

Executive Editor: Olga T. Kontzias

Assistant Acquisitions Editor: Amanda Breccia

Editorial Development Director: Jennifer Crane

Development Editor: Karen S. Fein

Creative Director: Carolyn Eckert

Assistant Art Director: Sarah Silberg

Production Director: Ginger Hillman

Production Editor: Jessica Rozler

Copyeditor: Susan Hobbs

Ancillaries Editor: Noah Schwartzberg

Photo Researcher: Alexandra Rossomando

Illustrator: Precision Graphics

Cover Design: Carolyn Eckert

Front Cover Art: Courtesy of WWD (top), Shutterstock Images (map), Getty Images (bottom left), and David Pearson/Alamy (bottom right)

Text Design: Ingrid Paulson

Page Composition: Mary Neal Meador

Library of Congress Catalog Card Number: 2010941993

ISBN: 978-1-60901-128-4

GST R 133004424

Printed in the United States of America

TP09

CONTENTS

EXTENDED CONTENTS

CHAPTER 4. CHINA 111

LIST OF TABLES

PREFACE

As domestic retailers outgrow their native markets, many begin to make plans for international expansion. In the past, they targeted mainly developed countries with cultures similar to their own. For example, many American retailers operate successfully in Canada and the United Kingdom. But the market has become saturated in the developed world, and the focus has shifted to developing countries in Eastern Europe, Asia, the Middle East, and South America. These markets offer great opportunities. But, they come with inherent complexities in terms of how to conduct business. It is important to understand each of these markets from a multidimensional perspective. Students who will be a part of this new trend after they join the workforce as well as retailers need to have a complete understanding of these emerging markets in order to succeed. This book covers aspects such as retailing formats and cultural influences that distinguish selected emerging markets. The main theme of this book is to understand retail as it exists in the emerging markets and various cultural and other factors that influence the retail setup.

Although many books cover some aspect of emerging markets, such as local retail formats or how to behave while doing business, there is no single book that is comprehensive in terms of providing a complete understanding of retail in emerging markets. While teaching courses on the global marketplace for retail industry, I felt a need for a text that would look at emerging markets and provide an understanding of how these markets are different from developed nations. That is what prompted me to write this book. It is designed for courses in international retailing and retailing in emerging markets, and can be used as a supplement for any other apparel-retail courses that require a global perspective. It is also designed for business-people who are interested in international expansion.

This text covers the most important aspects of conducting business in eight emerging markets that are consistently ranked in the top 20 in industry reports. The book is designed to help the reader understand the complexities of these markets and provide a detailed understanding of key attributes for conducting business. With emerging markets becoming crucial for international retail expansion, and with many retailers looking to set up offices in multiple countries, it is essential to be knowledgeable about emerging markets. The core chapters in this book are written by experts in retailing from the country being covered. Each contributor provides an understanding of the various concepts from a local perspective.

This is the only book that covers every topic regarding retailing in the top emerging markets specific to the apparel retail industry. Topics include the unique characteristics of consumers in a particular country, common retail formats, and regulations for foreign direct investment. Objectives at the beginning of every chapter should help students understand what they can expect to learn. Key terms are in bold and appear in the glossary for ready reference. Illustrations are provided to give the reader a better feel for foreign retail formats. A section in each chapter on retail careers should help students learn what it takes to work in these countries. Please note that all monetary references are in U.S. dollars. Case studies at the end of each chapter show how retailers have succeeded or failed due to certain characteristics of the concerned country.

ACKNOWLEDGMENTS

Writing this book has been a dream come true, and this would definitely not have been possible without the contribution and support from various people. Some of them helped me start it, whereas others were with me throughout the process.

First of all, I would like to thank all the contributing authors of my book. They were tremendously knowledgeable, supportive, and very enthusiastic about the book and contributing to it. Without their help, this book would not have been possible. I would like to thank Academy of International Business for being the source and helping me find all the contributing authors.

I am thankful to Jaclyn Bergeron at Fairchild Books, who helped me streamline the contents of the book and gave me very useful feedback for the first set of reviews. I would also like to thank Jennifer Crane and Alexandra Rossomando for their feedback and inputs. I also appreciate the reviewers of the proposal and manuscript and their feedback: Greg Arend, Nassau Community College; Dr. Joan Lynne Ellis, Washington State University; Sang-Eun Byun, Auburn University; Renee Cooper, Fashion Institute of Technology; Erin Parrish, East Carolina University; Dr. Jane Swinney, Oklahoma State University; Dr. Scarlett C. Wesley, University of Kentucky.

I don't know anyone else with more patience and attention to detail as Karen Fein. I am extremely thankful to her and give her a lot of credit for making this book look and read the way it does. I want to thank her for being so persistent about getting the best output.

There are some people who have made a major difference in my life and always inspire me to strive to be the best. I want to thank my brother, Sameer Halepete, and my major professor Dr. Mary Littrell for being my inspiration.

I want to thank my mom for giving me all the love, my dad for pushing me to do my best, and all my family for always being so supportive. Lastly, tremendous love, support, and encouragement from my husband, Sesh Iyer, made this book possible. My son, Sohum, who is wonderful in every way, helped by allowing me to work on this book through my maternity leave.

EMERGING MARKETS

1

Jaya Halepete
Mansi Patney

OBJECTIVES

After reading this chapter, you will

▶ Be able to define "emerging market"

▶ Understand the basic terminology of retailing formats

▶ Know the terms used for market-entry strategy

▶ Grasp the importance of understanding consumers in emerging markets

A developing market economy is an economy with a low-to-middle per capita income. Such countries constitute approximately 80 percent of the global population and represent about 20 percent of the world's economy. From developing economies, countries transition into emerging markets. Emerging markets are marked by forecasts of highest population growth and increasing income levels; these are usually countries that are restructuring their economies and offer great opportunities for trade, technology transfers, and foreign direct investment (Li, 2010). As apparel markets of developed countries have become saturated, their retailers have begun to focus on emerging markets for expansion. Even retailers that have not reached high levels of saturation at home are looking to expand into these emerging markets to gain

first-movers advantage, a sometimes insurmountable advantage gained by the first significant company to move into a new market.

It is important to note that the first-mover advantage refers to the first *significant* company to move into a market, not merely the first company. For example, Amazon.com may not have been the first online bookseller, but Amazon.com was the first significant company to make an entrance into the online book market.

Many research firms have been conducting analysis to understand emerging countries such as India, Russia, China, Indonesia, and Vietnam. These economies may have the best potential for apparel retailing; they have an expanding consumer base with higher disposable income.

A.T. Kearney is a Chicago-based global management consulting founded in 1926. A.T. Kearney focuses on the strategic and operational concerns of a CEO's agenda. The retail-apparel index (includes all the important drivers that make a market attractive to foreign investors) indicates the rank of a country as an emerging market attractive to foreign investors. A.T. Kearney calculates the apparel retail index by analyzing market size, prospects for growth, and consumer affluence, weighted 35 percent, 50 percent, and 15 percent respectively. Consumer affluence (the ability of consumers to spend on clothing) is calculated based on per capita clothing sales. The growth prospects number includes clothing sales, imports, clothing sales per capita, GDP per capita, and population growth. Based on the A.T. Kearney report and other research reports, this book covers Brazil, Romania, China, India, Russia, Turkey, Thailand, and Mexico (Table 1.1). Some markets remain as important emerging markets and attractive to investors for a longer time as compared to some others that mature and saturate very quickly. Based on a thorough research of important emerging markets in the current times and owing to space constraints, this book is restricted to these eight emerging markets.

Many large retail chains, such as Tesco (United Kingdom), Metro (Germany), Walmart (United States), and Carrefour (France), have already established themselves in developing countries in

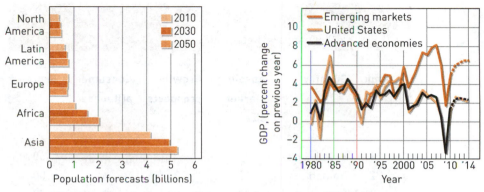

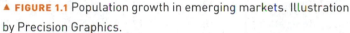

▲ **FIGURE 1.1** Population growth in emerging markets. Illustration by Precision Graphics.

various ways. Although these markets may not offer immediate profits due to problems such as poor infrastructure, widespread corruption, and a very diverse customer base driven by strong local culture, traditions, habits, and values, there is a potential of rewards in the long term.

The emerging markets' share of global gross domestic product (GDP) was about 45 percent in 2008 and is expected to grow to 51 percent in 2014 (Wooldridge, 2010). Since 2007, consumers in emerging markets have been spending more money than Americans. The potential growth rate of revenue, return on investment, and low cost of investment make emerging markets attractive to investors. But with increasing competition from many domestic as well as international players, the cost of investment in these emerging markets is increasing. Hence, it is becoming more and more important to make an entry and gain first-mover advantage.

Understanding the apparel retail market in emerging markets is a challenge that most international retailers face. In general, these developing countries have a large geographical spread, cultural diversity, and more than one language, which makes retailing extremely challenging for foreign companies. Other factors such as political situation, economic stability, real estate issues, market size, government regulations for entry, technical advancement, and consumer behavior all affect foreign retailers, who should grasp these

TABLE 1.1. 2009 Apparel Retail Index

Rank	Country	Absolute market size	Growth prospects	Consumer affluence	Score
1	Brazil	14	31	15	60
2	Romania	12	34	4	50
3	China	22	23	2	47
4	India	18	27	1	46
5	Argentina	12	27	8	47
6	Ukraine	11	34	0	45
7	Chile	9	21	14	44
8	Russia	15	22	7	44
9	Saudi Arabia	10	16	13	39
10	Turkey	8	27	2	37

Source: A.T. Kearney, 2009

challenges fully before making a decision to enter a foreign market. Due to the high level of risk involved in investing in an emerging market, retailers look for acquisitions (buying an existing company) rather than greenfield investments (a foreign company investing in a country by starting the construction from ground up).

This chapter covers some basic concepts that are essential for an understanding of these emerging markets.

EMERGING MARKETS FOR APPAREL RETAIL: WHAT MAKES THEM IMPORTANT?

Certain characteristics unique to emerging markets make them attractive to foreign investors. All these factors have to be thoroughly analyzed before investing in the market. Timing is very important in making the investment in these markets for various reasons:

- *Growing economy:* Emerging markets grow at a very fast pace. Taking advantage of increasing **gross domestic product** (GDP, which is the total value of all the goods and services produced in a country) and incomes in a country helps retailers become established and profitable quickly.
- *Reduced legislative burden*: To attract foreign investors, emerging markets are reducing regulations associated with starting a business. Many markets are changing their foreign direct investment policies to make entry easier for foreign investors.
- *Market saturation*: Some emerging markets were identified a decade or more ago, and many foreign investors have long since invested in them to have the first-mover advantage. Although some markets may be getting saturated, it is important to identify gaps in the market so that foreign companies can still consider investing to cover those gaps. So it is important to keep a lookout for the right markets to invest in at the right time.
- *Domestic competition*: Domestic retailers know their consumers much better than foreign retailers, making them the biggest threat. Domestic companies learn best practices from international retailers and combine them with knowledge of the local culture to become formidable competition for foreign retailers; however, the retailing environment in emerging markets is not as highly sophisticated in terms of technological excellence and high level of customer service as it is in developed nations like the United States.

CONSUMERS IN EMERGING MARKETS: A COMPLEX LOT

In 2008, the GDP for emerging markets such as India, China, and Russia was over 8 percent. In these parts of the world, less than 10 percent of the retail sector is organized (Moriarity, 2008) and consumption is growing. These factors make for compelling retail opportunities. The spending power of consumers is rapidly changing the retail industry in most of these emerging economies.

Multinational retailers seeking new sources of growth are watching the mass markets of Brazil, China, and India. Consumption is also on the rise in Mexico, Turkey, and Russia. As consumers in these nations have greater disposable income, they increasingly spend their money on items beyond the basic necessities (Meyers, 2007). Huge populations and strong economic growth have made them places of high interest in terms of market expansion.

Throughout the 1980s, most multinationals were reluctant to invest in low-income economies because they assumed that people with low incomes spent all their money on basic needs like food and shelter, with nothing left for goods and services. They also assumed that barriers to commerce such as corruption, illiteracy, inadequate infrastructure, currency fluctuations, and bureaucratic red tape made it impossible to do profitable business in these regions. For example, liberalization of trade policies in India began only around 1991. But today, many multinationals run successful businesses in developing economies due to improving conditions; these developing economies are no longer considered as low-income economies. Increasing income levels of the large middle-class population in these economies has fueled the retail market in the developing countries.

Due to the economic growth in sectors such as manufacturing and information technology, many families that fell under the low-income group now have jobs and are a part of the middle-class population. Thus, the middle-income segment has expanded and can represent up to 70 percent of the total population in some emerging markets (Heyde & Sundjaja, 2008). For example, in the large southern and eastern cities of China, consumer spending in the middle income segment has more than doubled since the mid-1990s and is growing rapidly (Moriarity, 2008).

Consumers in emerging markets are intensely interested in branded products. Products that have been customized for local customers attract intense interest. For example, brands such as L'Oreal have introduced fairness products (such as skin-lightening face creams) especially for the Indian market due to high demand for skin-lightening creams in the country. Brands must not be afraid to evolve. Consumers love brands that adapt and commit to emerging markets (Gilpin, 2009). Brands that seek a lasting commitment from consumers need to offer more than just the superficial excitement of their otherness. Brands that do not consider consumers' preference for their local culture will surely fail. Some brands also change their image (from high-end stores to low-end stores or the other way around) in emerging markets. For example, H&M is a mass-market retailer in the West. However, prices that are cheap in Europe and the United States are expensive for the average Chinese consumer; but with increased income levels, Chinese consumers today have higher disposable incomes. To acquire Chinese consumers, H&M has reinvented itself as a profitable player by offering clothes, shoes, and accessories unmatched in terms of style and (lower) pricing by local competitors (Gilpin, 2009).

It is important for foreign investors as well as domestic retailers to classify consumers into groups in order to understand them better and cater to their specific needs. In most emerging economies, consumers fall into four distinct groups:

- At the apex is the **global tier,** which consists of consumers who want products and goods to have the same attributes and quality as products in developed countries. For example, they shop for the same products at Louis Vuitton as consumers in developed countries do. They are well educated and well informed about global markets (Khanna & Palepu, 2005). Most companies that enter foreign markets try to cater to consumers in the global tier.
- The next set of consumers falls under the **glocal tier,** which consists of consumers who demand customized products of near-global standard and are willing to pay a shade less than global consumers do (Khanna & Palepu, 2005). In this group the competition between domestic and foreign companies intensifies. The domestic company understands the needs of the local consumers and can easily tailor the global product to suit. Foreign retailers need to spend time understanding the local consumers to meet their requirements. For example,

in Mexico, McDonalds has a McMolletes, which are refried beans, cheese, and pico de gallo served on an English muffin.

- The set of consumers who follow the glocal consumers falls under the **local tier**. These consumers are happy with products of local quality, at local prices (Khanna & Palepu, 2005). The local retailers of the emerging markets cater to consumers in this group because they understand the consumers and offer them local products at local prices.

- At the lowest tier lie consumers who can afford only the least expensive products. This tier is referred to as bottom of the pyramid (Khanna and Palepu, 2005).

A proper understanding of consumer types in the country where a retailer is interested in investing helps yield the right product and the right price, which in turn helps achieve success in the foreign market.

RETAIL FORMATS FOR ENTERING EMERGING MARKETS: DEPENDENT ON REGULATORY ENVIRONMENT

Availability of real estate in a country is one of the most important factors in attracting foreign investors (Expanding chains, 2008). Procuring real estate is important for retailers who want to build new stores rather than acquire existing ones. If a retailer cannot find a format that they are comfortable with due to unavailability or difficulty in obtaining prime location for a store, they are less likely to enter the market. There are many different formats to suit different retailers. Some formats are specific to a country (see individual chapters), but most modern formats are common in all the emerging markets. Some of the most common retail formats are:

Hypermarket: Hypermarkets are supermarkets and department stores combined together. Walmart is a great American example. These very large stores sell a wide range of products under grocery, household merchandise, apparel, and general merchandise, and usually have a selling area of at least 50,000 square feet (4,645 square meters) and ample parking. Able to buy in bulk, hypermarkets offer very good prices. They are often adjacent to towns and base their attraction on these prices and convenience to car-owning consumers, who can make many of their purchases in one place. Hypermarkets are widespread, especially in grocery retailing (Law, 2010).

Supermarket: A large, self-service store that carries a wide variety of food, household products, and other goods, which it sells in high volumes at relatively low prices (Law, 2010).

Cooperative store (consumer cooperative store): A store that is owned and controlled by members of the cooperative who use the products and not an individual owner. In this retail outlet format, members enjoy not only the benefits of good-quality products at fair prices but also a share of the profits (a dividend) based on the amount of each member's purchases (Law, 2010). Cooperatives vary in store type and number of members. These stores are beneficial for promoting products of small business owners or other less-powerful people (What is a cooperative, 2010).

Warehouse club (wholesale club; membership warehouse): A cut-price retailer that sells a limited selection of brand-name grocery items, appliances, clothing, and other goods at substantial discounts to members, who pay an annual membership fee (Law, 2010). These stores are normally established in warehouse-type buildings where merchandise is displayed without any frills. Sam's Club, a division of Walmart Stores, Inc., is an example of a warehouse club.

Main street stores: A store that is located on the primary street of a town. This street is where most of its shops, banks, and other businesses are located (Law, 2010).

Mom-and-pop store: A small retail business, such as a grocery store, owned and operated by members of a family and often located on a main street. In developing countries, mom-and-pop stores don't congregate on any specific street; they can be located anywhere, such as in regional markets, markets in residential areas, or markets in suburban areas (The Oxford American Dictionary of Current English, 1999).

- **Cash-and-carry stores:** A wholesaler that sells to retailers and other businesses at discounted prices on condition that they pay in cash, collect the goods themselves, and buy in bulk (Smullen & Jonathan, 2008). One needs to be a member of the store in order to make purchases. These stores sell products in bulk and the main customers are other business owners. For example, Metro (Germany) is an example of a cash-and-carry store where only business owners that are members can shop.

ENTRY MODES FOR EMERGING MARKETS: DEPENDENT ON REGULATORY ENVIRONMENT

A retailer chooses its entry format based on a country's regulations for venturing into new markets. The options include the following.

Franchising: A license given to a manufacturer, distributor, or trader that enables them to manufacture or sell a named product or service in a particular area for a stated period. The holder of the license (**franchisee**) usually pays the grantor of the license (**franchisor**) a royalty on sales, often with a lump sum as an advance against royalties (Law, 2009). The franchisor may supply the franchisee with a brand identity as well as financial and technical expertise. Common franchises are fast-food restaurants, gas stations, and travel agencies.

Joint venture: A joint venture is a contract between two companies to conduct business for an agreed upon duration of time. Companies get together in a joint venture to share each other's strengths, reduce risks, and be more competitive by using each other's skills in a marketplace. Joint venturers often carry on their principal businesses independently at the same time as the joint venture is functioning (Smullen & Jonathan, 2008).

Licensing: An agreement by which a company (the **licensor**) permits a foreign company (the **licensee**) to set up a business in a foreign market using the licensor's manufacturing processes, patents, trademarks, and trade secrets in exchange for payment of a fee or royalty (Black, 2003).

Direct investment: In this method of entry, the foreign company owns 100 percent of the company. Direct investments are made in different ways:

- *Wholly owned subsidiary*: A parent company holds a majority or all of the shares of a **subsidiary** and controls all of its functions. In a wholly owned subsidiary, the parent holding company owns virtually 100 percent of the common stock. There is no minority interest in the subsidiary. (Downes & Goodman, 2006; Smullen & Jonathan, 2008)
- *Acquisition*: An acquisition is the purchase of a company or asset. A foreign company may acquire a small or a large domestic company to enter the market depending on the size of the foreign company. The foreign investor does not have to worry about buying real estate and building from ground up (Moles & Nicholas, 2005).
- *Greenfield investment*: A form of foreign direct investment in which a parent company starts a new venture in a foreign country by constructing new operational facilities from the ground up. In addition to building facilities, most parent companies also create long-term jobs in the foreign country by hiring local employees (Clark, 1999).

REGULATIONS FOR FOREIGN DIRECT INVESTMENT: OPENING UP FOR TRADE

Foreign direct investment, in its classic definition, is defined as a company from a country making a physical investment into building a factory or setting up a business in another country. Smart investors consider a country's regulations for foreign direct investment (FDI) very carefully before investing in an emerging market. Most emerging markets are interested in attracting foreign investment and are working to make their FDI regulations simple and ensuring that their policies create a friendly business environment. The governments in emerging markets are also working to control corruption, eliminate unnecessary paperwork, and encourage transparency (where all laws and regulations are clearly defined and understood easily) (Foreign direct, 2010).

TOP GLOBAL RETAILERS: MARKET LEADERS

There are many successful retailers in the world. Some are successful in their home country and only present there. Some others are successful not only in their home country (for example, El Corte Engles in Spain) but also in all the countries where they are present (for example, Walmart, Metro). In this section, the top four global retailers, based on their domestic and international revenues, will be discussed.

WALMART

Walmart is the largest retailer in the United States. It operates over 4,150 retail facilities globally. Walmart provides general merchandise that includes family apparel, health and beauty aids, household needs, electronics, toys, pet supplies, fabrics, crafts, lawn and garden, jewelry, and shoes. It also runs a pharmacy department, tire and lube express, and photo processing center (Wal-Mart, 2010). Walmart is largely a discount retailer, and it sells products at the lowest possible prices. Its strategy is to expand by selling goods at low prices, thus outselling its competitors. The company's competitive strategy is to dominate every sector the company enters into. Walmart measures success in terms of sales and dominance over competitors. Internationally, the company's strategy has been to acquire companies and convert them into Walmart stores (Walmart,

2010). The company first expanded into Mexico, Brazil, Argentina, and Canada. They moved into Indonesia in 1996, but the stay in Jakarta lasted only about two years when it was burned in the 1998 riots and is now seeking re-entry into the market (Wal-Mart seeks, 2010). In 1996, Walmart moved to China. It subsequently tapped European markets such as Germany and the UK, as well as other Asian markets such as South Korea. Japan was the next stop, and by 2003, Walmart had established a network of 1,300 units in the overseas markets. The retail giant has succeeded everywhere but Germany and South Korea. The failures were mainly due to tough competition in the low-price segment and lack of understanding of the local culture in both the countries.

CARREFOUR

France's Carrefour is the largest retailer in Europe and second largest in the world. The company operates through four formats: hypermarket, supermarket, hard discount, and convenience stores. The group has over 15,500 stores that are operated by Carrefour or are franchise operations. Carrefour is present in 34 countries and is looking to further grow into China, Brazil, Indonesia, Poland, and Turkey. Depending on the country of operation, almost 90 to 95 percent of the merchandise sold in the store is sourced locally. Carrefour's main strategy is to gain customer trust in the company, the product quality, price, and service. Carrefour pioneered the hypermarket model, selling everything from household electronic items to fresh produce (Carrefour, 2010).

Carrefour has opened stores in many countries and eventually pulled out of many in a strategy to close down poorly performing stores to invest in more profitable countries. The countries where they pulled out from include Japan, Mexico, Russia, Switzerland, the United States, the UK, and China. Carrefour is also expected to pull out of some of the Southeast Asian market and is looking for a buyer. In 2010, the company opened several new stores in China and Romania, and its first cash-and-carry (where only business owners that are members can shop) store in India.

METRO

Metro group has over 2,100 stores in 34 countries in Europe, Africa, and Asia. Metro is Europe's third-largest retail chain after Carrefour and the UK's Tesco and the world's third-largest trade and retail group in terms of sales. This German retail giant's guiding principle is "as decentrally as possible, as centrally as necessary." The group started as a wholesale store in Dusseldorf in 1964, and transformed itself into Germany's largest retailer (Metro group, 2010). Though the company generated the majority of its sales from its home market, retail sales in Germany began to show a decline during the early twenty-first century due to a high unemployment rate, the country's wavering economy, a rise in inflation, and an increase in taxes. This led Metro group to operate in a high-cost environment with a low profit margin, which in turn had an adverse effect on the company's profits in Germany. To compensate for the declining sales in its domestic market, Metro pursued a strategy of expansion and internationalization through its cash-and-carry business model, and started focusing on emerging markets in Asia and Eastern Europe. Metro's focus on international markets has been an important factor in driving its growth in the light of the slowed growth in its home country. In its expansion, the company has a long-term focus on growing economies and consumers with high purchasing power (Metro group, 2010).

TESCO

Jack Cohen, who sold groceries in London's East End Markets, founded Tesco in 1924. By 2010, the company reached 95 percent of the UK population, providing items to an estimated 4,000 customers each day. It is the UK's largest retailer with more than 800 stores in eight countries, staffed by over 200,000 employees (Tesco.com, 2003).

There are two primary reasons for Tesco's success: first is the company's tremendous market penetration in the UK (95 percent) and European markets. The second is Tesco's commitment to supply its online visitors with a continuous stream of new, compelling offers and editorial information every time they visit the Tesco.com site (Tesco.com, 2003).

Tesco.com was launched in 1999 with a major relaunch in 2005. Tesco is the world's largest online grocery retailer and recognizes that product images and packet information are essential for online shoppers. Customers must be able to visualize products and have access to full label information to allow them to make more informed purchases (Tesco.com, 2003). Tesco has expanded in Central Europe and Asia. Tesco operates in 12 markets. By the beginning of the 1990s, Tesco had 371 stores in England, Scotland, and Wales—150 of which were superstores—and the company had become one of the United Kingdom's top three food retailers. On the international front, Tesco entered Thailand in 1998, South Korea in 1999, Taiwan in 2000, Malaysia in 2002, and China in 2004. The company's existing operations abroad were bolstered by several acquisitions, including the 2002 purchase of Poland-based hypermarkets HIT, the 2003 purchase of Kipa, a four-store hypermarket chain in Turkey, and the 2003 acquisition of the C, a chain of 78 food stores in Japan (Tesco Plc, n.d.).

FUTURE OF EMERGING MARKETS: CHALLENGING MARKETS

More than a dozen of the United States' top 20 retailers have focused their attention on emerging markets in their expansion plans. Retailers that invested early on in these markets are at a definite advantage over latecomers. Many factors, such as cultural differences, consumer behavior, local competition, and a business environment very different from home, make these markets challenging. But a proper understanding of the market and alterations that meet the market requirements can make a retail investment very profitable. Economists expect emerging markets to yield the world's biggest growth in the 2010s. These emerging markets are at various levels of maturity. Foreign retailers have just begun to enter some markets and have already established themselves in others. A foreign retailer needs to analyze each emerging market separately to determine the right moment to invest in it.

Case Study

TIMES ARE NOT AS TOUGH FOR SOME: CONSUMERS IN EMERGING MARKETS ARE LIKELY TO PERCEIVE THE RECESSION WILL BE SHORT

Despite the global recession kicked off in 2008, consumers in large developing markets viewed their medium-to-long-term prospects as strong. More consumers in India (51 percent), Vietnam (45 percent), China (34 percent), and Russia (31 percent) expected that the global recession would end in 2009 than consumers in other markets surveyed. One in two Indians believed the local economy would continue to show good growth, and that the global recession would have limited impact on their buoyant domestic market.

Some of this positive outlook is based on cultural differences. Indian investors have been safeguarded by the country's fairly new financial market, where savings accounts are the principal investment option for many consumers, mainly because few investment options exist overall. A.C. Nielsen is a global marketing research firm, with worldwide headquarters in New York City. According to Nielson's 2008 *Money Monitor,* Indians are more comfortable putting their money in fixed deposits and saving for a secure tomorrow than they are in spending for a comfortable today, a marked contrast with consumer attitudes in other, more developed markets.

In fact, Indian consumers were the most optimistic of all markets surveyed in 2008 with regards to their job prospects and personal finances over the next 12 months, with 75 percent optimistic that their job prospects were good or excellent and 77 percent expecting their personal finances to be in good or excellent shape in 2009. On the flip side, Korea and Japan were the most pessimistic, with a whopping 96 percent of Koreans reporting not so good or bad job prospects over the next 12 months, and 91 percent of Japanese expecting their personal finances to be not so good or bad.

Of the consumers who have cash to spare after paying basic expenses, cultural differences are stark in terms of how that money is spent. Three out of four (74 percent) people in Hong Kong and 70 percent of Singaporeans put extra money into savings, while 70 percent of Russians and 47 percent of Portuguese spend extra money on new clothes, a bright spot for the beleaguered apparel industry and a reminder of the optimistic attitudes in emerging markets versus the rest of the world.

The survey also found that there are a few places where consumers still plan on entertaining outside the home. Forty-five percent of Brazilians and Swiss spend extra cash that way, as do 44 percent of Russians. Russians are also the best hope for marketers of home improvement and new technology products, with 53 percent of consumers in that country planning to spend extra cash on their home and 52 percent planning to spend it on new technology products. For the travel industry, 53 percent of Chinese are planning to direct extra cash into holidays and vacations.

Just as many consumers react to the turbulent financial times by nesting at home, the tendency can also be strong for marketers to cut down on ad spending until the economic outlook brightens. Less adjustment may be necessary for global marketers with consumers in emerging markets, where attitudes remain positive, but for marketers targeting worried Western consumers, gaps and opportunities still exist. For example, whereas the "stay-in" trend is undoubtedly tough on bars and restaurants, it also creates openings for innovative premium and prepared foods and beverages designed for at-home entertaining.

Companies that continue to invest in their brands and products and stay engaged with their target market will come out of this downturn as winners. Consumers will remember which products best understood their needs during the slowdown, so brand investment has never been more important for securing long-term loyalty.

Source: Russo, J. (2008, December 5). Times Are Not as Tough for Some: Consumers in emerging markets are likely to perceive the recession will be short. Retrieved on December 15, 2010 from nielsenwire, http://blog.nielsen.com/ nielsenwire/consumer/times-are-not-as-tough-for-some-consumers-in-emerging-markets-are-likely-to-perceive-the-recession-will-be-short

Discussion Questions

1. Why is understanding cultural differences in emerging markets important for foreign investors?
2. What cultural aspect of consumers in emerging markets accounts for the less adjustment required by global retailers during down times in the economy?
3. What are the basic cultural differences between consumers of developed versus emerging markets?

REFERENCES

Anonymous (2003). Retrieved from http://www.rjmintz.com/general-partnerships.html

Anonymous (2009). Marketing Terms Glossary. Retrieved August 31, 2010, from http://www.marketingterms.com/dictionary/first_mover_advantage/

Black, J. (2003). *A Dictionary of Economics*. Oxford Reference Online. Oxford: Oxford University Press.

Carrefour (2010). Retrieved November 9, 2010, from http://www.carrefour.com/cdc/group/our-group/

Clark, J. (1999). *International Dictionary of Banking and Finance*. Glenlake Publishing Company: Chicago.

Downes, J. & Goodman, J. E. (2006). *Dictionary of Finance and Investment Terms*. Barron's, Hauppauge, NY: Expanding chains target emerging markets (2008). *SCT Week, 13* (37), p. 4.

Foreign direct investment policies (2010). Retrieved March 4, 2010, from http://www.economywatch.com/policywatch/fdi-policy.htm

"High street noun" *The Oxford Dictionary of English* (revised edition). Ed. Catherine Soanes and Angus Stevenson. Oxford University Press, 2005. Oxford Reference Online. Oxford University Press.

Heyde, R. A. & Sundjaja, K. (2008). Busting the myths about emerging markets. Retrieved March 5, 2010, from http://www.oliverwyman.com/ow/pdf_files/OWJ25-4-Busting_Emerging_Market_Myths.pdf

Khanna, T. & Palepu, K. G. (2005). Emerging giants: building world class companies in developing economies. Retrieved March 4, 2010, from www.hbr.org

Law, J. (2009). *A Dictionary of Business and Management*. Oxford reference online premium. Oxford: Oxford University Press.

Li, C. (2010). What are emerging markets? Retrieved November 9, 2010, from www.uiowa.edu/ifdebook/faq/faq_docs/emerging_markets.shtml

Gilpan, G. (2009, June 17). Insight is Everything. *Harvard Business Review*.

Smullen, J. & Jonathan, L. (2008). *A Dictionary of Finance and Banking*. Oxford Reference Online. Oxford: Oxford University Press.

Mangalorkar, R., Kuppuswamy, R. & Groeber, M. (2007). The BRIC promise.

Mexico "breaks the BRIC" to appear in the top four emerging
    economies (2008). Retrieved November 8, 2010, from
    http://www.gti.org/
    Press-room/Mexico-breaks-the-BRIC.asp

Metro Group (2010). Retrieved November 9, 2010, from
    http://www.metrogroup.de/servlet/PB/menu/1000083_l2/
    index.html

Moles, P. & Nicholas T. (2005). *The Handbook of International Financial Terms.
    Oxford reference online premium,* Oxford University Press: New York

Moriarity, M. (2008). Emerging opportunities for global retailers. Retrieved
    February 24, 2010, from www.atkearney.de/.../pdf_atkearney_bip_
    grdi_2008_1212762749d09c.pdf

Russo, J. (2008, December 5). Times Are Not As Tough for Some:
    Consumers in emerging markets are likely to perceive the recession
    will be short. Retrieved March 18, 2010, from
    http://blog.nielsen.com/nielsenwire/consumer/times-are-
    not-as-tough-for-some-consumers-in-emerging-markets-are-
    likely-to-perceive-the-recession-will-be-short/

Tesco Plc (n.d.). Retrieved November 9, 2010, from
    http://www.fundinguniverse.com/company-histories/
    Tesco-plc-Company-History.html

Tesco.com (2003). Tesco.com ensures online offer are as fresh as produce
    with Interwoven. Retrieved November 9, 2010, from
    http://www.interwoven.com.cn/documents/casestudies/
    tesco_august.pdf

Thailand's investment market retains its attractiveness (2008, May 9).
    Retrieved November 8, 2010, from http://www.nationmultimedia.
    com/2008/05/09/business/business_30072622.php

Walmart (2010). Retrieved November 9, 2010, from
    http://walmartstores.com/AboutUs/

Wal-Mart seeks re-entry into Indonesia (2010, November 4). Retrieved
    November 18, 2010, from http://www.thejakartaglobe.com/business/
    wal-mart-seeks-re-entry-into-indonesian-market/404947

What is a cooperative (2010). Retrieved November 16, 2010, from
    http://sfp.ucdavis.edu/cooperatives/whatis.html

Wooldridge, A. (2010, April 17). The world turned upside down. *The Economist*.
    Retrieved May 19, 2010, from http://www.economist.com/
    specialreports/displayStory.cfm?story_id=15879369

BRAZIL

2

Jaya Halepete
Luciana de Araujo Gil
Silvio Abrahao Laban Neto
Youssef Youssef
Flavia Silveira Cardoso
Wlamir Xavier

OBJECTIVES

After reading this chapter, you will

- ► Understand why Brazil is considered to be an emerging market
- ► Learn about unique characteristics of Brazilian consumers
- ► Gain knowledge about various traditional and non-traditional shopping formats in the country
- ► Understand the government regulations for foreign direct investment in Brazil

Many people agreed with Jeffrey Simpson, Canadian journalist and national affairs columnist for *The Globe and Mail,* when he wrote, "For a country with a tumultuous economic history, the first decade of the twenty-first century has been remarkably good: low inflation by Brazilian standards (4 percent to 5 percent), steady growth (4 percent to 5 percent), shrinking national debt, an

TABLE 2.1 Fast Facts about Brazil

Capital	Brasilia
Population	203.4 million
Type of government	Federal Republic
GDP: purchasing power parity: in US$	$2.013 trillion
Age structure	0–14 yrs: 26.7%
	15–64 yrs: 66.8%
	65 yrs plus: 6.4%
Religion	Roman Catholic: 73.6%
	Protestant: 15.4%
	Others: 11%
	Unspecified: 0.1%
Ethnicity	White: 53.6%
	Mixed Black and White: 38.5%
	Other: 1.6%

Source: CIAfactbook.gov

economy lifted by high commodities prices, and success in selected industrial sectors. Who would have thought a decade ago that Brazil would actually be lending money to the International Monetary Fund? Best of all, studies show a slow but steady diminution in income inequality. Poverty rates have fallen from 35 percent to 25 percent in a decade." Is Brazil the country of the future?

Slightly smaller in area than the United States, Brazil has the fifth-largest population in the world and the largest in Latin America. According to the World Bank, Brazil is the world's ninth-largest economy. By 2020, the majority of its population will be between the ages of 15 and 44, making Brazil one of the most important job and consumer markets in the American continent (Table 2.1).

Brazil has a wide range of natural resources. About 40 percent of the world's biodiversity is located in Brazil. Its continental dimension holds five important biomes: the Amazon (rain forest), the cerrado (savanna), the Atlantic Forest, the caatinga (dryland), and the Pantanal (swamplands). The Brazilian Amazon is the most important biological reserve in the world and holds 10 percent of the world's total freshwater reserves. Mineral deposits are also abundant in the country.

The Portuguese, who claimed Brazil in 1500 and ruled for more than three centuries, first brought the region into the global economy. Throughout the eighteenth and early nineteenth centuries, the Portuguese crown grew wealthy on the gold and diamonds they forced Native Americans and African slaves to mine. The colony became a constitutional monarchy in its own right in 1822. In 1889, a military coup established a constitutional democracy, which was destabilized by additional coups in 1930 and 1964. In 1985, the military returned power to civilian rulers, and a democratic regime was implemented. However, the international oil crisis in the 1970s plus a noncompetitive state-driven and somewhat closed economy have created a high inflationary business environment. In 1985, the indirectly elected president Tancredo Neves never took office. He was rushed to the hospital on his inauguration day where he died 39 days later. His vice president, José Sarney, took office definitively and tried through many different economic plans to control one of the world's highest inflation rates. Fernando Collor, the first directly elected president, took office in 1990. In an attempt to improve Brazil's competitiveness, he tried to implement drastic economic measures to control inflation, reduce government weight in the economy, and eliminate many legal restrictions to import goods such as cars and computers. Collor was impeached in 1992, accused of political corruption; his vice president, Itamar Franco, then took office. Under Itamar Franco, a set of economic measures, known as Plano Real, was implemented, and finally inflation started to be controlled and a stable foundation for economic growth was set. Since 2003 Brazil's economy has grown steadily at 5 percent per year (Brazil takes off, 2009). But the colonial legacy lives on in tremendous inequality among the citizens of the country.

▲ **FIGURE 2.1** Mercado Público located in Florianópolis Santa Catarina. Stores selling nonbranded apparel, mainly from China or locally produced. These stores still dominate the market targeting new and growing lower classes of consumers. Photo by Eduardo Trauer.

Highly unequal, although improving, income distribution is a critical challenge. Since 2003, the government's social policies have helped increase the minimum wage and boost retail sales. Brazil has a predominantly urban population (81 percent living in urban areas) and a very young population with an increasing disposable income. These changes have made Brazil a very attractive market for foreign investors. The private sector and the government have both been encouraging foreign investment by expanding and restructuring various sectors. Brazil is considered to be a very promising economy and was one of the first in the area to begin an economic recovery following the 2008/2009 crisis. The familiar quote says it all: "Brazil is the country of the future—and always will be." It seems, however, that with so many positive economic changes and an ideal customer base for retailers, the future has finally arrived and Brazil is an emerging market that has caught the attention of foreign retailers.

RETAIL INDUSTRY IN BRAZIL:
GIANTS AND DWARFS

Even with a large number of consolidations among retail businesses, small, independent outlets still dominate Brazil's retail landscape. Modern retail formats such as hypermarkets, supermarkets, and shopping centers are expanding very fast due to mergers, acquisitions, and foreign investment. Food retailing is by far the most developed retail segment in Brazil, where the French-Brazilian Grupo Pão de Açúcar, French-based Carrefour, and the U.S.-based Walmart dominate some Brazilian markets. However, in some capitals, and mainly in the interior of the country, small and medium players are dominant.

In an August 2010 article, Sara Andrade, fashion editor of *Vogue Portugal*, wrote, "Unlike [in] Europe or the U.S., where there are many high-street options like Zara and Mango, in Brazil most brands fall into two extremes: They have very low-profile brands like C&A, where you can get things of rather low quality at a really cheap price and, on the other end, designer brands like Maria Bonita and smaller independent labels that offer good quality and design at a high price point."

In 2008, Brazil's apparel retail industry generated revenues of $30.6 billion, representing a growth rate of 5.1 percent from 2004. Women's apparel was the most lucrative sector for the Brazilian apparel retail industry in 2008, with revenues of $14.6 billion, or nearly half of the total retail sales compared to 34 percent for menswear. In 2009, forecasters expected the Brazilian apparel retail industry to grow by 4.7 percent between 2008 and 2013 (Apparel Retail, 2009). Although multinational retailers, such as Timberland and Zara, serve the country's richer consumers, few global retailers, except for C&A, compete in its mass market, which is served mainly by small and medium independent stores, and large local single-format retailers accounting for more than 60 percent of the country's apparel sales (Artigas & Calicchio, 2007). Brazil is the most attractive apparel market for reasons of demographics and demand:

there is great potential for global apparel retailers," says Hana Ben-Shabat, a partner with global management consulting company A.T. Kearney.

With a per capita apparel consumption of $402 per year, six times what a Chinese consumer spends, Brazilian consumers may be considered extremely fond of shopping for clothes. The importance of individual identity among Brazilian consumers makes clothing retail an essential for them. Consumers are highly fashion conscious and celebrities tend to influence fashion trends in this country where more than 60 percent of the population is under the age of 39. Given income restrictions, Brazilian consumers look for good-quality products at the lowest possible prices, with credit playing a major role in the apparel market.

The apparel industry in Brazil is very competitive and has a significant number of local brands. The highly fragmented retail industry in Brazil provides an interesting opportunity for consolidation by retailers willing to understand and explore the idiosyncrasies of such a large and complex market ("Opportunities in Brazil," 2007). A study conducted by A.T. Kearney ("Emerging markets," 2009) ranked Brazil as the most attractive market for apparel retailing. This ranking considers among other factors the size of the market as well as the country demographics and economic perspectives.

Financial experts consider Brazil to be an extremely attractive market for retail expansion, and the most dynamic emerging market for the luxury retail sector. A better understanding of the Brazilian market requires an understanding of Brazilian consumers and the various formats in which the retail industry operates in Brazil.

CONSUMERS: DIVERSITY AND COMPLEXITY

Brazil has a vast territory, a diverse culture, and nearly 200 million inhabitants. Although the common Portuguese language and an excellent communications system (both TV and radio) have contributed to create some homogeneous tastes and behavior, local consumer habits are still very relevant. A closed economy and a low per capita income used to limit consumers' access to imported goods and brands, but the 1990s witnessed economic stabilization and inflation reduction. In the 2000s, the gross domestic product (GDP) started to grow at a low but steady rate, prices were reduced on imported goods (through import-taxes reduction), and consumers' credit became cheaper. As a result, the Brazilian middle class boomed.

Saving is not a common practice in Brazil. On the contrary, a substantial part of people's income is used to reduce debt. Financial institutions profit from anxious customers who pay interest of as much as 30 percent per year to own a new appliance or fashion apparel. Big retail stores use credit as a marketing tool to boost sales, and small ones need to offer credit services through credit card companies in order to compete.

Due to the presence of many informal businesses that do not pay taxes in total or partially, it is not easy to assess the Brazilian apparel industry, but Brazilian Textile and Apparel Industry Association (ABIT) reports that for 2009, 9.8 billion items were produced, $47.4 billion revenue, and 1.65 million jobs, of which 75 percent are female accounting for 3.5 percent of Brazil's total GDP. Unlike Asian countries, Brazil is not recognized as a cheap clothing exporter, and differentiated products such as Havaianas (the rubber flip-flop) and beachwear are sold in all continents at premium prices.

Brazilians are living longer, and a middle class is growing. The United Nation's *Centro Latinoamericano y Caribeño de Demografía* (CELADE) classifies Brazil as a country where the elderly population is increasing (ONU, 2008). In the 2000s, a 100 percent increase in the minimum wage and the acceleration of income-oriented social programs have reduced income inequality and given millions of consumers access to basic products for the first time. Those emerging consumers are not looking for exclusivity; they are looking for inclusion and belonging. As a result, several industries, including apparel, have had to increase production and reshape their product lines.

These new middle-class consumers have different preferences and priorities: sustainability issues, for instance, alter upper-class consumer behavior in many industries, but "the (emerging) C class [middle class] is not concerned about the environment, if they buy a low-energy-consumption home appliance, they are concerned about their wallet, not the world," as states Fabio Mariano, professor and partner of Insearch, a consulting firm which focuses on consumer behavior (Folha de Sao Paulo, 2010a).

Apparel stores in Brazil may benefit from the population's preference for similar fashions. Apart from designs and materials influenced by weather and cultural differences, a store in the northeastern region may carry a stock very similar to a store in the south, 2,000 miles away. Heloisa Omine, professor and former president of the Brazilian chapter of The Global Association for Marketing at Retail (POPAI), alerts her colleagues that "stores need to adapt to drag the attention of consumers from the emerging middle class, product displays must be accessible and enable self-service" (Portal Exame, 2010). Traditional regional apparel is usually restricted to special occasions.

Brazilian consumers' favorite place to buy apparel is the shopping center. In Brazil, 18.3 percent of all retail revenue is through malls. This industry's revenue in 2009 was $41 billion, distributed among 396 malls, over 70,000 stores, with 760,000 employees (www.portaldoshopping.com/br/). For Brazilians, the shopping experience is a social event. Shopping does not mean necessarily buying, for the visit to the mall encompasses meeting people (and even flirting), going to the cinema, and sharing meals. In big and violent cities, malls are safe islands where middle-class parents can leave their children for some leisure time. Usually people go to the malls in small groups: family, couples, or friends. But teenagers sometimes gather in parties of a dozen people or more, with no purchasing interests. In many cities small downtown shopping centers with a limited number of stores continue to thrive.

Through fashion, Brazilian people achieve group identity, social conformity, and distinction. Fashion is a means to show creativity and express sexuality (Mello et al., 2003). A 2007 survey

▲ **FIGURE 2.2** Mercado Municipal in São Paulo. Because the space is inexpensive and limited, the stores sell low-cost/high-margin products. Only food is sold in this market. © Didi/Alamy.

(Garcia & Miranda, 2007) identified the following motivations among Brazilian shoppers.

- Communication. Even fashion denial is a way to reject society's standards.
- Integration. Fashion style denotes the group someone belongs to.
- Individuality. Clothing distinguishes members of a specific group.
- Self-esteem. Clothing reinforces the buyer's self-regard.
- Transformation. People dress to be different.

Brazilian consumers differ significantly from consumers in most developed and many emerging markets. Some important differences for foreign retailers interested in entering the Brazilian retail market to keep in mind are (Artigas & Calicchio, 2007):

- About 80 percent of Brazilian consumers are very fond of shopping for clothes and they look forward to it. The clothes purchased are worn mainly for going out with family and friends.
- They are very fashion conscious, and local celebrities dictate the fashion trends. Local retailers in Brazil offer local fashion trends in clothing to their consumers.
- Brazilian consumers like to have a full range of merchandise to choose from, even if they don't intend to buy the high-end products. They want to treat themselves occasionally.
- Consumers trust local brands. The current multinationals have established a local identity by using local models in their advertising campaigns.
- Brazilians are more comfortable using credit than consumers in other emerging markets.
- They are very brand loyal to the brands associated with designers.
- They have special fondness for cotton apparel such as denim and T-shirts.
- Foreign brands are associated with wealth.
- Brazilian consumers are addicted to promotions. They look for promotions with attractive credit offerings, such as installment payments. These promotions are year-round, not seasonal as in other countries.
- Brazilian consumers demand good customer service in the stores. They prefer being known by salespeople, and like being extended credit without any formalities.
- They are known for comparison shopping. Brazilian consumers know the prices of twice as many products as consumers in other emerging markets. They visit several stores to compare prices before making a decision to buy.

WOMEN

Through fashion, human beings demonstrate their basic desires and instincts, and most fashion activity is related to social integration (Garcia & Miranda, 2007). Brazilian women in particular express their personalities not only with clothes but also accessories and jewelry. Fashion also may indicate social status, professional activity, and style (Leao, et al., 2007). In Brazil, women generally have an important role in apparel buying by shopping alone, without other family members. Teenagers and young adults usually rely on friends and fashion trends for their shopping decisions (Rubens, 2003).

Since the mid-1980s, Brazilian women's participation in historically male-dominated professions such as law, medicine, and engineering has increased. Their new incomes combined with their fashion consciousness have created a huge market for women's clothing. This market grew considerably in the first decade of the twenty-first century.

Soap opera stars and other TV celebrities are a powerful influence on the fashion choices Brazilian women make. Many Brazilian women stay abreast of fashion trends by reading magazines such as *Vogue, Caras, Manequim,* or *Nova* (the Brazilian version of *Cosmopolitan*) and when they go shopping, they are not shy. Sônia Hess de Souza, the CEO of Dudalina, an apparel manufacturer with 1,800 points of sale in Brazil, observed that "(Brazilian) women do not buy a single shirt, they buy two or three at a time" (Folha de Sao Paulo, 2010b).

MEN

Many Brazilian men don't own a suit, blazer, or jacket because they will never have the need to wear one. Casual business wear is the most common clothing worn by Brazilian men in both formal and social settings. Brazilian men dress casually in their tropical climate. In many places, a shirt and slacks are acceptable business attire.

There are signs that Brazilian men are increasingly concerned about personal aesthetics. For example, Brazil is the fifth-highest consumer of men's cosmetics in the world and the highest in Latin America. According to industry reports, men's cosmetics consumption is expected to grow by 9 percent in the Latin American region. Advertising and social expectations are changing the way men's cosmetic purchases are made. Instead of their wives, men are making these purchases for themselves. Most of these purchases are made in supermarkets.

CHILDREN

Children's apparel accounts for 24 percent of the industry's market share (IEMI, 2005) in Brazil. The mother, who used to make all decisions regarding her children's apparel, is starting to share the process with their other parent and the children themselves. Clothing is an opportunity for children and their parents to express themselves and leads to social integration (Frederico & Robic, 2006). Buying behavior has four primary drivers when it comes to children's apparel:

- ► Product quality
- ► Point of sale (store)
- ► Appearance
- ► Fashion

Appearance and fashion affect both children and parents, but quality and shopping convenience concern mainly parents. Brazilian retail and apparel brands devote significant advertising efforts to attracting children's attention, although there are several legal restrictions on advertising for children.

The children's clothing market has been growing at a steady pace in Brazil, generating revenue of $5.6 billion in 2008. By 2013, the value of this market is expected to reach $6.9 billion. Small stores with sole proprietors dominate the childrenswear market. The market does have a few large retail chains that account for a significant portion of the business. But a lack of brand loyalty in this sector leaves space for more retail chains in Brazil (Childrenswear in Brazil, 2009). An investor could very easily enter this sector through small-scale investment. Healthy growth in this sector is attracting foreign retailers. However, entrants should study the market carefully to avoid issues experienced by companies such as the French Petit Bateau and DPAM, and JC Penney (a tentative joint venture with Brazilian department store chain Lojas Renner). Unable to adjust their processes and products to local business practices, tastes, taxes, and income levels, these companies exited the market.

THE ELDERLY

The number of people over 60 is significantly high in Brazil (Ibge, 2008). Increased life expectancy is such a recent change that the fashion industry has not yet responded with products or services, but changes are already visible in other industries, such as tourism and hospitality. The elderly have slightly different motivations from younger generations for buying apparel in Brazil (Slongo et al., 2009):

- ▶ Comfort
- ▶ Self-esteem and vanity
- ▶ Emotional security
- ▶ Fitness to age and physical conditions
- ▶ Self-expression

For the elderly, clothing is symbolic and socially important. Health concerns may also drive apparel choices, not only because of attendant constraints on finances and mobility constraints but also because health issues change people's motivation. Key elements that influence elderly people in their apparel buying behavior are also different from young adults:

- ▶ Social group, friends, and family
- ▶ Fit to a special occasion or event
- ▶ Willingness to please someone
- ▶ Worries about their appearance and presentation

BEAUTY INDUSTRY IN BRAZIL

Brazil's youth culture is obsessed with beauty and celebrity. The country has two salons for every bakery, making beauty seem more important than bread (Research, 2005). Brazil is the third major consumer of cosmetics in the world and is the second-largest world market for plastic surgery (ABIHPEC, 2010). The Brazilian beauty fair Hair Brasil has more than 700 exhibitors and nearly 70,000 visitors. Natura, a domestic cosmetic company, is one of the most successful brands in Brazil. They sell through direct sales (like Avon in the United States), with more than 4,500 representatives in Brazil.

▶ Beauty Industry and Women

The average Brazilian woman devotes much of her time and money to her looks. This behavior is not limited to wealthy people; even in slums beauty salons are easily found. An average middle-class Brazilian woman has a manicure at least once a week, usually along with another body or hair treatment. The majority (65 percent) of Brazilian women have either wavy or curly hair, and fashion dictates straight hair. Hence, there is a huge market for hair treatment. A single hair treatment in a luxury salon, for a bride for instance, may cost thousands of dollars. A company called Higiia (www.higiia.com.br) offers plastic surgery financing programs for lower-income women, including a three-year payment plan.

Beauty products for black women, both services and cosmetics, represent another fast-growing market in Brazil. Several cosmetic lines have been released to fulfill the demand created by racial pride and consciousness. Although foundation and face powder are the leading black skin products, a wide range of makeup and accessories is available from several leading manufacturers, such as O Boticario, a Brazilian franchise, which offers beauty products through over 2,700 stores and is already present in 15 countries.

▶ Beauty Industry and Men

Previous generations linked pride in appearance to homosexual behavior. That attitude is gone. Men's health and beauty represents a promising new market. Men who until recently limited their grooming activities to a haircut and shave at the barber now have at their disposal professional treatments and dedicated salons, such as Garagem (http://www.garagemestetica.com.br/), a franchise with customers who spend 15 percent of their net income on beauty products. It is no longer hard to find men in beauty salons, taking care of nails or hair, or even in depilation sessions.

Young men in Brazil are leading important changes, and new beauty products for men come into play. As men usually do not set

▲ **FIGURE 2.3** A woman holds an advertisement for beauty treatments as she waits in line to receive treatment with Botox, hyaluronic acid, and other drugs. Such treatments are becoming very popular, with services being offered for low-income people through credit and at reasonable prices. AFP/Getty Images/Antonio Scorza.

aside as much time as women for their home beauty care, cosmetics for men are developed to consider not only gender and biological differences but also ease of application for convenience.

All of these previously mentioned factors make the beauty industry in Brazil a lucrative market for international investors.

LUXURY RETAIL IN BRAZIL

Brazil's GDP is expanding at the rate of 6 to 7 percent per year. It also has an increasingly affluent customer base. With a stable government and a strong currency, Brazil is working to improve its infrastructure and reduce income-distribution inequality to bring the country up to international standards.

The emergence of an upper class with stable earnings makes for an attractive consumer segment. Brazilians also spend more of their disposable income on fashion products than consumers in many other countries. Brazilians spend more money on designer clothing, luxury cars, and cruises than consumers from other nations. This hedonistic consumption is one of the main reasons so many international luxury retailers want to enter the Brazilian retail market.

Many foreign luxury retailers are entering the market on their own, but some are partnering with Brazilian companies, a smart move given the country's complexity in terms of income distribution, taxes, and logistics (Brazil: The allure, 2009).

It seems that Joãosinho Trinta, producer of Brazil's most spectacular Carnival, was right when he said "only intellectuals like misery; what poor people go for is luxury." Lack of cash does not deter Brazilians from purchasing luxuries (A Better Today, 2009). From 2000 to 2008, Brazil's luxury market growth was 35 percent (Strehlau, 2008), and it is expected to grow another 35 percent by 2015. Luxury stores such as Tiffany and Louis Vuitton make their highest profits from their São Paulo stores. In 2010, about 50 luxury brands planned to enter Brazil by 2013.

São Paulo is not the only market for luxury products, and many other cities have emerged for luxury retailers to consider, such as Rio de Janeiro, Belo Horizonte, Campinas, Brasília, and Rec-

▲ **FIGURE 2.4** A man walks past a showcase of Brazilian luxury store Daslu for men on sale at the high-class Cidade Jardim shopping center. Luxury shopping centers are expanding fast in Brazil and particularly in São Paulo. Cidade Jardim hosts Tiffany, Hermès, Chanel, and Furla stores. AFP/Getty Images.

ife. One of the most significant barriers to the luxury retail market is the escalated price of products with high import and local taxes and duties. Many products cost twice or three times their retail prices in the United States.

APPAREL RETAIL FORMATS: OLD AND NEW WITH A LOCAL TWIST

Similar to most emerging markets, Brazil has a wide range of retail formats, and Brazilian consumers tend to shop in many of them, regardless of their social or economic status. There are specialty retailers in urban markets, along with boutiques, discount stores, department stores, and street markets. Even as more organized retail formats enter the market, the unorganized sector is not affected much. Tax evasion and lean overheads may give the traditional retail formats a five percent point advantage in operating margins over organized modern retailers.

TRADITIONAL RETAIL FORMATS

Some traditional retail formats are still common in Brazil. They create competition for some of the large format stores by undercutting them on prices and selling right at their doorstep. The traditional classification approach, through store- and nonstore-based retail, may be used to classify retailing in Brazil.

▶ Store-based Retail

A physical store is the primary characteristic of store-based retail, which is further classified according to the following criteria.

- **Specialized small stores:** Small and medium-sized family-owned businesses that are mainly located on city streets and in shopping centers. According to the Brazilian Development Bank (BNDES) this type of store is predominant in the Brazilian apparel retail market.

- **Specialized retail network:** A network of stores controlled by a central headquarters with very little flexibility on price and promotion policies. Franchising is also an alternative to develop specialized retail networks. Such a network may be local, regional, or national and classified as small, medium, or large according to the number of stores in it. Examples of big Brazilian retail networks include C&A, Hering, Marissol, Casas Pernambucanas, Guararpes-Riachuelo (Lojas Riachuelo, Lojas Amrisa, Lojas Renner), and Lojas Marisa. This type of retail is mainly present in commercial galleries, malls, and shopping centers.

Non-specialized stores: Stores that carry a diverse mix of products, including:

- ▶ **Department stores:** Traditional American brands like Sears, Dillard's, and Mappin (a Brazilian company) have been replaced by specialized networks, such as C&A, carrying only apparel, accessories, bed and bath apparel, and health and beauty products. Casas Pernambucanas represents the closest example to a traditional department store by carrying some electronics.

► **Discount stores**: Medium-sized stores offering a limited mix of products including groceries, music, basic electronics, and basic apparel. Decor and service are very simple and prices are very aggressive. An example is Lojas Americanas.

Outlet stores: Big retail stores, far from urban centers, offering good deals and value to consumers.

Off-price stores: Stores that specialize in off-stock apparel, with big discounts to the consumers. This type of store can be located in or outside big urban centers.

Camelódromos: or popular markets. Small, popular street shopping centers present in almost every Brazilian city. Most products are low quality, very inexpensive compared to similar products, and sourced from China. Although popular and targeted to the low-income population, these markets are frequented by medium- and even high-income classes looking for replicas and cheaper imported goods.

Camelôs: Unregistered street traders who are part of many Brazilian neighborhoods. Camelôs are part of the "informal economy," a consequence of the complex tax system, high taxes, and weak fiscal controls. Camelôs present a great challenge to Brazilian policymakers; some studies demonstrate that informality impedes economic development and reduces competitiveness (Kenyon and Kapaz, 2005; Elstrod and Bebb, 2005).

► Nonstore-Based Retail

Nonstore-based retail is a format that focuses on consumers who have little time for shopping or who live far from urban centers.

▲ **FIGURE 2.5** Bambolina, a popular store located in Largo Treze commercial area in São Paulo. Mainly tailored to low- to medium-income consumers, these popular commercial areas include specialized small and even retail network stores. Abundance of low-price merchandise and credit are the most used sales tactics. They are very common in the majority of Brazilian large cities and attract customers from Latin America and Africa. Photo by Olivia Laban.

Personal sales: Sales made through direct contact between vendor and buyer. Sellers include:

▸ Registered street traders: Individuals who sell their products legally. They work mainly on streets with high pedestrian traffic or near office buildings.
▸ Door to door sales: This traditional approach is still very popular in Brazil, mainly in low-income areas: a door-to-door salesperson offers goods from his mobile showroom, which may be a van, a small truck, a motorcycle, or even a peddler's cart.

▲ **FIGURE 2.6** A Camelódromo holds small stores and is located in high-traffic areas selling a multitude of products from apparel to back-to-school products. This is a very popular format in many Brazilian cities. Photo by Eduardo Trauer.

▶ In-home store: An individual transforms part of his or her home into a showroom and regularly invites customers for coffee or tea parties that are followed by sales events.

▶ Network marketing: Consultants visit their customers' homes selling directly from manufacturers' catalogs. Similar to Avon or Mary Kay in the United States, the most well-known Brazilian equivalent is the local cosmetic and health and beauty aids brand, Natura.

Sales through direct marketing action (without personal contact): Sellers include:

▶ Catalogs: The twentieth century's high inflation rates prevented the development of catalog sales in Brazil. In any case, this sales format is decreasing in importance with the advent of the Internet and e-commerce.

▶ Teleshopping: This sales alternative is becoming popular in Brazil with some dedicated TV stations, as well as slots on regular TV stations. Many players use the infomercial approach, in which products are presented within an informative context. Some television retailers include Shoptime, Medalhão Persa, Shop Tour, and Polishop.

▶ Telemarketing: Telemarketing is very common in Brazil, mainly for magazine subscriptions and mobile phone services. When product images are mandatory, this format loses relevance.

MODERN FORMATS

Brazil has retail formats that are very similar to those in developed nations. In the food distribution sector modern retail formats like supermarkets and hypermarkets dominate. In the apparel industry the classic department store is not present: it was practically eliminated by high inflation and hypermarket competition. Some additional modern formats worth mentioning that reflect the structure of the market as well as changes in consumer behavior are as follows.

▶ Hypermarkets

These are large stores covering more than 52,000 square feet (5,000 m2) dedicated to a one-stop shopping experience. Hypermarkets are mainly located in big urban and suburban centers, easily accessed by car and public transportation, and require a significant parking area. Brazilian examples include Extra, Bourbon alongside international players such as Carrefour, and Walmart.

▶ Buyers Clubs

Buyers clubs are members-only stores similar to Costco in the United States. Examples include Dutch cash-and-carry operator Makro and Sam's Club.

▶Atacarejo

Atacarejo is a typical Brazilian format, blending wholesaling and retailing under the same roof with little or no service to customers. Whenever apparel is sold, the products are cheap and very basic. Brazilian retailers Atacadão and Assaí are some examples.

▶Convenience Stores

Convenience stores are a very popular format in Brazil, with stores located near or inside gas stations. The convenience store format has been modified to a hybrid format with stores becoming more like small supermarkets and fast-food restaurants.

▶Category Killers

The fragmented bookselling industry was the first retail sector to be impacted by the category-killer format. Atica, a publishing house, launched Brazil's first book megastores and sent a clear sign of the industry's consolidation. When Atica was bought by the French FNAC, other bookstores, like Siciliano and Saraiva, got the message and started revamping their networks by replacing small stores with larger ones that included other categories in their offerings, like electronics, computers, and videogames. The category-killer format is being developed in other categories like pet shops, furniture, and home decor.

▶Hard/Soft Discount

Europe's very popular hard-discount format is noteworthy for its absence in Brazil. The value proposition is based upon low prices, small stores with almost no service, and an assortment of 700 basic and high-quality private label grocery and housekeeping items with no national brands. The closest representative of this no-frills, value-driven approach in Brazil is Dia%, part of France's Carrefour Group. Dia% carries a very limited assortment with some national brands and a strong presence of private labels.

▶ Neighborhood Stores

The advent of the supermarket and hypermarket has reduced dramatically the mom-and-pop stores, mainly in big cities; however, time and convenience have become essential for many consumers pressed by busy schedules in the biggest cities. Additionally, the threat posed by hard and soft discounters has triggered actions from some retailers like Pão de Açúcar Group, which has revamped the old mom-and-pop grocery store with a new **neighborhood store** format—a small, conveniently located supermarket that carries an assortment customized for its location, which includes grocery, perishables, cleaning, and health and beauty products.

▶ e-Commerce

As access to computers and the Internet increases for Brazil's middle and lower classes, e-commerce is gaining momentum. However, the lack of standard sizes represents a strong barrier to apparel sales.

STORE OWNERSHIP:
THE CHANGING LANDSCAPE

As in most emerging markets, individual families dominate the retail business, from small, traditional formats to very large retail chains. Recent economic and political stability has led to the rapid expansion of capital markets. However, by May 2010 only six apparel retail companies had gone public. In other words, the industry is very fragmented. Four of the top five retailers in the country are public and their stocks are regularly traded on the Brazilian Stock Exchange (BM&FBOVESPA). The publicly traded are all Brazilian apparel companies: RIACHUELO (GUARARAPES), LOJAS RENNER, MARISA, and HERING. Casas Pernambucanas, another large Brazilian apparel retailer, is an example of a private, family-owned business.

Many local, regional, and national family-owned brands and their respective stores are respected for their creativity and design; however, a clear opportunity for process, productivity, and distribution improvement exists and is being explored by private equity funds and stronger brands through acquisition and consolidation. Companies like InBrands (encompassing Brazilian brands 2nd Floor, Bintang, Ellus, Fashion Rio, Herchcovitch: Alexandre, Isabela Capeto, Richards, Salinas, and SPFW) and BRLabels (Calvin Klein and Brazilian brands VR and Mandi) are acting as consolidators in this market by bringing technology, controls, and professional management to the companies while keeping the founders and creators at the product end. When this process is concluded, those companies are likely to become public.

FDI REGULATIONS:
CHALLENGING BUT IMPROVING

Brazil offers a challenging environment for foreign direct investment (FDI). In 2008, Brazil had the highest FDI in Latin America with an investment of $42 billion. Heavy taxation and regulatory requirements in Brazil are major deterrents for FDI by international retailers. Brazil has investment agreements with Belgium and Luxembourg, Chile, Cuba, Denmark, Finland, France, Germany, Italy, the Republic of Korea, the Netherlands, Portugal, Switzerland, the United Kingdom, and Venezuela (Doing Business, 2009).

To sustain high growth rates, Brazil needs FDI. There are no restrictions on FDI in the apparel retail sector. To attract more FDI, the government is working on domestic infrastructure. A company that is properly registered in Brazil is allowed to acquire real estate without any limitations. The retail stores are allowed to set their own hours for opening and closing. The government also has simple repatriation rules. A foreign company can take all the money earned in Brazil back to its country of origin as long as it is registered with Central Bank of Brazil and all taxes are paid (Legal Guide, 2007).

Some problems that foreign investors may face are the implicit costs of owning a business in Brazil, commonly known as "Custo

Brasil." Distribution, logistics, government procedures, and employee benefits all involve implicit costs. In addition to these expenses, complex customs regulations, an ineffective legal system, and a tax burden that increases the prices of imported products to 200 percent (Doing Business, 2009) create problems for foreign investors. Brazil is a relational country, a characteristic that is ingrained in the country's business culture. Successful companies build relationships with potential partners before entering the market.

INTERNATIONAL BRANDS: RISKS AND REWARDS

Songwriter Tom Jobim, who wrote "The Girl from Ipanema," liked to say, "Brazil is not for rookies." Many retailers successful in their country of origin have had to rethink and eventually abandon plans after entering the Brazilian market. Economic and political instability as well as a competitive market with many institutional voids have led to many of these aborted attempts. Companies that have quit the Brazilian market include the likes of Sears, JC Penney, Portuguese retail group SONAE, and Dutch food retailer AHOLD. Since the implementation of the economic measures known as Real Plan in 1994, the scenario has dramatically improved, and Brazil has become a destination for foreign investment in many areas, including retailing. International retailers have entered the market with different methods.

WHOLLY OWNED SUBSIDIARIES

Several successful companies have entered the market without any partnerships through wholly owned subsidiaries. Such companies, including Dutch wholesaler Makro, French home improvement chain Leroy Merlin, Spanish fast fashion apparel retailer Zara, Tiffany & Co., and Dutch popular apparel retail chain C&A, have started Brazilian operations from scratch and are growing organically. Other companies such as Carrefour have entered the market through this format and later accelerated their expansion through acquisitions.

ACQUISITIONS

This method is also a common way to enter the market. The French retailer FNAC bought Brazilian publishing house Atica store and the Chilean retailer CENCOSUD bought Brazilian companies G. Barbosa and Irmãos Bretas. Through such acquisitions, the foreign company does not have to spend time acquiring real estate or store space because they already have that from the existing stores of the companies they buy.

JOINT VENTURES

These are less frequent in Brazil. Walmart initially attempted a joint venture with Lojas Americanas but then decided on a wholly owned subsidiary with a mix of organic growth and acquisitions. Perhaps the most successful joint venture in Brazil is between French retail group Casino and Brazilian Grupo Pão de Açúcar, who have formed the largest Brazilian retailer operating supermarkets, hypermarkets, and electronics stores.

Except for the fast-food industry, there are no records of franchising as an entry strategy for retailing.

INFLUENCES ON APPAREL RETAILING: TV AND MUCH MORE

Two factors are key influencers in the apparel retailing industry in Brazil: the shopping mall culture and fashion.

SHOPPING MALL CULTURE

The development of the shopping mall industry in Brazil goes hand in hand with the development of the apparel industry. When shopping malls in São Paulo and Rio sponsored fashion shows in the 1990s, Brazilian fashion saw its biggest boom. Whereas shopping malls in most Western countries cater to blue-collar and middle-class consumers, this is not necessarily the case in Brazil.

Several corporations are transforming sites in upper-class neighborhoods of major cities into upscale malls with apparent success. In São Paulo, for example, three luxury malls coexist within a 15-mile (5 km) radius. These malls serve as entertainment centers as well as fashion outlets for most luxury brands. For instance, of the six Louis Vuitton stores in Brazil, four are in shopping malls.

FASHION INFLUENCES

Until the 1930s, Brazilians followed European fashion, with Paris setting the standard for women and London for men. Fashion magazines were mostly translations of top European publications. In the 1930s, Flavio Carvalho, a Brazilian architect and artist in Recife, led a movement to rescue native values and reinforce Brazil's tropical identity. Stylists slowly started to adapt global trends to the lifestyles and climate in Brazil. Clothes became more informal and more colorful.

Since the 1970s, the major laboratory for trendsetting has been the soap opera world, mainly the primetime shows on Brazil's main TV channel, Rede Globo. Whatever the lead character in a soap wears is what the middle class will want to wear. The 1980s saw the arrival of the local editions of major global publications such as *Elle, Marie Claire,* and *Vogue.*

In 1994, Brazil's first group fashion show was organized. It featured most of the top brands in Brazilian fashion and was sponsored by a cosmetic company named Phytoervas. Phytoervas Fashion ran for two years until, under the sponsorship of a major shopping mall, it converted into Morumbi Fashion. By 2000 it had evolved into São Paulo Fashion Week and left the mall for the Bienal Pavilion, the site of Latin America's most important contemporary art exposition. The leaders of Brazil's fashion industry selected the location to raise the show to the level of a world-class event, with attendant international press coverage (Souza Lopez, 2007).

Two fashion shows in Brazil draw attention from international media: São Paulo Fashion Week (SPFW) and Fashion Rio, both run by the domestic conglomerate Inbrands.

OTHER INFLUENTIAL FACTORS

Other factors influencing the development of the apparel industry in Brazil are:

- The strengthening of the Brazilian real, which favors:
  - The entry of global brands into the Brazilian market
  - International travel by members of the middle and upper classes, which raises their awareness of global brands
  - Discretionary income, which allows for more expenditure on fashion and apparel–
- Young Brazilian designers finding their way into the international fashion community (Ocimar Versolatto, Francisco Costa, Isabella Capetto, Tufi Duek, and Alexandre Herchcovitch, among others)
- Top Brazilian models becoming international fashion icons (Gianne Albertone, Shirley Malmmann, and Gisele Bundchen)

GETTING TO KNOW DOMESTIC COMPETITORS: LEARNING FROM THEIR SUCCESSES AND FAILURES

Savvy foreign retailers wanting to enter the Brazilian retail industry will investigate the competition and try to understand the reasons for their success. The following sections present the companies that must be part of such a study.

GRUPO PÃO DE AÇÚCAR (GPA)

GPA is the largest retail chain in South America. It reported sales of about $15 billion in 2009. GPA has continued to be successful and grow even in the face of tough competition from foreign retailers entering the Brazilian market. The company operates different retail formats (hypermarkets, supermarkets, convenience stores) and acquires competitors to remain in the forefront. Excellent customer service and broad geographic coverage make GPA highly successful.

▲ **FIGURE 2.7** Isabeli Fontana walks down the catwalk during Monange Fashion Tour at Via Funchal in August 2010 in São Paulo, Brazil. Latin Content/Getty Images.

LOJAS AMERICANAS

This retailer defies categorization; the chain sells confectionery, personal care, lingerie, and music CDs. It offers low prices at high-end locations. The stores are mainly located in shopping malls. They have a lot of promotions on seasonal products and offer credit, making expensive products accessible to a larger consumer base.

RIACHUELO

The company was founded in 1947 and operates more than 110 apparel department stores in 21 of the country's 26 states. They are also Latin America's largest apparel manufacturers. They sell women's, men's, and children's apparel. Again, the credit card has been important to their success. Many Brazilians thought of Riachuelo as the place their mother shopped until the store decided to renovate the brand to attract younger customers. Their customer base is predominantly dominated by middle and lower middle classes.

RENNER

Founded in 1922, the company has more than 120 stores with 94 percent located in premium shopping malls. The company targets customers on the medium to higher income strata. They sell private label apparel brands, private label cosmetics, accessories, and footwear. Their mission is customer "enchantment" to gain a competitive edge over their competitors.

MARISA

This retailer has 220 stores in 24 states. The chain differentiates itself by catering to lower- and middle-class women. Credit draws many customers, along with the lingerie and underwear. They mainly sell their own private label with a few exceptions. They have a fully automated distribution center and operate on a much higher profit margin than their competition.

HERING

Founded in 1880, with apparel retail activity since 1993, this retail chain operates more than 275 stores serving middle to upper-middle class. Most stores are franchised and their private apparel brand is available in more than 15,000 multibrand stores. They produce a wide assortment of premium-quality basic items, particularly T-shirts. O Boticario is a Brazilian cosmetics chain known for excellent sales assistance and good-quality products at low prices and a strong brand reputation among local consumers.

HOW MATURE IS THE RETAIL INDUSTRY? EVOLVING FAST

Although the Brazilian retail industry is highly fragmented, and 60 percent of it is made up of small local retailers, modern retail is well developed due to the entry of many modern retail formats in the late 1990s. Many statistical reports show that hypermarket sales are the highest in all retail categories. But these figures may arise from unreported sales by independent retailers seeking to evade taxes. Government interference makes entering the Brazilian market cumbersome. Registering a business takes 152 days compared to three days in the United States. Many jobs are being created, but most of them are in the informal sector. Street stores are still popular. A complex regulatory and tax environment increases the cost of doing business, and many people choose the informal method of retailing. Many high-end products, such as electronics, jewelry, and apparel, are made in China and enter Brazil illegally by way of Paraguay. Informal retailers purchase these products and sell them throughout the country. Because these retailers don't pay import tariffs and taxes, it is difficult for formal retailers to compete with them on prices (Treewater & Price, 2007).

The apparel sector is Brazil is still largely untapped by foreign investors because of the demand for products very different from the home market of many retailers. Brazilian consumers have a strong preference for local brands and fashions. Even low-income consumers are trendy and fashion conscious. Although the market is not mature with plenty of opportunities to explore, a foreign retailer interested in entering Brazil must understand consumer preferences, behavior, and regional differences; develop skills to compete against local retailers; learn promotional techniques that are season specific; and offer special credit terms like the local retailers. The success of some local retailers relies on a good understanding of the local consumers' preferences, strong brands, and modern manufacturing technology, as well as appropriate distribution.

BUYING FOR APPAREL RETAIL STORES: LOCAL SOURCING STILL DOMINANT

A foreign retailer who wants to import products into Brazil must pay the import duty, the industrialized product tax (federal tax), and the merchandise and service circulation tax (state government value added tax), as well as a number of smaller taxes and fees (Doing business, 2009). These costs make it difficult for foreign retailers to compete with local products in terms of pricing.

Retailers in Brazil buy from manufacturers and wholesalers. Both industries are highly fragmented in Brazil. More than 30,000 retailers generating 1.65 million jobs form the links in the textile production chain, including yarn manufacturers, fiber producers, weaving mills, and apparel industries (ABIT, 2010). With the liberalization of import regulations, more retailers are buying from countries with low labor costs, such as China. Because apparel production is labor intensive, low labor costs significantly reduce the overall price of the final product (Apparel retail, 2009).

RETAIL CAREERS: FLEXIBILITY AND CULTURAL BLENDING

Brazil is open to skilled and knowledgeable executives from all over the world joining the workforce in the country. A number of publications, websites, and recruiting companies have been established to help expatriates get jobs in Brazil. Many immigrants are coming into Brazil to look for jobs because the country has a well-organized work structure, high salaries, and standardized working hours (Brazil jobs, 2010).

The most popular association for retailing professionals in Brazil is APROVARE (http://www.aprovare.com.br/). Members in this organization create a professional network. Personal relationships are important in Brazil and personal recommendations make it much easier to land a job. Jobseekers can attend various career fairs posting jobs in different sectors of the retail industry.

According to recruiting company Michael Page International (U.S.-based recruitment consultancy), to live and work in Brazil a temporary residence visa will be required. A temporary visa for employment purposes requires a job offer from a company based in Brazil. The company will apply to the Immigration Division of the Ministry of Labor on behalf of the candidate. Educational qualifications or work experience, an employment contract, adequate means of subsistence, no criminal record, and a satisfactory medical examination are the main criteria for approval of an employment visa and all documents required must be translated into Portuguese. The application processing period is around two to three months, and the visa is issued for a specific job and is not transferable between employers.

Knowledge of Portuguese is essential for communication. Some websites that post job offerings in retailing are www.careerjet.com.br, www.zap.com.br/empregos, www.olx.com.br, and www.jobzing.com/brazil. Most companies publish opportunities for interns on their own websites, but some internship information is also available on websites such as http://www.olx.com.br/q/estagio/c-386 and http://empregos.trovitbrasil.com.br/est%C3%A1gio-comercio-varejo.

THE FUTURE OF APPAREL RETAIL: GROWTH, REWARDS, AND RISKS

Brazil is a popular destination for foreign investors. From 2007 to 2008, foreign direct investment increased from $35 million to $45 million. FDI has increased steadily, and the number reached $8 billion at the end of December 2009 despite the global economic slow-down (Prahalad & Liebertahl, 2003).

Consumers have brand loyalty largely toward designer brands. But there is a large market for discount apparel retail with private labels. Discount stores can capture that market by developing private labels to follow local fashion trends. European and U.S. apparel retailers and manufacturers must consider seasonality and fashion cycles because Brazil is located in a different hemisphere. The apparel industry is highly fragmented, leaving room for several small retailers (Apparel Retail, 2009).

Foreign retailers that first began entering the Brazilian market in the 1980s operated with an imperialist mind-set that considered Brazil a new market for their old products. They banked on incremental sales for their existing products. They did not see this emerging market as a source of technical and managerial talent for their global operations. Such blindness has been one of the main reasons for their limited success in the market.

Economic instability, high inflation, and exchange volatility also contributed to the failure of many foreign investments. Now that the market has become more predictable, success is more likely. Foreign companies also have to understand some local cultural norms, such as the art of *jeitinho*, the Brazilian way of getting around problems in business and in life (Arrivals, 2009).

The Brazilian retail market presents various challenges to a new entrant.

- New entrants often have to fight price wars initiated by existing retailers who lower their prices to compete with the new entrant.
- Despite the evolution of the democratic system, corruption is still a part of Brazilian life.
- Infrastructure is a work in progress. Many small, unpaved roads, an almost irrelevant railroad, and airports and air traffic control all need improvement.
- A huge amount of investment is required to complete the infrastructure and development projects under way (airports,

roads, public transportation, and deep-sea oil exploration, among others). A slowdown in FDI will slow the infrastructure development.

▸ Brazil has a high crime rate. Security is a state-government responsibility, and dealing with organized crime represents a major challenge to some cities. Some big cities have high crime and murder rates (Brazil, 2009).

▸ Brazil has a highly regulated labor market, making the cost of employment high and leading to a high level of unemployment in the formal sector.

▸ Taxes are high and not wisely spent or invested by the government. Such waste increases the cost of labor, services, and consumer goods.

The biggest challenge that a foreign retailer will face in Brazil is a need to develop new products or alter its current offerings to suit the local market. Brazil is a large country with considerable differences among regions. A preference for local fashion and the heavy use of credit in an underdeveloped market also pose problems for foreign retailers. The high level of trust for local brands among local consumers is another hurdle that foreign retailers will have to clear. Providing consumers with fashion that is associated with their local celebrities may help develop loyalty among Brazilian consumers. Hiring local staff to interpret the wants and needs of the local population will also lead to a strong foothold in the local market.

CARREFOUR TRAVEL DIARIES: BRAZIL

The Carrefour Group opened its first store in Brazil in 1975. At the time, the brand was just starting to build up its international operations, and hypermarkets had not yet been introduced into Brazil. The group's arrival in this market coincided with the launch of its own brand products in 1989 and the introduction of the hard-discount trade name Dia% in 2001.

The group's strength resides in strong brand awareness, its multiformat policy, and its participation in local communities. The company set up a centralized distribution channel to overcome problems caused by poor local infrastructure. Carrefour had to face some initial problems, but had the first mover's advantage. Carrefour TV commercials star Brazilian celebrity presenter Ana Maria Braga. Popular among Brazilians, Carrefour's emphasis on fresh products, including the Garantia de Origem range, organic products, and innovative items, provides the company with a major competitive advantage. Some 5 million people possess a Carrefour Card, launched in 1989.

Since 2004, Carrefour has updated its brand image, both in relation to its customers and its employees, and has restructured its supermarket network based on a new concept suited to local markets: Carrefour Bairro. Since its entry into the gasoline retail market in 2003, it has also been developing its sales of non-food products. By 2010 it had established 18 travel agencies and 50 pharmacies.

Already the country's leading hypermarket chain, the group became the number one mass retailer in the food market in terms of sales in April 2007. It has also acquired Atacadao, a discount hypermarket brand with 34 stores and sales of a little over US$2 billion (1.5 billion euros). This acquisition allows Carrefour Brazil to expand its operations into a new customer segment by offering some 6,000 food items at discount prices in stores with an average surface area of 6,300 square meters (20,669 square feet).

The Carrefour Group reported sales of a little over US$5 billion (3.8 billion euros, excluding tax) in 2006. It is one of the country's five largest private employers, with 48,000 men and women on staff. More than 19,000 new employees joined the group in 2006. Carrefour has also developed partnerships with more than 15,000 local suppliers. Brazil will become the second most important country for the company next year, overtaking Spain and trailing only France, achieving a goal set by management a year early.

"Brazil," Carrefour Travel Diaries, Retrieved on December 15, 2010, from http://www.carrefour.com/cdc/group/our-business/travel----------diaries/brazil.html

Discussion Questions

1. What steps did Carrefour take in Brazil to be successful?
2. What would be your general recommendations regarding entry formats to a retailer interested in entering the Brazilian market?
3. Based on what we now know about Brazilian consumers, what is unique about them that a retailer entering the Brazilian market should be cautious about?

Case Study 2

NATURA: GOING BACK TO NATURA

Natura has been trying to make its business dealings as attractive as the faces of its Latin American customers since 1974. The company's business acumen is impressive, and its commitment to corporate social responsibility sets it apart from its global competitors. Its programs for social and environmental change and the products themselves set high standards.

Natura's Ekos line of products, available since 2005, uses sustainable ingredients from special reserves in rain forests and savannas, maintained by small local communities. The products contain Brazilian berries and plants, such as guarana, Brazil nuts, mate verde, and cocoa. The nature reserves are monitored by independent bodies such as the nongovernmental organization Imaflora.

Natura is also careful not to let any community become reliant on producing any single ingredient, in case it is no longer needed. It tries to aid other forms of development in the area, such as handicrafts and ecotourism. "We have a concept called 'bem estar bem'—'well being well,'" explains Guttilla. "Well-being is about the harmonious relationship with oneself. But it is also about having empathetic, successful, and gratifying relationships with others and nature." Natura is also tackling other environmental issues. Some initiatives, such as its Rainforest Education and Recovery Project, have taken on the mammoth job of regenerating the damaged rain forest ecosystem. Others, such as the Rio de Janeiro Botanical Gardens initiative, have smaller aims. The company intends simply to help the gardens maintain and improve their medicinal plant beds.

Bia Saldanha, co-founder and marketing director of the Brazilian fair trade fashion brand AmazonLife, says she admires the Natura brand for its business practices. She believes that Natura is one of only a few Latin American brands that genuinely makes a positive difference for both its consumers and communities.

Natura's commitment to the environment resonates with consumers throughout the continent. Natura's Mexican operations opened in August 2005, and it is already present throughout Argentina, Chile, Peru, and Bolivia. The Latin American business outside Brazil grew 52 percent in 2009 to US$18.5 million in revenues. There are more than 27,000 sales employees in these countries.

Source: "NATURA: Going Back to Natura." *Brand Strategy* (2005): 28.

Discussion Questions

1. What does Natura's success tell you about Brazilian consumers?
2. What makes Natura stand out from other cosmetic brands?
3. Can Natura go global (beyond Latin America) with their current strategy?

REFERENCES

A better today (2009, November 14). *Economist, 393*(8657), 9.

ABIT - Brazilian Textile and Apparel Industry Association

Statistical Data Brazil—retrieved November 6, 2010, from http://www.abit.org.
     br/site/navegacao.asp?id_menu=13&IDIOMA=EN

Andrade, Sara. "Inside Brazil's Booming Fashion Industry—The Business of
     Fashion," *Vogue Portugal,* August 5, 2010.

Arrivals and departures (2009, November 14). *Economist, 393*(8657), 9.

Artigas, M. & Calicchio, N. (2007). Brazil: Fashion conscious, credit ready.
     McKinsey Quarterly, 4, 76–79.

Brazil (2009). Datamonitor

Brazil & Columbia: Apparel attitudes (2008). Retrieved January 7, 2010, from
     http://www.cottoninc.com/SupplyChainInsights/Brazil-and-Columbia-
     Apparel-Attitudes/Brazil-and-Columbia-Apparel-Attitudes.pdf?CFID=2
     363940&CFTOKEN=72793671

Brazil: The allure of the underdog (2010). Retrieved May 20, 2010, from http://
     beta.luxurysociety.com/articles/2009/10/brazil-the-allure-of-the-
     underdog

Brazil jobs (2010). Retrieved on February 23, 2010 from http://www.jobzing.
     com/brazil/

Brazil retail: time to e-shop (2009, September 28). *Business Latin America.*
     The Economist Intelligence Unit Brazil takes off (November 14, 2009).
     Economist, 393(8657), 15.

Capp, J., Elstrod, H. & Bebb Jones Jr., W. (2005). Reining in Brazil's informal
     economy. *McKinsey Quarterly,* 1, 9–11.

Doing Business in Brazil (2009). Retrieved January 7, 2010, from http://www.
     buyusainfo.net/docs/x_7220198.pdf

"Emerging Markets Offer Growth Opportunities for Apparel Retailers Battling
     Declines in Domestic Consumer Spending." Retrieved December 4, 2009,
     from http://www.atkearney.com/index.php/News-media/emerging-
     markets-offer-growth-opportunities-for-apparel-retailers-battling-
     declines-in-domestic-consumer-spending.html

Folha de São Paulo Newspaper (March 16, 2005). Retrieved October 21, 2010,
     from http://www1.folha.uol.com.br/fsp/dinheiro/fi1603200502.htm

Folha de São Paulo Newspaper (January 1, 2010a). Retrieved September 16, 2010, from http://www1.folha.uol.com.br/folha/ambiente/ult10007u673513.shtml

Folha de São Paulo Newspaper (August 30, 2010b). Retrieved September 16, 2010, from http://www1.folha.uol.com.br/fsp/mercado/me3008201023.htm

Hall, C. (2009). WWD List: Windows of Opportunity. Retrieved November 2, 2009, from http://www.wwd.com/retail-news/wwd-list-windows-of-opportunity-2199757/print/

Kenyon, T. & Kapaz, E. (2005). The Informality Trap. *Public Policy for the Private Sector – The World Bank Group*, Note Number 301, December.

Legal guide for the foreign investor in Brazil (2007). Retrieved January 7, 2010, from http://www.brasilemb.org/docs/Trade%20and%20Investment/guide_investors.pdf

Portal Exame. Retrieved September 16, 2010, from http://portalexame.abril.com.br/gestao/noticias/lojas-classe-c-devem-ter-estetica-propria-596591.html/

Prahalad, C. & Lieberthal, K. (2003, August) The End of Corporate Imperialism. *Harvard Business Review*. Vol. 81 Issue 8, p. 109.

Research: Reaching Brazilian consumers (2005). *Brand Strategy*, p. 48.

Treewater, E. & Price, J. (September 2007). Navigating Latin American distribution channels. *Logistics Today, 48*(9), p. 1.

Poland
Slovakia
Ukraine
Hungary
Moldavia
Romania
Serbia
★Bucharest
Bulgaria
Black Sea

BUCURESTI
MALL

ROMANIA

3

Liviu Voinea

Andrada Busuioc

Irina Ion

OBJECTIVES

After reading this chapter, you will

▶ Identify the main characteristics of the Romanian apparel retail industry, including competition, market maturity, the tax system, consumers' preferences, and international brands

▶ Understand the competitive forces that drive the apparel retail industry in Romania and the factors that support them

▶ Find peculiarities about traditional and modern retail formats in Romania

▶ Identify future opportunities that this sector provides to international business

Romania is located in southeastern Central Europe, home to beautiful Black Sea beaches, emerald forests, medieval monuments, and the striking Carpathian mountain range. About 60 percent of the Romanian vocabulary is Latin based and overall, Romanians are considered similar to Italians or Spaniards (Table 3.1). Although Romania is an upper-middle-income country, it is one of the lowest-income

TABLE 3.1 Fast Facts about Romania

Capital	Bucharest
Population	21.9 million
Type of government	Republic
GDP: purchasing power parity: in US$	$254.7 billion
Age structure	0–14 yrs: 15.5%
	15–64 yrs: 69.7%
	65 yrs plus: 14.7%
Religion	Eastern Orthodox: 86.8%
	Protestant: 7.5%
	Roman Catholic: 4.7%
	Unspecified: 0.9%
	None: 0.1%
Ethnicity	Romanian: 89.5%
	Hungarian: 6.6%
	Roma: 2.5%
	Ukrainian: 0.3%
	German: 0.3%
	Russian: 0.2%
	Turkish: 0.2%
	Other: 0.2%

Source: CIAfactbook.gov

countries in the European Union. High levels of corruption, left over from the communist era, hinder the growth of business. Nevertheless, in its transition from a communist country to a democratic republic and EU member, this nation only slightly smaller than the state of Oregon has come a long way.

In the aftermath of World War II, Romania became a communist republic. Nicolae Ceaușescu, Romania's most prominent communist leader, tried to detach as much as possible from the Soviet Union's influence, successfully in some cases, not so in others. The communist regime remained in force until the Revolution of 1989. In the meantime, the country's economy turned from agriculture to industry, with around half of the total investments aimed toward industry and especially nuclear plant construction, electronics, and arms (during that period Romania was the fourth-largest European arms exporter). Around 58 percent of the national revenue was generated by the industrial sector. In the 1990s, Romania underwent a series of political and economic reforms for market liberalization and democratization. Romania joined the European Union in 2007 and is likely to adopt the euro by 2015.

Romania borders the Black Sea, which is, along with the Danube River, an important resource for international commerce. Romania has seen a major growth of about 340 percent in the retail industry. The population of approximately 22 million people and the increase in individual incomes make Romania an extremely promising market.

THE RETAIL LANDSCAPE: A HIGH POTENTIAL MARKET

Romania is the seventh-largest market in the European Union (which includes 27 markets) and one of the states with the highest growth rates in the region (7.1 percent in 2008). It is also highly attractive for investors, for reasons that are underlined in what follows, but also because Romania is a large market with approximately 21 million consumers, with an increasing purchasing power and a taste for fashion. A proof of the attractiveness is the amount of foreign direct investment in Romania, which reached $12.5 billion in 2008 (National Bank of Romania, 2009).

Retail is among the sectors that have attracted large amounts of foreign investment since the late 1990s. The Romanian retail market, including sales of cars and fuel, was worth $86 billion in

2008. Food products accounted for close to 24 percent of this total and nonfood products the rest. Excluding cars and fuel, the largest nonfood categories were DIY (Do It Yourself) products, clothing and footwear, consumer electronics, and cosmetics and toiletries (PMR Publications, 2009). Overall, retail sales in Romania grew at a much more sluggish pace in 2008 than in 2007, dropping sharply from 31.4 percent to 22.6 percent over a 12-month period. According to PMR Publications (2009), a British-American company that provides analysis of the business climate in the region Central and Eastern Europe, this downward trend is likely to continue, with growth slowing to 15 or 16 percent due to the global financial and economic crisis that started in 2008 and a decrease in consumer spending. The Romanian government had come up with a policy of a flat tax rate of 16 percent in 2005, which was a big tax cut for the upper middle class. This increased the consumption of imports and created a big trade deficit. With a falling demand for Western European products, Romanian exports suffered.

The retail market in Romania is estimated to have reached $138 billion in 2010 (Carrefour Romania, 2009), almost 150 percent more than it was in 2007. The investments of international retailers reached almost one billion dollars in 2010, the highest level in Central and Eastern Europe. The markets that have been traditionally attractive, such as Poland, the Czech Republic, and Hungary, have become saturated, so Romania and its neighbor Bulgaria are the new points of interest for international retailers.

Foreign direct investment (FDI) inflows reached the Romanian retail sector much later than other Central and Eastern European countries. The first entry of foreign retail chains in Central and Eastern Europe was in the Czech Republic, Hungary, and Poland in the 1990s, and in 1997 in Romania when the German chain Metro opened its first Metro Cash & Carry in Bucharest, the capital of the country. Starting with 2000, a rapid expansion of foreign retailers began, as Carrefour (France), REWE (Germany), and Cora (Belgium) entered Romania. The big French retailer Carrefour entered the market with a $51 million investment. At that time, the proportion between modern and traditional formats was 10 percent to 90 percent (GFK Romania, 2009).

As in other transitional economies with few significant domestic retailers, foreign chains have easily become dominant players in the Romanian retail sector. Before 2009, there were 62 hypermarkets and 560 supermarkets in Romania, but the number of inhabitants per store (hypermarket and supermarket) remained high (52 compared to 6 in France, for example) (Carrefour Romania, 2009).

The expansion of global retail chains in Romania was not uniform across regions. Bucharest and its surroundings along with the Western region (close to Hungary) were the initial focus of their entry. In 2005, the regional distribution of outlets was still uneven (Javorcik, 2009). Expansion strategies of the foreign investors differed. The cash-and-carry market has a longer tradition than the hypermarkets, starting with Metro's first entry in 1997. In 2008, the most active segment in terms of new entrants was clothes and footwear. Three major clothing retailers opened stores for the first time in Romania in 2008—Puma (Germany), LPP Fashion (Poland), and Peek & Cloppenburg (Germany). Although traditional stores still dominate the Romanian market (57 percent) (GFK Romania, 2009), the modern retail formats are gaining more and more field.

In Romania, small local businesses dominate traditional retail, whereas foreign companies control modern retail in almost all sectors—DIY, clothes, footwear, cosmetics, jewelry, beauty products, toiletries, textiles and apparel, and especially grocery. The only exception is the electronics segment, where the three most important players are Romanian.

Even though traditional stores still dominate the retail market in Romania, two forces are changing that: increased interest among foreign investors, who are rapidly developing modern retail formats; and Romanians' increased disposable income, which has oriented them toward consumption. Modern retailing is developing mostly in the nonfood industry, whereas the traditional trade is losing share. Moreover, Romanian consumers are increasingly adopting the purchasing habits of Western Europeans. Price remains the first reason for buying, but other criteria have become important, like the accessibility of shops, the range of products offered, the brand, the quality, and so on. For example, Romanian consumers enjoy shopping at outlets because they offer high-quality products at low prices; consequently, hypermarkets and supermarkets are increasingly preferred over small grocery outlets in urban areas (Euromonitor, 2008).

The Romanian retail market is likely to keep its high potential even as the global economy suffers. Romania ranked eighth among the 56 most attractive destinations for retail investors in 2010 in Europe, the Middle East, and Africa (CB Ellis, 2009). Although Western European countries dominate the first ten positions, there are three exceptions—Poland, Romania, and Russia. About 26 percent of 220 retail companies interviewed indicated Romania as a point of interest for expansion in 2010.

The current development of the retail market in Romania, including the apparel and textile industries, is strongly influenced by its communist history. For nearly 50 years, the communist regime prohibited private property, which killed competition in all the consumer goods industries. This policy educated consumers not to have too high expectations on goods, to accept them as they were, a vision that seems incomprehensible to a capitalist consumer. More than this, products were often unavailable, so that people had to develop informal networks to obtain them, like greasing the palms of store owners. Basically, there was no "consumer behavior" to speak of in the period between 1947 (the installation of communism in Romania) and 1989 (its fall). There was no market—because planned economies, like the Romanian one, do not function with this principle. Instead, the state is the producer and the distributor of all goods, products, and services, from meat and health to cars; it establishes the prices, the supply, the needs of the consumer, their salaries, and so on. Communism almost annihilated consumerism or entrepreneurship. In time, the Romanian consumer has changed in the capitalist period that started in the 1990s.

CONSUMERS: GROWING INCOME AND GROWING MIDDLE CLASS

There are signs that consumer-spending patterns in Romania are starting to converge with those typical of a modern economy, although it is generally accepted that consumption patterns resemble those of a developing country. Since 2000 Romanian consumers' buying power has risen.

Malls attract mostly young people looking for entertainment and middle-class shoppers looking for a better quality of products. Meanwhile, hypermarkets are attracting all categories of consumers with their low price offers and diversity of products. The time constraints imposed by modern living are leading consumers to want shopping and leisure activities at a single location.

What makes Romania a typical developing country in terms of consumption is that an important share of income is dedicated to food purchases. Food products accounted for 37.58 percent of total consumption in 2009, with nonfood at 44.05 percent, of which 4.9 percent was dedicated to apparel and textile products (National Institute of Statistics, 2009). Therefore, the demand for food products is likely to be more sensitive to income rise and increase faster than the demand for other manufacturing products (Javorcik, 2009). In general, demand for clothes and footwear depends on disposable income. The key question for foreign investors is how much of this new demand will be supplied by local firms and how much will be imported?

As consumers, Romanians care most about patriotism, the environment, and fair trade. For an equivalent price, Romanian consumers will choose fair trade products and those that protect the environment. Retailers, therefore, have every interest in explicitly informing shoppers about the procedures used to verify compliance of the products they sell with environmental and fair trade standards. Two-thirds of Romanians prefer homemade products, although this does not apply to apparel. This trend is becoming keener as they get older. Most (two-thirds of the population) of Romanians would not buy products manufactured using child labor, and are aware of the carbon impact of imported goods. However, 37 percent of Romanians favor price over any other concerns (Deloitte, 2009).

The Romanian apparel market is distinguished by:

▶ The growing income of the Romanian middle class
▶ Growth of fashion consciousness among Romanian men and women, along with a willingness to experiment with fashion
▶ Apparel brands' considerable expenditure on advertising and marketing
▶ Increased exposure of the Romanian population to television and other international media
▶ Increased demands of Romanian consumers for quality and fashion
▶ Growth in number of magazines discussing new fashion looks and celebrity styles
▶ Increased foreign travel among Romanian consumers

Romanians buy 80 percent of the goods they consume at full price and the rest is purchased during promotions, much like buyers in developed countries (Circulation snapshot, 2009). Since 2008, the financial crisis has had two noteworthy effects on consumer demand in apparel:

1. Anxiety has curbed the propensity to consume. Romanians are relatively pessimistic regarding their incomes and job security.
2. New criteria for buying have appeared. Consumers want to purchase less, but they still want to buy better. They are making new trade-offs that favor practicality over frippery; the durable

over the ephemeral; conscious, well-planned purchases over impulse buying; and innovations that offer something substantially new, not merely cosmetic changes. Successful apparel retailers are attentive to these choices when they select their product ranges and the messages they communicate.

For Romanian consumers, especially in poor economic times, low prices and sales are key factors for purchasing. Usually brand is an important criterion for buying apparel; however, brands have been losing ground to cheaper products.

WOMEN

Romanian women are known for being preoccupied with fashion and beauty. Moreover, their increasing incomes, arising from their deeper integration into the labor market, have led women to shop for clothes as an entertainment activity, like women from more developed economies. Young, urban Romanian women buy smart, casual clothes for work.

The Romanian consumer usually prefers to buy from large retailers because of the brands, price, and variety. It is not unusual for Romanians to buy apparel from grocery retailers that have developed their own apparel brands (for example, Carrefour) because they offer lower prices. Price remains important for Romanian women when purchasing clothes.

MEN

In Romania, women have been the primary apparel purchasers, but Romanian men are learning about image and fashion. Aesthetics is not a traditional priority for the Romanian man—a tendency that is changing, with more and more men being attracted to fashion. For both women and men, buying preferences vary significantly according to their environment (urban versus rural) and their income.

▲ **FIGURE 3.1** Picture taken in the hypermarket Auchan, showing Romanian brands Elmiplant and Gerovital competing with foreign brands L'Oreal, Nivea, and Garnier.

Romanian brands count on lower prices, as can be seen in the picture, but also on a high and long experience in the Romanian cosmetics market; Gerovital is a brand of Farmec, a Romanian company founded in 1889, and Elmiplant in 1992. Photo by Irina Ion.

BEAUTY INDUSTRY IN ROMANIA

There are some gender differences when it comes to buying beauty products. Men tend to buy few beauty products, mainly for cultural reasons, whereas women love to shop for them. Women tend to use homemade cosmetics, owing to traditional consumption patterns, a desire for natural products, and cost—homemade products are much cheaper than store bought. In any case, Romanian women do show interest in beauty products, and they use them according to their budget constraints.

In general, the beauty products market in Romania is currently developing. Ten years ago, the majority of the companies offered only classical products to the market, without niche products; for example, there were no men's organic products. The main companies in the market are Oriflame, Avon, the Romanian Farmec (the largest Romanian beauty products producer), Gerocossen (Romanian), Elmiplant (Romanian), and many brand, luxury products, such as Lancome and Dior. Romanian products are price competitive in comparison with foreign products, which consumers appreciate very much. Also, they are associated with high quality, even for foreigners. Estimates of the CEO of Oriflame Cosmetic Romania evaluated the beauty market in 2008 at 600 million euros (approximately $835 million). Many specialized retail beauty shops have opened, the most well known being Sephora.

CHILDREN

Most Romanian consumers buy children's clothing depending on price; brand is not important to them when it comes to childrenswear. There are high-income families who want their children to be fashionable, but overall, Romanian families are more concerned with price and price-quality ratio, and much less with brands.

LUXURY RETAIL IN ROMANIA

The majority of wealthy Romanians live in the capital city of Bucharest. The city now has many luxury brands such as the Italian Emporio Armani, Ermenegildo Zegna, Paul & Shark, and Gucci. The Calea Victoriei Boulevard in Bucharest is where all these stores are located and the street is becoming a destination for luxury brands. The luxury market in Romania developed considerably in 2008 when many international luxury retailers entered the market through multibrand stores.

There have been many failures in the Romanian luxury market, for various reasons. Romanians who travel to Paris and Milan to shop for luxury goods are familiar with the latest offerings. Unfortunately, some of the multibrand stores that sell luxury brands sell last season's merchandise and sometimes even counterfeit

merchandise. Some luxury brands have attempted stores in hotels. Louis Vuitton opened their store in a JW Marriott hotel gallery. It turned out to be a wrong choice because their customers did not frequent the hotel gallery. Also, the store sold ready-to-wear merchandise that was made in Romania. Like many other emerging countries, Romanians are very sensitive to the country-of-origin label, and they believe that anything made in their country is inferior to what is made in the West. Some luxury brands that entered the market in 2008, such as Salvatore Ferragamo, did not do well because of poor timing; it was the beginning of the global economic crisis. The brands, such as Escada Couture, closed in 2008 because they entered Romania through a franchise agreement, and the franchise owners did not know how to handle the brand in Romania.

There have been many problems with luxury retailers entering the country in part because Romania is seeing the rise of a large counterfeit luxury market. But even with all these problems, many luxury retailers are looking at the Romanian market for investment. "Hermès and Burberry have been looking at the Romanian market for some time and are looking for spaces to open monobrand stores through local franchises. They are discussing with potential investors. These two brands could enter the Romanian market towards the end of next year," says Oliver Petcu, general manager of CPP Management Consultants (Emporio Armani, 2010).

APPAREL RETAIL FORMATS: MALLS TAKING OVER OLD-FASHIONED SHOPPING

In terms of retail formats, more and more Romanians prefer to shop in malls, shopping centers, or outlets over traditional stores. People who opt for the "old-fashioned" way of shopping mostly have low or medium to low incomes because products sold in these shops are usually cheap, or at least cheaper than the ones in shopping centers or malls.

Apparel retail formats are classified by the type of consumer they cater to, along with whether they are traditional or modern. The traditional formats cater to low- and, at most, medium-income consumers, and the modern formats target the medium-to-high- and the high-income consumers.

TRADITIONAL FORMATS

These are formats that have been in existence since the beginning of the 1990s.

▶Stands in Markets (Open or Closed Markets)

Stands in markets and streets offer, in general, the cheapest products on the market, usually at very low quality. Most of these

▲ FIGURE 3.3 38 store is the equivalent of a U.S. dollar store. It sells everything for one single price (1 euro). The products sold in the store are mainly Chinese products. Photo by Andrada Busuioc.

products come from China, which explains the very low prices. But vendors prefer Turkish and Polish goods, especially when it comes to clothes. China is the main source for underwear, pajamas, and sportswear; Poland is well known for its blouses for women and pullovers for women, men, and children. Of the several Turkish imports, the most popular are the leather jackets. Products are usually sold with no receipt, putting market stands in the informal economy (the economic activities that are neither taxed nor regulated).

▶ Stands on the Streets

These are not a formal format for retail because selling on the sidewalk is usually done with no legal authorization. Most clothing items found here are underwear, sportswear, and winter essentials such as hats, gloves, and scarves. These stands are usually placed in crowded areas such as plazas, but also near bus stations and subway entrances. Their target consumers are people with minimum to low income, so most of their products come from China.

▲ **FIGURE 3.4** Red Dragon, a popular shopping destination in the storages. They are mainly wholesale markets where smaller vendors purchase products to sell on the streets or in the 38 stores. Products can also be purchased for personal use. Chinese products dominate this market. Photo by Andrada Busuioc.

▶ The "38" Store

Similar to dollar stores in the United States, **38 stores** promote a single price for all the items sold, including clothes. In mid-2000, this price was one euro, which at that time was worth around 38.000 lei. Even though the exchange rate varies, the shops have kept their original slogan, "All for 38." All of the clothes in these stores come from China.

▶ The Secondhand Store

Secondhand stores evolved in the years after the fall of communism as the only places that sold clothes from Western Europe. Secondhand shops offer both no-name and brand-name items at very cheap prices. There are several price policies—per kilogram, per product, a single price for all products, or a single price for each category of product. Vendors usually set a single price for a kilogram of clothes or the same price for every item when they are dealing in very cheap, no-name clothes. Vendors differentiate prices among categories or items to indicate brands, whether they are medium- to high-income or luxury brands. Although these clothes are secondhand (new clothes being a very rare exception), they are usually associated with high quality.

▶ The Storages

The storages are an agglomeration of stands, usually used as the supply point for market stands, street vendors, or 38s, or for personal use. They can be found outside big cities, but most storage vendors prefer a site in the Bucharest suburbs, which they call Europe. Europe consists of several storages, such as Red Dragon, which carries products mostly from China but also Poland and Turkey. Although the vast majority of the stands sell to individuals, most of the shopping done there is for reselling. The storages are located in the suburbs, making them hard to reach for city dwellers, and they close around 1 p.m., before most employed people get off work. They are very crowded places on Saturdays and Sundays when most people can shop, and the difference between the prices in "Europe" and the ones in the market or street stands is usually small enough that shoppers don't care.

▶ Traditional Stores

These are fading away because stands, hypermarkets, and supermarkets carry the same products. After the fall of communism, the vast majority of middle-class Romanians preferred them for their Polish and Turkish products, which were associated at that time with high quality. In the 1990s, traditional store owners sourced directly from these countries, but now they can buy them from the storages. The very few traditional stores that still exist are located mostly in small towns. Traditional stores that are present in big cities such as Bucharest try to sell Romanian-made

▲ **FIGURE 3.5** Romanians look on as a model presents a wedding dress made by Romanian fashion designer Doina Levinta at the Expo Marriage wedding fair, February 2008 in Bucharest. AFP/Getty Images/ Daniel Mihailescu

products that are not established brands. These stores target the middle class.

MODERN FORMATS

These formats have developed since the late 90s and have a well-defined structure. They are usually chain stores.

▶ Hypermarkets and Supermarkets

Hypermarkets and supermarkets sell products from brands that are not well known, designed for medium-income consumers. They also sell groceries, usually relegating clothes to a basket and not offering shopping assistance. The main attraction for people buying clothes at hypermarkets and supermarkets is cheap prices. Most sophisticated consumers do not buy clothes from a hypermarket or supermarket.

▶ Department Stores

These are losing popularity, especially in the big cities, as they are replaced by shopping centers. They are usually an agglomeration of stands selling no-name products, usually sourcing from the storages, which offer Chinese, Turkish, or Polish clothes. Stands that belong to small, Romanian clothing manufacturers can still be found, but they are rare.

▶ Discount Concept Stores and Outlets

These are becoming more and more popular because brand clothes can be found at low prices. The relatively cheaper apparel outlets—stores where products can be bought at the manufacturer's selling price—are located mostly on the outskirts of large cities. There are three main types of discount concept stores and outlets: discount concept stores, brand outlet stores, and outlet malls. Discount concept stores sell both brand and non-brand clothes. Consumers like not only the cheap prices but also their offer of brands that have not yet entered the Romanian market. Usually, the brand clothes come from foreign countries' past seasons, with tags still showing the initial price in euros or British pounds. Although brand outlet stores are very popular among consumers who shop them, Romania has only a few (mostly sportswear, such as Nike or Adidas) as most brands with outlet formats sell sufficiently through other means in Romania. The third format, the outlet mall, gathers brand shops selling previous collections at discount prices. The first outlet mall in Romania, Bucharest's Fashion House Outlet Center, just opened in 2008. The outlet concept is still developing in Romania because although people value it, the discounts offered are usually low and in some cases, they do not justify the travel to suburbs where these stores are located.

▶ *Shopping centers and malls*

There are two kinds of shopping centers—the shopping centers themselves, and the so-called commercial galleries in hypermarkets and supermarkets. The main difference is that whereas in the commercial galleries almost all of the shops are brand shops, selling only products of a certain brand (the same format as in malls), shopping centers feature multibrand shops. Moreover, no-name clothes can be sold in some shops, especially if the shopping center is located in a small town. Many towns in Romania have shopping centers, which were transformed by the privatization of communist-era department stores.

Malls and shopping centers flourish in Romania, as a rising number of Romanian consumers develop a taste for shopping as a leisure activity, especially those residing in the capital and a few other large cities. About 20 malls opened in Romania in 2008 and another seven in the next two years. Developers have oriented toward cities with over 100,000 inhabitants. Fashion retailers prefer malls to street locations, since malls receive more visitors, up to 35,000 people per day during weekdays and 40,000 on weekends.

However, some retailers choose to open outlets on streets with high pedestrian traffic.

▶ Single Brand Apparel Stores

These can still be found, especially on shopping arteries, and are the preferred mode of selling by both popular Romanian and foreign brands. The concept of shopping on Main Street is not very well developed in Romania. As in developed countries, the advantage is that it attracts pedestrians who didn't necessarily intend to shop. Moreover, these streets are located in the city centers, so they are not only easy to reach (unlike malls or shopping centers) but also very visible, and attract people to have a look on their way to work, for example. This is the format of choice for the luxury brands, which are located mainly in two kinds of places in Bucharest—the dedicated streets (such as Calea Victoriei Street and Dorobanti Street) or in the shopping galleries of five-star hotels (such as JW Marriott Bucharest Grand Hotel). Louis Vuitton, Escada, and Max Mara are just a few examples. However, there are very few spaces available for retailers on the main commercial streets in Bucharest and other major cities, and rents are high.

▶ Internet

In apparel purchasing, the Internet is mainly used to research and compare, more than to buy. Two-thirds of Romanians go online to find products to buy, select places to shop, and compare prices efficiently. On the Web, supply and demand are met more easily than they are on the street. Price, a key motivator for the purchase decision, has become more transparent thanks to the Internet. Older consumers mainly use the Internet to research and compare prices, whereas men and individuals aged 35–54 use it for purchases. Clothes rank fourth of all the products bought on the Internet in 2008, after books and magazines, movies, and software products.

▲ **FIGURE 3.6** A model presents an outfit by Romanian designer Ingrid Vlasov during ready-to-wear Spring/Summer 2010 fashion show in October 2009 in Paris. AFP/Getty Images/Francois Guillot.

STORE OWNERSHIP:
A MULTINATIONAL PLAYERS MARKET

Multinational players dominate most retail channels, such as hypermarkets, supermarkets, discounters, and DIYs. The segments dominated by local companies are specialist retailers, such as durable goods, pharmacies, leisure, and personal goods. But there are some fragmented categories, such as clothing and footwear, which do not have a clear leader. This situation is likely to change as economists anticipate a large amount of foreign investment, already initiated by a number of European companies.

When speaking of ownership in the Romanian apparel retail industry, a distinction needs to be made among the different types of retail brands, formats, and owners themselves.

ROMANIAN OWNERS

Romanian owners of a business in apparel retail are widespread, but the type of ownership differs significantly. Outlets of Romanian-owned manufacturers are either funded by a single person or were privatized after the fall of communism. The first category includes large, well-known brands such as I.D. Sarierri or Jolidon, and small designers such as Agnes Toma and Nichi Cristina Nichita. Designers that participate in international fairs and exhibitions, such as Irina Schrotter or Agnes Toma, are well known in the domestic fashion industry. The companies in the second category are usually joint stock companies, owned by one or several strategic investors and other small investors. For example, almost 75 percent of the Romanian producer and retailer Braiconf is held by small investors (Bucharest Stock Exchange, 2009). Another form of Romanian ownership is the franchise, usually used for international brands (such as Zara, Intersport, or Stradivarius). Some franchisers focus on luxury brands; for example, Rafar, the fashion division of Romanian holding company RTC Holding, brought Franco Ferre in 2010. Franchising, in comparison with direct control of the retail business, is the predominant option in Romania.

FOREIGN OWNERS

Foreign owners are either international brands that decided to enter the Romanian market directly, through Greenfield investment, or a franchise. Greenfield investors include the German brand NewYorker, which invested $1.3 million to open a store in 2009. LPP Fashion, a Polish company, operates Reserved and Cropp Town, whereas the Spanish group Industria del Diseño Textil (Inditex) operates Bershka, Stradivarius, and Oysho. Marinopoulos Group is a Greek company that operates the franchise for Gap, Banana Republic, and Marks & Spencer, whereas Azali Trading, belonging to a Lebanese investment group, brought Zara and Pull & Bear. Azali Trading is the owner of the franchising for the brands Zara, Pull & Bear, and Sunglass Hut in Romania. It was created in 2004 and received from Inditex the right to operate the brands in the country.

There are also international investors that took over manufacturing companies at privatization, such as Textila Oltul, whose main shareholder is the Belgian company Drapantex.

FDI REGULATIONS: EQUAL TREATMENT TO ALL

There are no government regulations for entry into the Romanian market. The foreign investment regime is designed to attract foreign investors. Romanian legislation follows basic EU principles, namely freedom of forms and procedures for investment; free market access in all areas of economic activity; equal treatment applied both to domestic and foreign investors, residents or nonresidents; the right of foreign investors to repatriate profits derived from investments, after the payment of taxes and legal fees; and the protection of investments, through guarantees against nationalization, expropriation or other measures with equivalent effect (Romanian Government Emergency Ordinance, 2008). There are no specific investment requirements for starting a company in Romania. The procedure requires fulfillment of legal formalities such as obtaining the approval of a judge and the registration at the National Trade Register Office and the National Agency for Fiscal Administration (Romanian Agency for Foreign Investment, 2009).

INTERNATIONAL BRANDS: FRANCHISING IS IN

There are two ways for international brands to enter the market: through franchising, and through a Greenfield investment. Foreign companies overwhelmingly choose the first one (Table 3.2).

FRANCHISING

Franchising is the most popular way for international brands to enter the Romanian market because foreign brands don't need any money to franchise. The foreign company makes a profit at a low risk.

A problem with this kind of business approach is that it can create an inefficient production and distribution chain. For example, in textiles, it is estimated that 80 percent of Romanian production is CMT (cut, make, and trim) for export markets. Most of this percentage is represented by arrangements in which a company, named beneficiary, provides raw materials to another company, named executor, to be processed according to the beneficiary's specifications. Romanian companies produce for such international firms as Sweden's H&M, Dorothy Perkins, Holland's C&A, or Naf-Naf in this manner. The produced goods are then shipped to the company that outsourced, only to come back to Romania as supplies for the stores. It is possible in a Romanian C&A store, for example, that many clothes labeled "Made in Romania" have not been sourced from Romanian producers but rather imported from the mother company. The additional transportation costs are reflected in the final price of the goods.

TABLE 3.2 Foreign Retailers—Their Turnover and Brands in Romania

Rank	Retailer	Turnover in Europe 2008 billion €/$[1]	Brands	Present in Romania Starting from the Year
1	Marks & Spencer	12.0€//17.28$		Yes, 1999
2	Inditex	8.2€//11.8$	Zara, Pull and Bear, Massimo, Dutti, etc.	Yes, with the exception of Uterqüe
3	H&M	7.4€//10.65$		Will open in Spring 2011
4	C&A	6.3€/(2009) /8.69$		Yes, 2009
5	Next	4.1€//5.9$	Superdry, Lipsy Miss Sixty, Firetrap, etc.	Yes, 2008
6	Debenhams	3.3€//4.75$	Products of different designers	Yes, 2007
7	Esprit	3.1€//4.46$	Accessorize, Adidas, McCartney, ALDO, Avangarde, etc.	Yes, 2006
8	Peek & Cloppenburg	1.7€/(2007) /2.31$		Yes, 2008
9	Benetton	1.7€//2.44$		Yes, 1994
10	Etam	1.0€//1.44$		Yes, 1994

1. The values in dollars are calculated for 1€ =1.44$,for 2008, 1€ =1.36$ for 2007 and 1€ =1.38$ for 2009, based on the average official exchange rate at http://www.bnro.ro/ Baza-de-date-interactiva-604.aspx

Source: www.retail-index.com

GREENFIELD INVESTMENT

Greenfield investment is not a popular choice owing to high costs and risks. The investor has to set up a company from the base—rent or buy a place, handle the supply, distribute, and sell the products, hire the staff, get through all the legal forms, and so on. New Yorker entered the Romanian market through a Greenfield investment in 2007 and had developed up to seven stores by 2010. The average sum invested for opening a New Yorker store is around $1,200 per square meter (approximately $109 per square foot). The majority of well-known foreign fashion retailers operate in Romania.

The vast majority of Romanians are well aware of the quality of a product or service, its origin, and the trademark under which it is sold. A 2003 survey conducted by the Bucharest marketing and consulting agency Daedalus Consulting showed the following preferences among Romanian consumers:

- Germany, Japan, and the United States for technology products
- Italy, France, Germany, and the United States for clothing and footwear
- The United States, Japan, Germany, and the Netherlands for electronic and domestic appliances
- France for cosmetics and wine
- Russia for vodka
- The Netherlands for dairy products
- The United States for cigarettes
- Brazil and Colombia for coffee (Nicolae, 2007)

INFLUENCES ON APPAREL RETAILING: DOMINATION OF GLOBAL RETAILERS

Romanian apparel retailing has been influenced by various factors. There has been an increase in retail area, especially malls in the city as well as on the outskirts, and foreign competition has increased. Challenges in the retail sector include limited competitiveness within Romanian apparel brands, not many organized retail areas other than malls, high cost of weak infrastructure, low degree of sophistication among Romanian consumers, dominance of franchising instead of direct control of business, and the aftermath of the 2008 financial crisis.

After a long period of depression, Romania's consumer market grew spectacularly from 2000 to 2010. Romania's retail market in 2009 was a developing one, with important international players established in the country. There is still room for diversity and competition from Romanian retailers. Important Romanian retailers are almost absent from distribution channels, in comparison with foreign retailers. The Romanians are either small units, with no real capacity to have their say in the market, or larger companies that distribute their own manufacturer's brand. Because foreign retailers dominate the market, its development is at the mercy of the international financial markets, and has had much slower growth rates since the boom leading up to 2008 (PRM Publication, 2009). Still, the market is expected to remain relatively dynamic. New international retailers, such as C&A, have established footholds in Romania, and others, such as H&M, are evaluating this expansion option.

Generally, global retail chains transform the retail sector and affect the supplying industries in the host economy. In Romania, as in other countries, global retail chains differ from indigenous retailers not only in terms of scale but also because of their access to advanced technologies, modern management strategies, and global sourcing networks. One current trend is that suppliers, instead of selling their product to a large number of small retailers, may deliver larger quantities to retail outlets. Also, global chains create economies of scale and increase competition, due to their ability to source products from abroad. As retail chains become more important, their bargaining power with suppliers grows. Moreover, being able to import products rather than purchasing them locally allows global retail chains to demand that suppliers lower prices. By increasing competitive pressures on suppliers, cutting distribution costs, and offering easier access to information and a larger market, global retail chains may stimulate productivity growth in the supplying industries (Javorcik, 2009).

In the case of Romania, the competitive pressures of foreign apparel retailers haven't lead to a real consolidation of domestic retailers, so the market is still dominated by global apparel retail chains.

Romanian textile and apparel products have undergone significant changes since the Agreement on Textiles and Clothes (ATC) came to an end on January 1, 2005, and Romania acceded to the European Union (EU) in 2007. The Asian countries, direct competitors of Romania, have far lower labor costs, so this fragile Romanian advantage came to an end by 2007, which also brought fewer opportunities to operate CMT activities. Moreover, low labor costs were correlated with low productivity before 2007 (workers were paid little and they worked little), so the beginning of a new period of development of the sector was also jeopardized by low productivity patterns. In Romania, difficulties in obtaining skilled workers will continue to drive labor costs up. Romania's level of productivity is, together with Poland's, far below the average of the 27 countries of the European Union (86 percent and 63 percent below respectively). With lower salary levels than all European countries, except Bulgaria in some industries and periods of time, Romanian enterprises had little incentive to move from a labor-intensive mode of production and toward productivity-enhancing investments (AD Little, 2008).

Perhaps the most impressive peculiarity of the Romanian retail sector in apparel is the development of the domestic, Romanian supply of apparel. It is marked by a significant level of limited competitiveness of apparel products. As a result, the sector has not produced brands, and it is not competitive in prices. The textiles and apparel sector were mainly unable to create powerful brands, but instead they specialized in activities CMT for third parties.

The lack of a well-developed industrial design school with a business focus has also contributed to the weak state of domestic apparel manufacture and retail. There is an established Faculty of Textiles, Leather and Industrial Management in Iai in northeast Romania (http://www.tuiasi.ro/facultati/tex/). Despite its national prestige, there is room for more such educational institutions. Moreover, the level of specialized education has decreased for specific textile skills such as dyeing, sewing, and so on, and for related skills such as mechanical engineers to conduct maintenance. Good Romanian designers are rare. This is one reason why local companies have an average of two collections per year, whereas international companies have six per year. Interestingly, textiles and apparel across the EU were the industries showing the strongest decline in shares of low-skilled employees over the period 1999–2005 (Landesmann, 2009).

Due to Romanian retailers' inability to create fashion and image, they have failed to create brands that can be recognized by local as well as foreign consumers. The sector also lacks efficient support services, such as quality control, transportation, storing facilities, and information regarding the market and the identification of and connections to new distribution channels.

The lack of appropriate retail areas, except malls, remains an important problem. In Bucharest, for example, several neighborhoods are adequate for the establishment of a shopping district. But each of them has limitations: They are not pedestrian friendly, or they don't have a sufficient level of traffic, or are under construction, or the rents are prohibitive. Luxury apparel stores face problems because of the lack of an established shopping district, which in the cities of Western Europe is generally the old part of the town. In the case of Romania, the old parts of cities and towns have not been properly preserved.

High expenditures on logistics are a problem in apparel retailing and are mainly due to poor infrastructure, like roads or expansive store spaces.

Salaries have grown in the past years and so has Romanians' purchasing power. Romanian consumers have a relatively low degree of sophistication, which makes them less educated consumers.

Because of this, they will be tempted to be less strict in making purchases; in other words, the Romanian consumer will compromise on image, color, or quality of the textile.

With the 2008/2009 financial crisis, retail sales in the textile and clothing industry deteriorated for the first time since the 1990s. Despite a reduction in consumer prices, European consumption made by individuals as consumers is estimated to have decreased by 1 percent in the clothing sector. Indeed, the EU27 retail turnover slightly decreased both in value and volume (-0.4 percent and -0.1 percent). The difficulties faced by sectors that would buy textiles (for example, construction, automotive, and housing), in combination with increasing production costs, hurt the textile industry (Adinolfi, 2009).

In Romania, the textile and apparel sector was also affected by the decline in demand both foreign and domestic, especially foreign since Romanian products are mainly exported. According to a 2009 survey, clothing retail will be one of the sectors most affected by consumers' shaken confidence; 49 percent of global consumers and 59 percent of Romanian consumers will spend less on new clothes (Nielsen, 2009). Romania is, in fact, one of the most pessimistic Eastern European nations in times of crisis.

CULTURAL INFLUENCES ON TEXTILE AND APPAREL RETAILING

Whereas modern cultures, especially those of the West, favor individualism and exchange such resources as money, information, and products, traditional cultures such as Romania's tend to be more collectivist and exchange such resources as love, status (for example, you reward somebody by appointing that person in an important position), and service (Lascu, 1996). As the only country in the region with a language derived from Latin, Romania has experienced isolation from its neighbors; consequently, Romanians have banded together, and their values are socially determined. They are a homogenous group, in terms of race, nationality, ethnicity, religion, and traditions. Research has linked ethnicity with buying habits, but the importance of ethnicity in Romania is low in terms of consumer preferences, due to its homogeneity.

There are no significant differences in apparel preferences among the three historical regions of Romania (the south, called the "Romanian country"; the one situated in the center of the Carpathian Mountains, "Transylvania"; and the eastern part of the country, "Moldavia"). At the most, the western population in Romania has more demanding consumers, due to being closer to the western markets.

Located at the intersection of Western modernity and Eastern tradition, Romania has kept its cultural homogeneity intact, culling from Balkan, Russian, and Western influences. The Balkan culture can be observed in consumers' preference for traditional retail stores, street markets, bargaining, and so on, although it is hard to dissociate such a preferences from low incomes that only allow purchasing from the cheapest retailers.

For nearly 50 years, competition and selling were dormant in Romania in the communist sphere of influence. Retail was also significantly different in the communist era, in all the areas of activity. First of all, the marketing and advertising components were practically absent from the functions of the firm. In fact, firms—or private property—were prohibited and products and services were produced and distributed by the state in Romania. Consumers enjoyed a very restricted diversity in all the goods and the price was set up by the state. Moreover, products were very difficult to find, especially in food and in the late years of communism (starting in the 1980s). State-owned shops had modest infrastructure. A few Romanian brands were on the market, produced in state-owned factories.

In the 1990s, the opening of the borders facilitated an intense traffic of products: first at the Hungarian, ex-Yugoslav, and Bulgarian borders, and afterwards with more distant countries like Turkey, Poland, and Greece, as well as some Middle Eastern and Asian countries. Large warehouses sold mostly Turkish, Chinese, and

▲ **FIGURE 3.7** Locals line up for fruits in Sibiu, Romania. Under communism, there was a restricted supply of food that resulted in people lining up outside the grocery store to buy vegetables, fruits, and bread. National Geographic/Getty Images/Winfield Parks.

Arab products wholesale, whereas street vendors offered the boutique experience, as did luxury shops established by some Western entrepreneurs (Nicolae, 2007).

FASHION INFLUENCES ON TEXTILE APPAREL RETAILING

Romanians like to wear fashionable apparel, and they adapt easily to Western tendencies. Broadly speaking, Romania does not have a tradition in fashion, or in beauty products, so the need to be fashionable is satisfied mainly by foreign products and brands.

The freedom of expression found after the fall of communism, together with people's high exposure to television, has

▲ **FIGURE 3.8** These stands sell traditional Romanian clothing that is worn during traditional dance or musical performances. The products are handmade by local artisans. Photo by Marian Lungu.

brought image to the fore of Romanians' preoccupations. The Romanian public's fashion awareness is an important determinant of apparel retailing.

Moreover, Romanian consumers like brands so much that they prefer to buy imitations over nonbranded apparel. The market for fake products manufactured in Turkey or other Asian countries is considerable in Romania, although public statistics for it are missing.

DISTINCT FEATURES OF APPAREL RETAILING

The apparel retailing sector in Romania is the expression of a growing market, although affected by reductions in demand due to the 2008/2009 financial crisis.

The Romanian apparel retail market is dominated by foreign products and brands and also by foreign retailers. As in other developing countries, foreign retailers sell branded and modern fashions, whereas domestic ones sell more modest, traditional clothes.

One peculiarity of Romanian apparel retail is the lack of a Romanian internationally well-known brand. It is somewhat paradoxical that Romanian manufacturers and retailers have not managed to create brands because in Romania the textile and apparel industry is a leading export sector. Even after 2005, when exports in Romania started to decline due to the liberalization of foreign markets for China, textiles and apparel stayed among the top export sectors because exports were based on CMT activities, in which Romanian factories manufactured products from famous international brands, using foreign raw materials, design, marketing, and branding. Textiles are mainly imported to Romania, transformed into clothes products with higher value added, and re-exported. Third parties contract CMT production, then distribute the products under their brand. The textile sector as a whole is very dependent on the foreign trade (National Institute of Statistics, 2009). In the manufacturing industry, low personnel costs should somehow compensate for lower productivity levels. Textiles have the highest labor costs, followed by leather and apparel. Reliance on cheap labor costs has made Romania vulnerable to salary increases and to the recent trade liberalization (in 2005 and 2007), with countries competing on a low cost basis.

Artisan products are a distinctive niche in Romanian retail. They consist mainly of traditional Romanian clothing, worn for folk dancing and singing performances or for exhibitions. Other artisan products include home decorations, carpets, and dolls. Foreign consumers value their crafting by hand.

GETTING TO KNOW DOMESTIC COMPETITORS: LOCAL IS GOOD, TOO

The domestic fashion market increased by an average of 15 percent yearly from 2006 until its contraction of 35 percent in 2009, according to an estimation of the CEO of a fashion company. The internal apparel and textile market is not as extended as the export sector.

Among the most well-known big domestic apparel retail chains in Romania are Jolidon, I.D. Sarrieri, and Braincof. Both Jolidon and Sarrieri are producers of undergarments, well established in the Romanian market. Sarrieri is associated with luxury products, with more exquisite design and higher prices than Jolidon. Jolidon carries a line of men's underwear, whereas Sarrieri does not. Jolidon developed as a single brand, and I.D. Sarrieri has two: Sarrieri and Body Up. Perhaps one of the most important strengths of these two competitors is the fact that they are domestic in a country where consumers are pleased to buy trusted and fashionable products from their countrymen. Romanians equate both companies with good quality and, in the case of Jolidon, fair prices. It is one of the most well-known Romanian brands and has gained a following of loyal customers.

HOW MATURE IS THE RETAIL INDUSTRY?
FAR, FAR AWAY

The developing Romanian retail apparel market is far from reaching the point of maturity. Signs of an underdeveloped market are not only the prevalence of the traditional retail formats or the low level of competition, but also the structure of ownership (few shareholders).

The number of malls and shopping centers (around 80 in 2010) is estimated to grow, as numerous developers announced their plans to enter the market. Moreover, several projects were under construction and scheduled for completion in 2010/2011. There are several outlets on the market, but the concept is far from what it is supposed to mean—the discounts are symbolic and attract very few customers.

Since 2000, many well-known brands have entered the Romanian market, but some of the more important players have not. The sensitive point is the luxury segment, where just a handful of famous brands can be found and only in multibrand stores. Most international brands have entered the market through franchise, suggesting a higher comfort level with low-risk formats for expansion into Romania.

The number of local brands is small and constitutes a low percentage of market share. Most local producers work in the CMT system, and just a few sell directly on the Romanian market. Some national brands have expanded abroad, such as Jolidon, and of these some, such as Sarrieri, a luxury lingerie producer, have become well known.

Some Romanian companies have, in association with Romanian designers, opened stores in a different country. For example, Pascu & Pascu GBR, along with several Romanian producers and designers, have opened "original Ro," a store that sells Romanian items in Karlsruhe, Germany.

An interesting program is a contest designed to promote Romanian designers' creations in international markets. Organized by the International Center for Commerce (Geneva, Switzerland) and the Romanian Ministry for Small and Medium Enterprises, Commerce and Business Environment (FEPAIUS, 2009), "I did it my way" is a competition open to designers whose brands are at least four seasons old. Designers are invited to send videos, and the winners are reproduced on a DVD for distribution to the mass media and consumers via the Romanian embassies.

BUYING FOR APPAREL RETAIL STORES: DEPENDENT ON FOREIGN SUPPLIERS

Romania sources apparel and textiles from the world's leading exporters. The European Union supplies Romania with most of its textile and apparel products, with 67.45 percent of its imports coming from the EU. Within the EU countries, Romania sources most goods from Italy (33.87 percent) and France (8 percent) because of traditional economic relations among the countries and affinities, and similarities in consumer preferences. It will be difficult to assess whether this is the effect of trade diversion or to geographical proximity. Trade diversion is a concept used in international economics and trade, and it is opposed to trade creation. In general, trade creation means that a free trade area (FTA) creates trade that would not have existed otherwise. As a result, supply occurs from a more efficient producer of the product. In all cases trade creation will raise a country's national welfare. Trade diversion means that a free trade area diverts trade away from a more efficient supplier outside the FTA toward a less efficient supplier within the FTA. It is interesting that EU is the major supplier of Romania even after liberalization of the market in 2005, when imports from China were liberalized. Imports from China accounted for only approximately 18 percent of total imports, although China is a low-cost competitor for the EU products, as it is for Romania.

RETAIL CAREERS:
ATTRACTIVE CAREER PROSPECTS

In 2008, the demand for labor in apparel retail grew, although it registered a slight decrease in 2009. The year 2008 brought a fundamental change in the concept of retail: a more client-oriented approach. This approach means that there is a need for a more direct contact with the product for the consumers and also a more personalized treatment for them. This, in turn, modifies the buying impulse of the buyers, making them buy more. As a result, the retail area registered growth not only in customer service positions (especially cashiers) but also acquisitions.

The positions most in demand for apparel retail specialists are development director, buyer (purchaser), logistics specialist, internal auditor, and tax specialist. These people are hard to find, either because there are not so many in the market, or they would rather pursue careers in banks, consulting companies, or other environments they consider best for their professional development.

Unskilled workers in apparel retail, such as shop assistants and cashiers, earn between 140 and 420 euros monthly (approx.

$190 and $570 respectively), 369 ($500) being the net average salary in 2008 (National Institute of Statistics, 2009). Apparel retailers also offer positions in human resources, legal, security (at least in companies that do not outsource this service), logistics, managerial, and so on. The salary packages for purchasing managers (also known as buying managers or commercial managers) can vary between 1,500 and 2,500 euros ($2044 to $3407) a month, and is usually accompanied by a large package of benefits. Overall, retail salaries are growing, but without a corresponding relation to employees' productivity.

In the capital of the country, Bucharest, salary levels are the highest, and in small towns, rural areas, and the north of Moldavia (in eastern Romania) the lowest salaries are registered.

The retail sector as a whole saw an average personnel fluctuation of an estimated 10 percent, particularly among middle and top managers, in the last three years. More than 50,000 people work in retail chains, a figure comparable with that of doctors in Romania (about 48,000) or the equivalent of half of the personnel in the armed forces. Romania has the world-class Faculty of Textiles, Leather, and Industrial Management in Iai, in northeast Romania (http://www.tuiasi.ro/facultati/tex/), but needs more schools. University studies, which take three years, culminate in the Romanian system with a graduation license diploma (diploma that indicates that one has finished university studies) as they do throughout the European Union. Internships depend mainly on the policy of individual firms and availability. We can observe the emergence of companies that offer training courses for design, but which may or may not offer official (governmental) certification for these occupations. Multinationals have made internships common practice in Romania.

FUTURE OF APPAREL RETAIL: STILL OPEN FOR INVESTMENT

In Romania, textile and apparel retailing will have to adjust to the competitive forces of an open market. It has to pass gradually from the CMT system to develop its own design and marketing functions in order to have a more favorable position on the value chain and for businesses to benefit from their own brands. This implies that besides better training systems for designers and other personnel, it is important to strengthen the chains from the producer of raw material to the producer of final product.

For the perspective of foreign investors, conclusions are of two types. For the foreign investors already established in Romania, there is the benefit of the first movement that came when the market was lacking competition. Their major disadvantage was poor infrastructure and low purchasing power, now improved, but in any case, not comparable with that in other EU developed countries. For foreign investors still outside the Romanian market, there is room for their products because competition is still low.

Case Study 1

BRAICONF:
LOOKING TO THE GREENER PASTURES

Braiconf is Romania's largest producer of shirts and blouses. It both sells under its own brands (Braiconf, Sergio) and supplies for the major brands and fashion houses (Max Mara, Valentino, Versace, Armani, Kenzo). It is a Romanian company, established in 1950 as part of the communist regime's planned economy.

Romanian employees bought the company in 1996, through a privatization initiative called MEBO (Management and Employee Buyout). In 2010, 25.1 percent of the company was held by Bank Julius Baer, a Swiss private banking group, and the rest (74.89 percent) by small investors (Bucharest Stock Exchange, 2010).

COMPANY PERFORMANCE

The company's strategy, based mainly on exports, had deleterious effects on the company's performance over the years until 2000. At the start of the twenty-first century, this strategy brought success. Foreign clients, who were looking to outsource, were attracted by cheap Romanian labor, as well as the fact that Romania had already abolished trade barriers for commercial trade within the EU.

The company's performance was in line with market conditions—high turnover and high profits, until 2005. In that year the exchange rate changed dramatically; exports became expensive as the local currency started to strengthen. The effects were immediately visible on Braiconf's profits.

Moreover, international competition got tougher, as other countries became attractive for outsourcing (especially such Asian markets as China, Taiwan, and Bangladesh). Braiconf had not anticipated the shift in the currency evolution. The company's strategy, based mainly on exports, became distressful instead of successful.

NEW STRATEGY

Braiconf realized the need for a new strategy and turned to the internal market. The company launched three new collections in Romania, designed for women, and promoted them by means of special public relations events. It expanded its network of shops to 17 stores by the end of 2008 and expanded their products.

The new strategy did not generate the high profit rate the company had when it was focused on exports, but it allowed Braiconf to remain on the market, to recover the losses, and to consolidate its position on the local market. The company sets a good example of successfully using diversified strategies for diminishing risks.

Discussion Questions:

1. What are the advantages and the disadvantages of the CMT activity for a Romanian apparel company that is both producer and retailer?
2. What market strategy (CMT, export, focus on the internal market, entering the foreign markets, and so on) should this kind of company adopt to minimize financial risk?
3. Given the current economic trends (Romanian and international), what kind of strategy could maximize the company's profits and why?

Case Study 2

SECUIANA: FROM DUSTY TO STYLISH

Secuiana is the main producer of trousers in Romania. Founded in 1968, they specialize in producing trousers exclusively for men, through their Adam's brand.

The history of the company is somewhat similar to that of Braiconf. It was privatized through MEBO in 1992 and starting with that year it had a continuous development trend. Because it was focused on exports, the troubles in the production of CMT determined the company to pay increasing attention to the domestic market by developing a proper chain of stores, a circle of internal customers, brand awareness, and strengthening their brand's image. In 2009, Adam's products were sold through a network of 36 shops and five franchises. The company plans to expand in the next years with six to eight stores per year. In 2008, over 60 percent of turnover was made on the Romanian market and this percentage is still growing.

COMPANY'S STRATEGY

One of the main problems Secuiana faced after the fall of communism in 1989 was its own image, associated with old-fashioned, "dusty" products. Secuiana was a famous name during the communist period, but only due to the lack of competition on the domestic market—a small number of local producers (the retail was made through state-owned department stores) and close to zero foreign competitors, as their entrance on the Romanian market was blocked by the state. Moreover, most of the clients associated the "made in Romania" products with low quality, or at least lower quality than those produced abroad. (The perception still exists today for some of the customers.)

Therefore, Secuiana focused in the early years after the fall of communism on the foreign market, taking advantage of the high demand for outsourcing, the profitability of CMT activity, and of the exports due to the favorable exchange rate. All this time, the company learned not only how to design and produce stylish clothes, adapted to the demand, but also how to sell them and how to attract customers. The brand launched for the domestic market, Adam's, had nothing to do with the old Secuiana, and the clothes were not at all like the ones locally made. Even the brand name, Adam's, sounds foreign. The shops also looked as though they were owned by a foreign retailer—large spaces with modern arrangement and attractive showcases, and the concept used was more that of a shopping assistant than of a vendor.

Adam's targeted the medium- to high-income customers and those who demand a higher quality level. The production was adapted to small-volume products that required high complexity. Secuiana decided to change the structure of the workforce by increasing the focus on distribution, marketing, and services related to sales and in the detriment of the production sphere. This way, Secuiana became well known on the Romanian market for its modern, stylish clothes and shops.

Discussion Questions

1. Why can a "history" of over 20 years be a burden for a Romanian company?
2. How did the Romanian companies benefit from the CMT activity, aside from the financial component?
3. Which are some of the elements that can contribute to the success of a Romanian apparel retailer?

REFERENCES

Arthur D. Little (2008). Study for the World Bank. *Romania Competitiveness Project Sector Analysis: Light Industry.*

Adinolfi, R. (2009). The EU-27 Textile & Clothes Industry in the year 2008. *Presentation for the Euratex General Assembly.* Retrieved November 20, 2009, from www.euratex.org/system/files/.../Economic+Situation+2008_+Adinolfi_0.pdf

Bucharest Stock Exchange (2009). *Companies and securities,* Retrieved December 3, 2009, from http://bvb.ro/ListedCompanies/SecurityDetail.aspx?s=BRCR

Carrefour Romania (2009). *Press release.* Bucharest.

CB Richard Ellis (2009). Bucharest Retail Market View. *CB Richard Ellis Reports.*

Circulation Snapshot (2008, September 22). *Ziarul Financiar.* Retrieved November 20, 2009, from http://www.zf.ro/companii/retail/in-retailul-de-moda-romanii-au-prins-gustul-promotiilor-ca-in-occident-20-din-produse-se-vand-la-reduceri-3210532/

Delloitte (2009). *Delloite, X-2009. The Rebound?* Retrieved November 20, 2009, from http://www.deloitte.com/assets/DcomRomania/Local%20Assets/Documents/EN/CB/ro_CountryReportChristmas_111609.pdf

Emporio Armani and Zilli in Bucharest this year, Hermes and Burberry on the lookout (2010, March 17). Retrieved October 14, 2010, from http://www.romania-insider.com/emporio-armani-and-zilli-in-bucharest-this-year-hermes-and-burberry-on-the-lookout/#

Euromonitor (2008). Retailing in Romania. *Euromonitor International Report.*

FEPAIUS (2009). *Press Release.* Retrieved November 20, 2009, from http://www.fepaius.ro/citeste/38/+_I_DID_IT_MY_WAY_+_Concursul_Filmului_de_Moda_din_Romania_+_Prima_Editie_+_.html

GfK Romania (2009). Press release. *Modern trade covers 43% of the Romanian consumer goods market,* Retrieved November 20, 2009, from http://www.gfk-ro.com/public_relations/press/multiple_pg/004680/index.en.html.

Javorcik, B. S. & Yue, L. (2009). Global Retail Chains and Their Implications for Romania. *Working paper, Forum for research in Empirical International Trade,* 9, 20, 22.

Landesmann, M., Leitner, S., Stehrer, R. & Ward, T. (2009). Skills and Industrial Competitiveness. *Research Reports, 356,* 46.

Lascu, D. N., Manrai, L. & Manrai, A. (1996). Value Differences between Polish and Romanian Consumers: A caution against Using a Regiocentric Marketing Orientation in Eastern Europe. *Journal of International Consumer Marketing, 8–3,4,* 127–129.

National Bank of Romania (2009). Foreign Direct Investments in Romania—annual report 2008. *Periodical Publications.*

National Institute for Statistics (2009). Data Base Tempo Online.

Nicolae, M. (2007). Romanian Consumer Behavior. *Presentation for the School of International Business & Economics.* Retrieved November 20, 2009, from http://www.fem.uniag.sk/Elena.Horska/texty/ROMANIAN_CONSUMER_BEHAVIOUR.ppt#259,3,Introduction

Nielsen (2009). *Nielsen Global Consumer Confidence Report.* Retrieved November 20, 2009, from http://www.nielsen.com/

PMR Publications (2009). *Modern Retail Market in Bucharest, far from saturated.* Retrieved November 29, 2009, from http://www.ceeretail.com/76350/Modern_retail_market_in_Bucharest_far_from_saturated.shtml

PMR Publications (2009). *Romanian retail affected by global crisis, but the prospects remain bright.* Retrieved November 29, 2009, from http://www.pmrpublications.com/press_room/en_Romanian-retail-affected-by-global-crisis_-but-the-prospects-remain-bright.shtml

Romanian Agency for Foreign Investment (2009). *Investment Legal Framework.* Retrieved November 23, 2009, from http://www.arisinvest.ro/en/investment-legal-framework/

Romanian Government. (2008). *Emergency Ordinance no. 85 from June 24, 2008.* Retrieved November 23, 2009, from http://www.cdep.ro/proiecte/2008/600/00/3/oug603.pdf

CHINA

Laubie Li
Jun Ying Yu
Xin Liang Gu
Ai Tian Zhang
Chuanlan Liu
Jaya Halepete

4

OBJECTIVES

After reading this chapter, you will

- ▶ Understand why China is considered an emerging market
- ▶ Comprehend the unique characteristics of Chinese consumers
- ▶ Understand the market structure of Chinese markets
- ▶ Know the regulations for foreign direct investment

In just 30 short years, the world has witnessed the transformation of China from an underdeveloped, agriculture-based economy into a global manufacturing hub. The capacity of the People's Republic of China to cope with rapid change is astonishing. A powerful central government is said to be the reason for this communist nation's effective and systematic collateral transformations. The irony is that, in spite of a strong central government, there exists intense competition among provinces and cities. The competitive nature of the provincial or city relationships in turn has fostered a culture of competition at the firm level. Chinese firms are always prepared to compete with local and international competitors, which is reflected in a booming retailing industry that is riding on the wave of an expanding middle class.

Over the course of two millennia, China was home to many of the world's great emperors. Its transition to modernity was exceedingly difficult. In the nineteenth and early twentieth centuries, its people endured civil unrest, famines, and foreign occupations. After World War II, Mao Zedong's communist government imposed strict regulations on people's everyday lives, and millions died due to poor economic planning. Mao's regime ended with his death in 1976, and by 1978 Deng Xiaoping was at the helm. He and others leaders reset China's course toward market-oriented economic development. Living standards improved dramatically. For the first time, Chinese people congregated around the televisions and other modern conveniences that began to appear in their villages.

Since the 1980s, China has transformed from an economy that was largely closed to international trade to a more open market. It has the second-largest economy in the world in terms of gross domestic products (Barboza, 2010). China's rapid economic growth has had a great impact on the global economy. In 1978 Deng Xiaoping opened China to trade with the outside world, and since then the economy has grown tremendously. Between 1978 and 2007, the country's gross domestic product (GDP) grew at an average rate of 11.29 percent per year, an increase of 67 fold, outperforming any country in the world. China surpassed Germany as the world's third-largest economy in 2008, only behind the United States and Japan (Chuang, 2009).

China's population of 1.3 billion people excites and attracts many investors, as does their private savings rate of 50 percent of their GDP (Table 4.1). In March 2010, China's foreign exchange reserves exceeded $2.4 trillion. Despite overtaking Japan in August 2010 as the second-largest economy in the world, however, China's per capita income ranked 103 in the world, with a value of $3,687, as compared to $37,800 for Japan, according to World Bank data in 2009. In economic terms, China is not even a middle-income coun-

TABLE 4.1 Fast Facts about China

Capital	Beijing
Population	1.338 billion
Type of government	Communist state
GDP: purchasing power parity: in US$	$8.748 trillion
Age structure	0–14 yrs: 19.8%
	15–64 yrs: 72.1%
	65 yrs plus: 8.1%
Religion	Daoist (Taoist): 20–30%
	Buddhist: 18–20%
	Christian: 3–4%
	Muslim: 1–2%
	Nonreligious: 40–60%
Ethnicity	Han Chinese: 91.5%
	Zhuang, Manchu, Hui, Miao,
	Uighur, Tujia, Yi, Mongol,
	Tibetan, Buyi, Dong, Yao,
	Korean, and others: 8.5%

Source: CIAfactbook.gov

try. The income disparity and consumption power of the Chinese varies from class to class and from city to city, making a standardized national retailing strategy, including that for apparel, almost impossible to implement.

The appreciation of the Chinese yuan (Ren Min Bi, or RMB) and property prices since 2008 have induced people to consume more. Economists estimate that during 2006–2011, the disposable income of mainland Chinese (excluding Hong Kong and Macau, which are special administrative regions) will grow by 9.4 percent per year. Assuming this level of economic performance continues, China will become the largest economy in the world by 2030

(Chuang, 2009). The Communist Party's Eleventh Five-Year Plan (an economic development initiative with a different agenda for each five-year period), adopted in 2006, called for economic growth to be driven by domestic demand, rather than on international investments and trade as it was in the first decade of the century. The Party has put in place policies that support this plan, including the speeding up of urbanization by increases in infrastructure, transport, and housing investment; improving the medical and social security system; increasing education subsidies; reducing agricultural taxes; improving agricultural infrastructure; setting urban minimum income levels; and lowering tax breaks.

Manufacturing has been the hottest sector in the Chinese market since it opened to world trade in 1978. At the same time, free market retailing became legal for the first time since 1949, and China's retail sector took off. In 1992, the government's deregulation of retailing and opening of the local retailing market to foreign companies, on a trial basis, induced further penetration by foreign apparel retailers in the country (Au, 2000). The number of retail outlets, including those with foreign ownership, increased substantially during the 1990s. Different formats of retail outlets emerged, and competition in the apparel retailing market became much more intense (Kwan, Yeung and Au, 2003).

THE RETAIL LANDSCAPE:
A LUCRATIVE MARKET FOR INVESTMENT

Retail sales in China grew by 16.9 percent in 2009 and by 18.2 percent in the first five months of 2010. Recovering consumer confidence is improving retail sales, thereby keeping China a very lucrative market for further investments. In 2009, the Chinese apparel retail industry was forecast to have a sales value of $106.2 billion (RMB 725 billion) by 2013, an increase of 25 percent over 2008 (Datamonitor, 2009).

China's apparel market is the third largest in the world, with 17 percent of earnings coming from organized retail. An average consumer spends $45 to $90 on apparel a month, which is considered very low in comparison to other developing countries. With an increase in middle-class consumers in urban areas, the spending on apparel is expected to increase. There is a trend of increased spending on clothing among Chinese consumers. The growing affluence of middle-class China has created an increased interest in foreign brands rather than higher preference for domestic products, thereby intensifying competition.

China's clothing retail sales are through a diverse mix of exclusive stores, franchises, and Internet sales channels. Shopping malls and supermarkets account for most sales, although the sales volume of new clothing retail channels continues to grow.

China's apparel market has become increasingly attractive to foreign retailers due to the growing number of consumers keen on high-quality foreign brand apparel (Zhao, 2003). The potential of the Chinese market is even greater since China joined the World Trade Organization in December of 2001, granting foreign companies easier access to its 1.3 billion consumers (Hainan News Net, 2003).

CONSUMERS: IMPROVING QUALITY OF LIFE

As economic conditions in China continue to improve, consumption of textile, apparel, and beauty products increases correspondingly. Understanding Chinese consumers helps foreign investors to provide them with the right product mix. As quality of life improves among Chinese consumers as a whole, their expenditure on apparel is on the rise.

Consumers of apparel and beauty products today tend to be in their twenties and thirties. Although younger consumers are more sensitive to price than older consumers, younger consumers do purchase high-end clothing, brand-name beauty products, or even luxury items. In addition to an improved material life, the Internet has helped to lower the consumer's age. Chinese consumers in the 25–45 years age range are more likely to do non-shop shopping than those who are in their fifties.

Since the 2000s, quality has become a more important factor, which is affecting the purchasing behavior of Chinese consumers. A large number of people prefer to buy clothing made in France, Italy, or the United States instead of locally, and they want to buy products with foreign brand names. Consumers prefer foreign brands not only because they like the quality and styles but also because the lifestyle indicated by the labeled country of origin appeals to them. Therefore, the influence of country of origin or brand is significant.

The consumption of garments and beauty products via multiple channels is becoming popular. Consumers choose traditional retailers when they need to buy social or work clothes, but also buy basics, fad, and fast fashion from non-shop retailers for convenience, wide selection, and low prices.

Some unique features of Chinese consumers that a foreign retailer needs to know in order to cater to them are:

- The middle class, which will be the main customer group in the 2010s and 2020s, is becoming highly brand conscious.
- Chinese consumers are showing greater interest in casual wear. They are increasingly aware of fitness, and casual clothing aids in leading the active lifestyle associated with being fit. Many Chinese offices have also changed their dress code to "smart casual," increasing the demand for this category of clothing.
- Consumers are looking for trendy clothing that is fashion forward. As in many developed nations, apparel sold in China has a short life cycle.
- Function (such as protection from the environment) is becoming as important as factors like color and comfort to Chinese consumers. Chinese consumers consider innovative fabrics in their apparel purchase decisions (anti-perspirant finish on fabrics for running clothes).
- Chinese consumers give higher preference to comfort than fashion.

- More and more Chinese consumers want to express individuality. They like their clothing to express their status, taste, and sense of fashion.
- Chinese consumers display an increased interest in richer and sharper colors to differentiate themselves from others.

WOMEN

Retailers interested in investing in China need to understand the emotional and rational behavior of Chinese women and cater to their needs to be successful in the market (Silverstein & Sayre, 2009). In general, Chinese women are optimistic and enthusiastic about their personal lives, communities, and the world. China's one-child policy, implemented in 1979, has allowed these women an opportunity to pursue higher education and to do well in life. Nevertheless, Chinese women have learned from their parents how to live frugally. They do not like to spend too much money on shopping, take loans, or spend on unnecessary purchases. They prefer to invest and save their money. However, the savings pattern is changing, with women spending a bigger portion of their salaries than before. Almost 78 percent of married women make grocery and apparel purchases for the family and 65 percent of women spend 60 percent of their salary (The rise of female consumerism, 2007).

Chinese women like to spend on products that lessen their workloads and free up their time. They are also unsatisfied with the type of lingerie available in the market and are willing to spend more on it. The purchasing power of Chinese women is on the rise, with highly educated women earning and spending more and empty nesters having more disposable income than before.

MEN

"A total of 80 percent of wealthy male Chinese consumers are aged between 18 and 44, have an annual household income of more than 250,000 yuan ($37,550), are well educated and are open to the acquisition of luxury products," says Kunal Sinha, Regional Cultural Insights Director for Ogilvy & Mather's Asia Pacific office (Yip & Chang, 2010).

Chinese men spend money to splurge as well as to express their masculinity. Spending money is also another way for Chinese men to display power. They do not like shopping around for deals, are repeat purchasers, and stick to brands that they like. Hence, it is important for retailers to build a brand image. Chinese men are also very quality conscious and look at every aspect of a garment from fabric to craftsmanship. Men also like to mix and match pieces, which has encouraged the growth of the accessories market (Performance of China's, 2006). Menswear in China is an untapped market, hence a very important market for retailers to focus on.

CHILDREN

China has the largest population of children in the world, which makes them an important customer base for retailers to target. Chinese children also have higher economic power than children in other developing economies and as only children (due to the government's one child per couple policy) have a unique influence on their parents and grandparents (Cheng 1993, Shao & Herbig, 1994). They have more discretionary income than children of any other country (McNeal & Yeh, 2003).

BEAUTY INDUSTRY IN CHINA

After tourism, automobiles, and real estate, beauty is the fourth-largest industry in China. Skincare products are the most popular beauty product sold in China, accounting for almost 71 percent of the total sales in this category, followed by makeup and fragrances. Anti-aging and skin-whitening products make skincare the most popular category. It is very different from the American beauty industry, in which skincare products represent only one third of sales. The aging

Chinese population is ready to spend extra money on anti-aging skin-care products, so high-end brands do well in China.

Historically, Chinese women have not worn makeup, and so they are not well educated regarding its usage. With growing Western influence, Chinese women are showing greater interest in learning how to wear makeup. Makeup, although not an important category at the beginning of the century, is picking up and is expected to become an important category in the 2010s. Cosmetic surgery is fairly common among Chinese women. The most common procedures are making the eyes rounder, narrowing the nose, and lengthening the legs.

Chinese men have also started taking a greater interest in their appearance. They understand that good looks will help them

▲ FIGURE 4.1 L'Oreal SA brand men's cosmetic creams and lotions displayed for sale at a supermarket in Shanghai, China. Sales of men's health and beauty merchandise in China are set to overtake North America in 2010 and will probably grow about five times faster until 2014, according to data from Euromonitor International. Bloomberg via Getty Images.

in various aspects of their lives and have started spending on skincare products. Although skincare is the best-selling category among all the beauty products for men, products for hair and overall grooming are expected to become popular in the next decade.

Beauty retailers focus on traditional services such as whitening, breast enlargement, weight loss, hair dyeing, and hairdressing. The women's beauty market is already intensely competitive. As for the men's beauty market, demands are expected to increase with developing interest in beauty and nutrition. With the Chinese economy growing at a fast pace, the beauty industry is expected to continue to grow.

LUXURY RETAIL IN CHINA

China is the world's second-largest luxury goods market, after Japan, with consumers spending between $5 and $6 billion. Luxury consumption is growing rapidly in China's main cities such as Beijing and Shanghai in which the income level is relatively higher than median. Even during the world financial crisis of 2008 and 2009, luxury consumption in China grew at an amazing speed. In China, a high consumption rate does not equal a mature consumption culture. Quite a lot of consumers in China do not understand the connotation of "luxury" well; for example, most Chinese consumers cannot tell if "Ralph Lauren" is a luxury brand or casual and sportswear. The driving force behind conspicuous consumption and the associated success of Western brands may have its roots in a desire among some parts of the Chinese population to emulate successful Western cultures by buying luxury products (Dickson et al., 2004).

Improving income levels and advertising promote China's luxury consumption. The one-child generation is highly individualistic and self-indulgent. They like to set themselves apart by purchasing and using luxury goods. The urban Chinese consumers are very brand-conscious and like to wear luxury products with large visible logos (Seckler, 2009). This generation also has parents who have been saving money and grandparents who dote on them with expensive gifts. Almost 75 percent of the luxury product consumers in China are under 40, much younger than those in the United States and Europe. Lower food prices give Chinese consumers more disposable income than Westerners.

Statistics are not available to show how apparel features in the overall sales of luxury goods in China; however, almost every luxury apparel brand has outlets in China. For example, in Plaza 66, one of Shanghai's most popular shopping malls, 80.4 percent of merchandise sold comprises world-famous brands, such as Chanel, Dior, Louis Vuitton, and Escada.

APPAREL RETAIL FORMATS: BEING REVOLUTIONIZED BY MODERN FORMATS

Most foreign apparel manufacturers need to use China's existing distribution channels to access the domestic market. The structure of distribution channels in China, particularly the channels for foreign brand apparel products, is different from those in free markets like the United States and other developed countries. Foreign retailers are constrained by the Chinese government in many different ways, such as slow implementation of regulations. Collaboration with Chinese companies within Chinese borders for manufacturing as well as retailing is usually recommended as the best way for a foreign retailer to be successful in China (Zhang et al., 2002).

Multiple retail formats, such as big department stores, exclusive stores, mail order, discount stores, warehouse stores, and shopping centers, co-exist in China. The success of a retail format depends partly on region. Apparel companies are experimenting with different approaches to selling and marketing their products. New retail formats are leading a quiet revolution.

Department stores have the largest share of clothing retail sales because such store formats sell high-end and middle-high-end apparel merchandise to consumers who have higher incomes than most Chinese consumers. Chain stores tend to concentrate on middle-high and middle-end clothing. General merchandise stores, warehouse stores, and supermarkets are popular outlets for middle- and low-end clothing. They form the fastest-developing retail sector, due to lower operating costs. Convenience and price advantage have made online, telephone, mail order, and other nonstore sales another integral part of China's retail formats. Wholesale and retail outlets operated by garment manufacturers or low-end suppliers from the cities primarily service the rural markets.

TRADITIONAL FORMATS

Open-air markets and street stores pre-date modern formats in China and continue to be popular.

▶ Open-Air Markets

Open-air markets can be found along major commercial streets, around major trade centers, or in shopping centers. Open public places or parts of major streets convert to open-air markets at specific times of day, some of which are seasonal. There are morning and evening open-air markets. Morning open-air markets usually start around 6 a.m. and finish by 9 a.m., attracting people who participate in morning exercises (which many Chinese do in large groups) and then shop early for the day's groceries. Such open-air markets are restricted to neighborhood residents. Vendors sell basic apparel merchandise at low prices at such markets. Evening open-air markets usually start after regular office hours, and close around midnight or even later depending on whether there are still customers around. There are many booths selling produce, meat, spices, canned goods, clothing, and hardware. Open-air markets are good places to find last season's or contractor's over-run clothes at discount prices. Besides local consumers, they also attract tourists.

▶ Street Stores

Urban and small-town consumers alike shop in street stores, which may be present on any street. They sell many different categories of

▲ **FIGURE 4.2** A customer inspects a multicolored umbrella at an open-air market in Beijing, China. The Asian Development Bank urged China to step up efforts to boost domestic consumption as a means of steering the nation away from its heavy dependence on exports and investment. AFP/Getty Images.

products, but mainly grocery or other convenience items. Most stores are part of renovated residential apartments. Owners of these ground-floor apartments renovate their apartments to be street stores, and either run the stores themselves or rent them out for others to run. Sometimes a street store is just a window on the side of a building. Some street vendors sell clothing or other products from small temporary stalls or stands. Apparel is mainly sold through stores lined along the streets.

MODERN FORMATS

Modern retail formats such as department stores, supermarkets, convenience stores, and warehouses are emerging and becoming popular in China.

▲ **FIGURE 4.3** Street side store, Beijing. This is a popular retail format in China where the first floors of many apartment complexes are renovated and converted into shops. These may be temporary stalls or become well-established stores. Photo by Mukesh Gajra.

▶ Department Stores

From the Chinese consumer's perspective, shopping at department stores means buying high-quality products (Zhu, 2008). Large department stores are popular venues for shopping in China. Urban residents normally do not have large living spaces. They like to shop in department stores as a leisure activity or a brief break from home when it's too crowded. In China, department stores sell general merchandise including both soft lines such as apparel and hard lines such as furniture. Some department stores even include supermarket selling groceries. Most department stores allocate a large space for selling apparel merchandise. Apparel merchandise retail sales through department stores seem to be the main contributor to total apparel sales, accounting for 30 to 40 percent of total store sales.

Department stores are ideal outlets for famous fashion brands, geared to customers who are looking for high-quality products. Foreign-owned department stores in China usually possess a good image and marketing experience, and are, therefore, popular product outlets for apparel companies. Department stores that originate from Asian countries, such as the Japanese Yohan, Isetan, and Seiyu, the Malaysian Parkson, and the Taiwanese Pacific, are good examples, as is the French Printemps. Printemps has claimed the consumer base of luxury goods in China by opening an up-market version of its international department store format. However, in order to adapt to local supply conditions, it deviates from its normal practice and in China it relies on licensees operating their own areas in the stores.

For department stores, the main revenue comes from "joint operation," which means that department stores provide premises to brand agents to set up and operate counters or showrooms, while collecting payments through the storewide cash register. Joint operation constitutes 80 to 90 percent of total department store sales. Sales generated directly from other divisions of department stores are secondary to joint operation. In addition, department stores work with vendors on consignment (where a retailer pays the vendor only after the goods are sold and can return unsold merchandise) and on general sale (where a retailer pays the vendor before the merchandise is sold, based on payment terms agreed upon by both).

▶Supermarkets, Convenience Stores, and Warehouses (Membership Clubs)

Supermarket-style outlets have a much shorter history than department stores in China. The first supermarket or "free-to-choose market" in China was established in 1981 at the Guangdong Friendship Store in Guangzhou. When China started "open-door" reform, the coastal province of Guangdong, home to one of the world's major ports, as well as the country's most populous and prosperous province, was the guinea pig for testing a market

▲ **FIGURE 4.4** Dongang Department Store, Beijing, China. The department store opened in Beijing in 1998, reputed to be the largest shopping mall in Asia. It is Beijing's most modern shopping plaza with 14 levels, 60 escalators, 40 passenger elevators, and five glass-sided sightseeing elevators. © OJPHOTOS/Alamy.

economy. The initial supermarket took only foreign exchange certificates; therefore, normal local residents could not shop at supermarkets. The first renminbi-based supermarket was subsequently opened in 1982, also in Guangzhou, and others began to appear in Beijing, Hangzhou, Shanghai, and other parts of China. Nearly all of the supermarkets in those days were operated as subsections of local department stores. The success of the trial in Guangdong province laid the foundation for free market retailing in the world's most populous country. Apparel sales in China as a result have been a direct beneficiary of this development.

In China, supermarket-style outlets can be divided into three groups according to size. Each group has specific market positioning when it comes to apparel sales. Large-scale comprehensive supermarkets sell low-grade underwear, shoes, coats, and other essentials. They are price-driven markets for consumers with little concern for brands. Good examples of such comprehensive supermarkets include French-based Carrefour, American-based Wal-mart and Sam's Club, Germany's Metro Cash & Carry, and the Dutch company Makro. However, it is worth noting that exclusive brand outlets selling apparel merchandise are joining this group of supermarket stores. The second group of supermarket-style outlet stores is medium-sized domestic supermarkets, such as Lianhua and Nonggongshang, Hualian-Lawson, and Kedi, which are mainly franchised convenience stores selling a very limited stock of cheap apparel, such as socks, underwear, and pajamas. The third group of supermarkets is warehouse clubs or membership clubs. They are usually small in size and specialize in specific types or styles of apparel, such as sports or casual.

▶ Specialty Stores, Company-Owned and Franchised Chain Outlets

Many Chinese garment companies have replicated European formats directly. Company-owned chain stores and franchises are common in China. Chinese firms have also picked up the vertical integration concept developed by the Spanish fashion brand Zara. For instance, YiShion, the well-known casual wear brand, is operated as a vertical integrated apparel business. YiShion's parent company started as a manufacturer, taking contract orders from foreign manufacturers or retailers. In 1997, the company launched its own brand YiShion to be in charge of the whole market chain to increase its profitability.

The Hong Kong–based Giordano operates a large chain of small apparel stores in the former colony. In China it has developed a new store concept. Its stores are much bigger, offering more varied assortments of apparel merchandise. In addition, whereas it owns its Hong Kong stores, its Chinese stores are operated by franchisees. The new format has become the base for its Asian expansion.

Stores that specialize in casual wear are very popular in China. This format was initially introduced to mainland China by Hong Kong–based retailers. The first groups of specialty store retailers opening stores in first-tier cities such as Guangzhou, Shanghai, and Beijing included Giordano, Bossini, and Jeans West.

A few years later, Chinese domestic entrepreneurs established their own brands and opened stores across other cities. Specialty stores are mainly privately owned and located in major commercial streets or inside department stores, shopping malls, or shopping plazas. Most specialty store retailers use franchising to expand their market and earn more market share. In addition, both domestic and foreign specialty stores sell online.

▶Fashion Boutiques

Fashion boutiques specialize in selling higher-priced items in small quantities. Since 1990 high-end fashion boutiques have become increasingly popular in major cities. Boutiques are mainly located on major commercial streets in first-tier cities such as Beijing, Shanghai, and Guangzhou. Boutiques are all privately owned businesses. Domestic fashion boutique retailers are increasingly investing in developing and promoting brand names to differentiate themselves from competitors.

▶Designer Stores

In the early 1980s, French designer Pierre Cardin introduced the **designer store**—the format of a store carrying products of one single well-known brand to China (Mitchell, 2002). Several years later, many well-known international labels, including luxury brands, started entering the Chinese market. Louis Vuitton opened its first store in a Beijing hotel in 1992. With increasing sales of foreign luxury goods in China, many luxury brands have opened stores in China. Giorgio Armani, Chanel, Givenchy, Bentley, Hermès, Maserati, Kenzo, and many other clothing designers all have boutiques in China ("Louis Vuitton opens Beijing flagship store," 2005).

▶Hypermarkets

French retailer Carrefour introduced the format of hypermarkets, which has been well received by Chinese consumers. Since 1995, Carrefour has kept the lead position among foreign retail companies in China. In 2010 it operated 156 stores in 45 major cities of the Chinese mainland, with over 50,000 employees. Hypermarkets are

▲ **FIGURE 4.5** Office workers walking past an advertisement for Emporio Armani brand. Luxury products are most popular among younger consumers who are only children (due to China's "one child" policy) and have higher disposable income. AFP/Getty Images/LIU JIN.

taking hold in China thanks to the lure of low prices, convenient one-stop shopping, accessible locations, and the integration of other retail facilities such as restaurants, cinemas, and coffee-houses that can turn a shopping trip into a day out. Among the companies, leading this industry growth are Walmart/Trust-Mart (US), Carrefour (France), Tesco (UK), and RT-Mart (Taiwan). Domestic retailers adopted this format very quickly. In 2010, the largest hypermarket retailer in China was Shanghai-based Lian-hua Supermarket Holdings Co. Ltd. Hypermarkets are privately owned or public corporate ("Hypermarket culture booms in China", 2010). In China, supermarkets mainly sell low-price and basic apparel products. The majority of hypermarket shoppers buy necessities, except for clothes. Even though all hypermarkets have a clothing department, product assortments are mainly the basics, therefore not very attractive to customers who are looking for fashion merchandise. In addition, Chinese consumers are not used to buying apparel products from hypermarkets or supermarkets ("Hypermarket apparel sales are struggling," 2004).

▶Manufacturers Outlet

The joint-venture retailer, Yansha department store, opened its first manufacturer's outlet in China, Yansha Outlet, in Beijing in 2002. Yansha Outlets feature over 200 brands like Versace, Prada, and CK, and they offer mostly new but off-season products. Urban Chinese who prefer brand products have embraced this format. Chinese consumers favor outlets because they offer authentic brands and products, discount prices, easy accessibility, and convenient parking. Outlets are only located in major cities, such as Beijing, Shanghai, and Chongqing, and provincial capitals such as Hangzhou, Suzhou, Harbin, and Hefei.

▶Apparel Wholesale Market

The **apparel wholesale market** format is a hybrid retail format combining the functions of manufacturer's showroom, wholesaler, and retailer. Such markets are located at commercial sites with low rent. Wholesale-market customers include retailers and individual consumers. Wholesale markets carry a wide range of different categories of apparel merchandise, including high-end, moderate price, and low-end products. Vendors from all over the country not only sell products to retail buyers and individual consumers but also take production orders and look for franchisees to expand their businesses. Many foreign retailers' Chinese contractors sell their overrun or returned merchandise in wholesale markets. Chinese consumers, especially middle- or lower-class consumers, favor this retail format. They can find the latest styles at relatively low prices through bargaining or buying more items. For instance, Qipu Lu Wholesale market is the largest wholesale market in Shanghai. The market is actually a cluster of small vendors offering the latest styles of all categories of apparel products at low prices. Both retail buyers and consumers can buy merchandise at wholesale prices based on the amount of purchase. Retail buyers and consumers negotiate with vendors. Such markets attract the most apparel shoppers not only from local areas but also visitors.

►Secondhand Luxury Brand Boutique

Retailers started selling secondhand apparel products in the late 1980s. By 2010 many boutique stores selling secondhand luxury brands saw increasing sales. **Secondhand luxury brand boutiques** target savvy consumers who desire luxury brands but cannot afford or are not willing to pay full price. Such retailers obtain inventory by buying from different distribution channels.

▲ **FIGURE 4.6** Apparel wholesale market format located in Qipu Lu, Shanghai. It is a Chinese-style retail format, a hybrid retail format combining functions of manufacturer showroom, wholesale, and retail. Such markets are located at commercial sites with a low rent. Wholesale markets have retail buyers and consumers as customers. These markets carry a wide range of categories of apparel merchandise, including high-end, moderate price, and low-end products. Photo by Mukesh Gajra.

They also sell products for individuals on commission. Sometimes celebrities send their used luxury items to secondhand luxury brand boutique stores. Retailers carefully select every item based on brand, style, and quality. All the used items have to be in good condition. The prices are set by owners and are priced at 40 percent to 60 percent of original prices. The normal commission rate is 15 to 20 percent of sales. If the item cannot be sold, owners pay 5 percent of the prices as a display fee. Some celebrities even open such stores to sell not only their own used items, but also second-hand luxury items collected from their social network. The normal commission rate is 15 percent of sales.

▶Online Retail

Online retailing has developed rapidly in China. According to China Internet Network Information Center (CNNIC) reports, in the first

▲ **FIGURE 4.7** Secondhand luxury boutiques have become very popular in China among the people who want to own high-end brands but cannot afford them. The products sold in these stores are obtained through various distribution channels such as celebrities. AFP/Getty Images/ SAMANTHA SIN.

six months of 2009, over 100 billion purchases took place online. CNNIC reports estimated that annual Internet purchases would reach RMB 2,500 billion (USD 374 billion) by the end of 2009, of which 61.5 percent were for online purchases of clothing and home accessories, an increase of 12.6 percent compared with the previous year. Jonathan Lu, president of Taobao, a popular Chinese online auction site, says, "We are excited about the prospect of growing China's online fashion market through a partnership with world-leading casual wear brand UNIQLO. UNIQLO's decision to join the lineup of global companies already operating online stores on Taobao underscores the continued growing strength of online retailing in China, as nearly 100 million people have elected to purchase goods, such as apparel, via the Internet rather than through traditional brick-and-mortar retail."

STORE OWNERSHIP: CONSOLIDATION AND INVESTMENT PHASE

Given the difficulty in separating apparel retailing from general retailing in China, any discussion of ownership of apparel enterprises has to spring from ownership in the retail industry.

DOMESTIC ENTERPRISES

To modernize China's retail industry in response to foreign competition, large domestic retailers (especially those located in the same cities) have consolidated among themselves or taken over small operators to form retail chains. These actions have received strong support from the Chinese government as a means to promote the development of indigenous retail chains. Both Lianhua (United China) and Hualian (China United), the two largest retail chains in China, have pursued this growth approach by providing management to franchised stores and supplying merchandise thereto through their corporate distribution networks. To fend off foreign competition, two of Beijing's largest retailers—Wangfujing

Co. Ltd. and Dong'an Group—merged in 2000 to form the capital's first super-retailing group, Beijing Wangfujing-Dong'an Group Co. Ltd. (China Economic Review, 2000; Fang, 2006).

Retailers originating from Hong Kong, Macao, and Taiwan have mainly invested in exclusive or franchised specialty stores, which require low investment and, hence, involve low risks. Examples are Jeans West, Giordano, Crocodile, and Goldlion, all of which are owned by Hong Kong interests. With their familiarity with the social environment in China and knowledge of the local culture and cost-effective ways of operating in China, these enterprises have made big investments in department stores and supermarkets.

FDI REGULATIONS: OPEN WITH DEEP COMMITMENT

China's retail sector totally opened up to foreign direct investment in December 2004. With these new regulations, foreign retailers do not have restrictions on the number of stores or their locations in China.

When China joined the World Trade Organization (WTO) in 2001, the Chinese government began to lift restrictions on foreign direct investment gradually, and this greater level of liberalization has enabled international retailers to pursue expansion in China. In turn, these retailers have strongly influenced modern retailing techniques and have introduced new formats into the Chinese market. At the same time, China experienced a series of economic and distribution reforms, including reducing the degree of government protection to domestic retailers, and domestic retailers found themselves forced to compete with foreign retailers. By 2006, the distribution sector opened up further. Most strikingly, China has agreed to open up the entire market of logistical chain and related services to foreign enterprises, including inventory management; assembly, sorting, and grading of bulk lots; breaking bulk lots and redistributing into smaller lots; delivery services; refriger-ation, storage, warehousing, and garage services; sales promotion, marketing, and advertising; and installation and after services including maintenance and repair and training service. No other WTO member has made such deep commitments in this sector (Mattoo, 2003).

INTERNATIONAL BRANDS: PROVIDING RESPITE FROM DAY-TO-DAY WAY OF LIVING

Foreign retailers in China do business in a variety of formats. Those from Asian countries have mostly adopted a department store for-mat, which provides the much-needed psychological escape from crowded living conditions in China. The Japanese Yohan, Jusco, Sogo, Isetan, and Seiyu, and the Malaysian Parkson are good exam-ples. European and North American retailers came after these Asian retailers and introduced hypermarkets (Carrefour), cash-and-carry warehouse retail stores (Metro, Makro, Ikea), discount department stores (Walmart), and membership clubs (Sam's Club, Pricesmart, Metro, and Makro), all of which also provide a respite from cramped housing (Dawson, et al., 2003).

INFLUENCES ON APPAREL RETAILING: A NEW GENERATION AND A NEW WAY OF LIFE

The retail industry in China has some unique features that one must understand to be successful in this country. Culture, technol-ogy, fashion, apparel exhibitions, and fashion magazines are the major factors that influence apparel retailing in China.

CULTURAL INFLUENCES

As people around the world worried about the financial crisis and its economic effects, luxury consumption in China reached new heights, thanks to the government policy to boost domestic consumption. A March 2009 *New York Times* article declared China the world's fastest-growing luxury consumption market. It is hard for many people to understand how a developing country has become the world's second-largest luxury consumption market. It's cultural. The prosperity of China's market economy has brought dramatic changes in urban consumers. For one thing, they have become more eager to "keep up with the Joneses." The new generation is tempering traditional attitudes about consumption. "The philosophy is 'enjoy life today' against the old Chinese custom of saving, saving, saving," notes Lawrence Lau, management controlling director of L'Oreal, China. New ways and old together constitute the unique Chinese apparel consumption concept. Consumers choose particular products or brands not only for function or performance but also as expressions of specific personality and social status.

Chinese consumers regard "face" (*mianzi*) highly. They transmit social status through dress. Luxury products are a way to strengthen one's identification with a high class, which is attractive to Chinese consumers. The rich use luxury to express themselves and the rest use whatever luxury they can afford to give the appearance of wealth.

TECHNOLOGICAL FACTORS

The Chinese government has realized the importance of advancing its technology for economic development. Although information technology has not been widely applied in China's brick-and-mortar retail market, some apparel retailers have adopted systems such as online electronic cash registers (ECRs), electronic point of sales (EPOS), cash-free payments, and electronic security. Foreign retailers can use their sophisticated technology in China to gain an upper hand in this area.

FASHION INFLUENCES

The influences of fashion on apparel retailing are huge. The mass media has emerged as one of the most powerful forces shaping consumer attitudes in China. Consumers acquire information about fashion through many channels, such as fashion exhibitions, fashion shows, and fashion magazines. Movie stars or celebrities are often featured in the advertisements of domestic brands. Regarded as fashion innovators, consumers look to them for correct ways to wear apparel. Understanding and catering to this group of consumers can increase the rate of adoption of a particular fashion style and thereby increase sales (Muzinich et al., 2003).

APPAREL EXHIBITIONS

Apparel and fashion shows and fairs have significant influence on fashion trends. Since 2000, more and more international apparel and fashion shows have been held in China, significantly broadening the perspectives of Chinese consumers. Shanghai is gaining a reputation as a global fashion center, and a fair share of China's television programming consists of local models striding down catwalks. The Annual China Fashion Awards organized by trendy Shanghai broadcaster Channel Young is starting to gain international clout. But not all broadcasts are up to global standards. Shanghai has plans to develop its fashion business and aims to join the ranks of Paris, New York, and Milan. To achieve that goal, Shanghai must improve its ability to host international fashion exhibitions and communicate effectively.

FASHION MAGAZINES

Fashion magazines are important channels through which fashion information is transmitted to the public. Since *Vogue* hit Chinese newsstands in 2005, a lot of other high-end fashion magazines, such as *Cosmopolitan* and *Elle*, have arrived. The Chinese fashion

▲ FIGURE 4.8 Guo Pei's Thousand and Two Nights collection at a fashion show in National Stadium during China Fashion Week, Spring/Summer 2010. Shanghai is becoming one of the fashion capitals of the world, and the Chinese fashion shows are becoming popular all over the world. Getty Images/Victor Fraile.

magazine market has become highly competitive, which is very good for spreading fashion information.

GETTING TO KNOW DOMESTIC COMPETITORS: GEARING UP FOR COMPETITION

The major competition for foreign investors in China's retail market are domestic privately owned companies, other wholly owned foreign companies, and state-owned enterprises. Bailian Group, a state-owned retail company, is the second-largest retailer in China. The parent company of this group operates department stores, grocery stores, hypermarkets, and convenience stores. The company has adopted foreign retail formats and hires managers from foreign competitors in order to remain competitive. Such state-owned retailers have been catering to Chinese consumers since long before foreign competitors entered the market, which strengthens their position.

METERSBONWE

Metersbonwe is one of several successful domestic apparel brands that may be major competition for foreign retailers entering the Chinese market. As a domestic casual clothing brand that responds to market changes with innovative approaches, Metersbonwe saw an enormously successful first decade in the new century. Positioning itself as a "young and energetic" purveyor of casual wear, the company has established itself as the top domestic brand with a target market of young consumers from 18 to 25 years old, mostly high school and college students. It offers fashionable products at affordable prices. Among its many pioneering moves, the most important has been the adoption of a franchising business model. Metersbonwe strategically focuses on design, marketing, and distribution, and outsources manufacturing and most of its retail sales through franchising. During the first five years after its establishment in 1995, they expanded gradually, growing by

▲ FIGURE 4.9 Metersbonwe is the highest-earning store for casual clothing in China. The retailer has used franchise outlets for expansion and has been strengthening the brand's image to effectively respond to the increased level of competition from many new entrants in the casual wear sector. © TAO Images Limited/Alamy.

approximately 50 franchising stores annually. By 2009, according to its official website, Metersbonwe had more than 3,000 stores in China. Among all the stores, around 87 percent were franchising stores. Its annual sales reached 7 billion (RMB) ($1.05 billion). Metersbonwe owns the largest market share of casual apparel in China (Metersbonwe.com).

After the first five years, several domestic brands started duplicating Metersbonwe's success by using its business model, benchmarking its marketing strategy as well as positioning their brands to compete in the same target market. At the same time, foreign brands such as Zara and H&M have been competing for this corner of the Chinese apparel market. Under attack on two fronts, Metersbonwe has taken a series of actions to strengthen its brand and market competitiveness.

Metersbonwe has been focusing on distribution channel development. The franchising business model helped the retailer in two ways. Using franchising to expand its market saved the cost of opening new stores. Metersbonwe supplies the products, and franchises keep 25 percent of sales. All the franchisees work hard to increase sales, helping this retailer to develop and maintain market share. In addition, outsourced manufacturing has saved them money.

SEMIR GROUP

Established in 1996, Semir group is another successful private apparel business in China. The retailer targets young consumers, including middle school, high school, and college students. Semir also focuses on developing its distribution channel through franchising. The group has around 130 manufacturers as its suppliers or vendors. Semir focuses its resources on product development, quality control, and distribution channel expansion. The group relies on its brand to increase its market share and total assets. With an established brand based on style, quality, and value, Semir has recruited franchisees in more than 200 cities in

China. They have also started expanding into the global market, in such countries as Russia, Vietnam, and other emerging markets.

YISHION

YiShion has established itself as a nationally famous casual clothing brand. YiShion targets the same groups of consumers as Semir and Metersbonwe. YiShion produces and sells menswear, women's wear, and childrenswear. It relies on high-quality garments, an advanced computer-aided design production system, and well-established distribution channels. In 2010, there were more than 3,000 franchised stores across all 23 provinces in China.

Unlike other casual apparel brands, YiShion is a vertically integrated enterprise. They do product design and development and have their own production facility and distribution channel. Their headquarters are at Donguan in Guangdong province, which is one of the country's largest apparel production and distribution clusters. YiShion hires employees to open stores in different provinces as well as recruit franchisees. They are also expanding internationally into countries such as Iran, Jordan, Kuwait, Malaysia, and Oman, as well as other emerging markets in Asia and Africa.

HOW MATURE IS THE RETAIL INDUSTRY? STIFF COMPETITION YET OPEN MARKETS FOR INVESTMENT

Ever since the Chinese retail opened up to foreign investors, domestic retailers have undergone major restructuring to get ready for the intense competition expected from the international retail chains. Some domestic retail chains also hope to improve their valuation in case an international retailer is interested in acquiring them. The domestic retailers' strong relationship with their suppliers makes them stiff competition. Successful international retailers find a niche in the Chinese market. An international retailer interested in entering the Chinese market needs to find the right strategy and investment vehicle if they are to prosper.

International brands are becoming popular in China. Whereas only a small proportion of the Chinese population can afford expensive, imported brand apparel items, consumers with increased exposure to foreign fashion through the media are becoming more receptive to international fashion styles and trends (China's beauty market, 2005). Demand for imported brand products is growing also due to changes in buying behavior and increasing purchasing power. Although Chinese registered local brands have also developed quickly (there are at least 100,000), only 0.3 percent of them are considered well known among Chinese consumers (China National Commercial Information Centre, 2006). Typical examples are Yonger, Firs, and Li Ning. It is generally agreed that foreign apparel brands occupy the high end and middle end of the market.

International brands set the pace of the contemporary Chinese apparel business. It wasn't until 2001 that brand name products started to become household words, and by 2006 the luxury brands had gained Chinese consumers' attention. China's premier cities are beginning to mature in terms of retail stores, so retailers are focusing on second-tier cities, that is the provincial capital cities with populations of less than two million, such as Changchun, Shijiazhuan, Ulumqi, and third-tier cities, which are those coastal cities with better developed economies and relatively higher consumer purchasing power, such as Qinhuangdao, Weihai, and Beihai. For international retailers that are interested in expanding into the Chinese market, it would be wise to consider second- and third-tier cities for expansion.

BUYING FOR APPAREL RETAIL CHAINS: IT'S ALL AT HOME

Since 1960, the internationalization of markets, competitive advances in product, process, and business technologies, and changing consumer requirements have brought about radical and continuous change in the textile and apparel industries. A few of the transformations over this period have included the emergence of large, powerful retail groups; widespread integration and then de-integration in textile manufacturing; the emergence of diversified apparel companies without factories; and the development of new channels to market, such as the Internet (Kilduff, 2000). All of this has made the Chinese apparel manufacturing an important part of the retail industry.

China is an important international hub of sourcing for apparel retailers. Its role is becoming increasingly important because of its ability to gauge its products to apparel consumption trends. Retail chains in China use the Chinese manufacturing industry for their low-end products, and luxury brands import from their own manufacturing setups abroad. Country of origin plays a very important role in luxury brands among Chinese consumers. Many of the international retailers (such as Walmart) in China source their products from within the country, which helps reduce the costs associated with importing.

RETAIL CAREERS: REGULATED ENVIRONMENT

Despite the country's opening up since 1978, China still has a relatively centralized manpower planning system that regulates the labor market. In general, a worker has to obtain an employment permit to enter the job market. Jobs are classified into 66 directory entries by the Ministry of Labor and Social Security, and one must undergo training and obtain professional qualification certificates under the Chinese Labor Law and Vocational Education Law to get an employment permit. In China, individuals have the opportunity to pursue careers in the retailing industry as vendors, store employees, and buyers.

For a foreigner interested in working in China, the employer has to apply for approval and for a People's Republic of China

Employment License. The company may hire a foreigner only in case of special needs and only if a domestic candidate cannot fill the position. The foreigner has to also meet some basic regulations, such as be older than 18 years of age, have professional skills, have no criminal record, and have a valid passport. The regulations for foreigner's employment in China promulgated jointly by the Ministry of Labor, Ministry of Public Security, Ministry of Foreign Affairs, and the Ministry of Foreign Trade and Economic Cooperation of the People's Republic of China can be found at the government website at http://www.gov.cn/english/2005-08/29/content_27366.htm.

THE FUTURE OF APPAREL RETAIL: ON THE WAY TO BECOMING A FASHION CAPITAL OF THE WORLD

The apparel retailing industry in China has experienced significant transformations since the country opened its doors to the world in 1978. In step with China's economic growth and integration with a globalized economy, and in response to rising expectations of the "newly rich" consumers, the industry underwent changes in terms of firm ownership structure, retailing format, and distribution channels. However, given the disparity of income between cities and the countryside and between different classes of people in the country, the development of apparel retailing in China will follow a hybrid model reflecting a combination of price-sensitive, fashion-sensitive, and brand-sensitive approaches.

Most Chinese believe in moderation. They are usually fashion followers, not innovators. Traditional Chinese culture frowns on full self-expression, but a new generation has started to develop its own ideas. They have the courage to express themselves in public and transmit their style and personality through their dress. Personalized consumption is replacing blind following. In a campaign to showcase Shanghai's creativity in the lead-up to its 2010 Expo, this "Sin City" declared its aspiration to become the Fashion

Capital of Asia. Because Shanghai is already a popular venue for fashion shows and apparel exhibitions, the declaration signals the coming of age of China's proactive stance on the apparel industry, including retailing. The government support given to local designers in Beijing, Shanghai, and Guangzhou may pave the way for China to become a fashion capital in the years to come.

Case Study 1

LI NING: ANYTHING IS POSSIBLE

The 1980s Olympic gymnastics champion Li Ning founded Li Ning Co. Ltd. in 1990. Capitalizing on the Chinese fashion culture as "followers" and riding on the casual and sportive trends, he positions himself as the hero that ordinary people look up to, making athletic shoes and sporting apparel (Chaney, 2008).

Trying to become the Nike and Adidas of China, Li Ning's logo and slogan resemble those of the two well-known international brands. The "brand confusion" and "nationalism" strategies seem to work well for Li Ning in the emerging market of China. In 2006, Li Ning posted revenues of US$418 million, and total profits of about US$39 million. As of March 2007, there were 4,297 Li Ning retail stores. The company directly owns some of the retail stores; others are franchised. It is a multibranded store that has entered into agreements with various companies for research and development and production of sporting equipment.

However, Li Ning's products seem to do well primarily in sports shoes sales, due to price advantage. In 2005, Li Ning entered a joint venture with Aigle, a French sports apparel company, in order to position itself up market. The objective was to capture customers who matured with Li Ning into their middle age and who could afford to dress themselves to look "successful" and "active." In 2010, the company had third position in the country in terms of sales after Nike and Adidas (About Li Ning, 2010).

Since 2007, Li Ning has also collaborated with the Chinese National Basketball Association, the China University Basketball Association, the China University Football Association, and the Association of Tennis Professionals, the last being the breeding ground of most Chinese sports heroes (Balfour, 2008).

In 2010, Li Ning set up its U.S. headquarters in Portland, Oregon, the heartland of Nike. The company opened its first American store on January 4, 2010. Their move was mainly to tap local talent and then work toward competing with the big brands directly.

Despite these efforts, Li Ning still faces significant competition from international brands, which have featured internationally renowned Chinese sportsmen such as basketball star Yao Ming and track star Liu Xiang in their brand marketing. The company has had a growth of 37.5 percent in the last three years and projected revenues of over $1 billion in 2010.

Discussion Questions

1. Discuss the strategy used by Li Ning to become successful during the initial launch phase with specific focus on their understanding of the Chinese consumers.
2. What do you think is the company's expansion strategy? Is there anything you recommend the company should do different to suit the Chinese market?
3. What do you think the company should do in order to become number one in terms of revenue?

Case Study 2

THE KEY TO SUCCESSFUL BRANDING IN CHINA

Many marketers complain that the Chinese are not brand loyal. Consumers in China, they moan, will latch onto a new brand one day only to discard it in favor of a competitor the next. Exasperated marketers argue that confronted with such mercenary consumption patterns, they cannot understand their core markets. Although there is some truth to the complaint that Chinese consumers switch brands frequently, it is not a function of Chinese culture, as some may suppose. Rather, Chinese consumers remain fickle because China is in a phase of its development where companies bombard consumers with vastly more choices than they had even a decade ago. Another problem is that multinational companies have not always done an adequate job of identifying and understanding their core markets in order to target them effectively.

Clarins and L'Oréal are two hugely popular personal care brands around the world. However, their China stories are very different. L'Oréal and its associated brands are very successful, and they have developed brand loyalty with Chinese male and female consumers. One 43-year-old chief financial officer of an investment bank told us in an interview, "I only buy Lancôme as it makes me feel young and beautiful." On the other hand, Clarins has struggled when trying to target male consumers.

The mistake that Clarins has made is to use models for their advertising campaigns to whom the typical Chinese male cannot relate. Already nervous that caring about their appearance means that they are not manly, Chinese males have been put off by Clarins' advertising campaigns. To advertise male grooming products, Clarins chose ethnically diverse, metrosexual models that presented an image most Chinese men could not identify with. When viewing ads, potential buyers were confused as to why and how they would want to look like the models using Clarins products.

L'Oréal has been much more successful recently through its choice of Korean movie stars for its male cosmetic brand, Biotherm. These Korean stars exhibit a look, style, and personality that Chinese men aspire to and that Chinese women wish their boyfriends would exhibit.

Clarins is not alone in portraying its brand in an odd light to Chinese consumers. Too many brands launch advertising campaigns centered around preppie blond models lounging on sailboats. In a country where sailboats and the Hamptons are not in the popular imagination, this advertising tack does not work.

Many of the brands Americans use are ones that people chose because their parents used them. Often young adults use Tylenol or Colgate because their parents introduced them to the brands when they were young. In China under Mao, there was little brand choice, so today's youth are trying brands without any teaching by their parents. But these Chinese youth are becoming very savvy as they determine what they like and what they do not.

To develop a brand successfully in China, it is not enough to take a short-term outlook and try to sell into every available market. This risks eroding long-term prospects. It is better to first define what your brand is supposed to embody and then work to support that image. Multinationals must understand that Chinese consumers in the first-tier cities of Shanghai, Beijing, and Guangzhou will soon be as brand savvy as any in New York, London, or Paris. And consumers in the second- and third-tier cities like Chengdu and Dalian will move with lightning speed to catch up with international trends.

Source: Rein, Shaun, "The Key to Successful Branding in China," Bloomberg *BusinessWeek*. Retrieved on December 15, 2010, from http://www.businessweek.com/globalbiz/content/sep2007/gb20070925_202489.htm

Discussion Questions

1. What makes the brand loyalty issue a major concern in China?
2. What do international retailers need to know about Chinese consumers in order to offer them the right merchandise and use the right promotional techniques?
3. Are Chinese consumers really not brand loyal? Discuss what aspects of a country's culture may make consumers more loyal than those from other nations.

REFERENCES

About Li Ning (2010). Retrieved October 10, 2010, from
    http://www.lining.com/EN/company/inside-1_1.html

Au, K.F. (2000), "Market wide open," Textile Asia, August, pp. 73–6.

Balfour, F. (2008, May 1). China's Li Ning toe-to-toe against Nike and Adidas.
    Retrieved October 10, 2010, from http://www.businessweek.com/
    magazine/content/08_19/b4083051446468.htm

Barboza, D. (2010, August 15). China passes Japan as second-largest economy.
    Retrieved October 10, 2010, from http://www.nytimes.com/2010/08/16/
    business/global/16yuan.html?ref=david_barboza

Bruce, M., Daly, L. & Towers, N. (2004). Lean or agile—A solution for supply
    chain management in the textiles and clothing industry? *International
    Journal of Operations and Production Management, 24*(2), pp. 151–170.

Chaney, J. (2008). College student Li Aihua wears his tattered, gungy Li Ning
    basketball sneakers with pride. Retrieved October 10, 2010, from
    http://www.reuters.com/article/idUSHKG13709320080221

Cheng, C. (1993). Little emperors make big consumers. *China Today,* 42 (April),
    47–49.

China Economic Review (2000). Beijing stores announce merger. *China
    Economic Review*, October.

China National Commercial Information Centre (2006), *Industry Series on
    China's Apparel Market 2006*, Li & Fung Research Centre, Li & Fung
    Group, Hong Kong.

China's beauty market (2005, August 4). Retrieved October 6, 2010, from
    http://www.hktdc.com/info/vp/a/cepa/en/1/3/1/1X009S7H/Closer-
    Economic-Partnership-Arrangement—CEPA—Obsolete-/China-s-
    Beauty-Market.htm

Chuang, Y. (2009). The Rise of China and Its Implications for the World
    Economy. 38th Taiwan U.S. Conference on Contemporary China, Session
    IV, pp. 2–33.

Christopher, M. (2007). New directions in logistics. In Global logistics—New
    directions in supply chain management, 5th ed., Kogan Page.

Datamonitor: Apparel retail in China—Industry profile 2009.

Dawson J., Mukovama M., Choi, S. C. & Larke, R. (2003). The International-
    isation of Retailing in Asia. London: RoutledgeCurzon, p. 117.

Dickson, M. A., Lennon, S. J., Montalto, C. P., Dong, S. & Zhang, L. (2004).
    Chinese consumer market segments for foreign apparel products.
    Journal of Consumer Marketing, 21(5), pp. 301–317.

Fang, H. (2006) Comparative study and optimization in the field of clothing
    retail in direct selling model, Southwest Jiao Tong University.

Hainan News Net (2003). Chinese people's new consumption after the WTO (in
    Chinese). Retrieved February 15, 2010, from www.hnxw.com/200110/
    ca38355.htm

Hayes, S. G. & Jones, N. (2006). Fast fashion: A financial snapshot. *Journal of
    Fashion Marketing and Management, 10*(3), pp. 282–300.

Hypermarket apparel sales are struggling: More window shoppers than
    purchasers (2004). Retrieved April 15, 2010, from http://sports.eastday.
    com/eastday/2004qsy/node7342/userobject1ai723147.html

Hypermarket culture booms in China (2010). Retrieved February 15, 2010,
    from http://www.talkingretail.com/news/industry-news/7164-
    hypermarket-culture-booms-in-china.html

Kilduff, P. (2000). Evolving strategies, structures and relationships in complex
    and turbulent business environments: The textile and apparel industries
    of the new millennium. *Journal of Textile and Apparel, Technology and
    Management 1*(1), pp. 1–10.

Kwan, C. Y., Yeung, K. W. & Au, K. F. (2003). A statistical investigation of the
    changing apparel retailing environment in China. *Journal of Fashion
    Marketing and Management, 7*(1), pp. 87–100.

Louis Vuitton opens Beijing flagship store (2005). Retrieved April 1, 2010, from
    http://www.chinadaily.com.cn/english/livechina/2005-11/21/
    content_496633.htm

Mattoo, A. (2003). China's Accession to the WTO: the Services Dimension.
    Journal of International Economic 6(2), 299–339.

McNeal, J. U. & Yeh, C. H. (2003). Consumer behavior of Chinese children:
    1995–2002. *Journal of Consumer Marketing, 20* (6), 542–554.

Mitchell, S. (2002). All about pierre cardin: An brief biography of Pierre Cardin,
    his life, his work, and his business empire, from http://www.essortment.
    com/lifestyle/pierrecardinfa_solw.htm

Muzinich, N., Pecotich, A. & Putrevu, S. (2003). A model of the antecedents and consequents of female fashion innovativeness. *Journal of Retailing and Consumer Services, 10*(5), pp. 297–310.

Performance of China's apparel product sectors (2006). Retrieved October 25, 2010, from http://www.idsgroup.com/profile/pdf/industry_series/ISissue7.pdf

Seckler, V. (2009, November 25). China's luxury scene growing with young adults. *WWD, 198*(111), p. 10.

Shao, A. & Herbig, P. (1994). Marketing implications of China's little emperors. *Review of Business,* 16 (Summer/Fall), 16–20.

Silverstein, M. J. & Sayre, K. (2009). Women want more. HarperCollins Publishers, NY.

The rise of female consumerism in China (2007, August 7). Retrieved October 25, 2010, from http://www.womenofchina.cn/Data_Research/Latest_Statistics/18158.jsp

Yip, K. & Chang, B. (2010, August, 12). Male big spender splash their cash in China. Retrieved October 25, 2010, from http://www.asianewsnet.net/home/news.php?id=13079

Zhao, H. (2003). China's apparel market is entering a brand-based competitive era (in Chinese). Market Daily. Retrieved February 15, 2010, from http://enjoy.eastday.com/epublish/

Zhang, L., Dickson, M. & Lennon, S. (2002). The distribution channel for foreign-brand apparel in China: structure, government's role, and problems. *Clothing and Textile Research Journal, 20*(3), pp. 167–80.

Zhu, J. (2008). A Comparative Study on Apparel Marketing Channels between China and South Korea. Beijing Institute of Fashion Technology, master thesis.

INDIA

5

Jaya Halepete

Mansi Batra

Vaishali Jadhav

OBJECTIVES

After reading this chapter, you will

- ► Understand the characteristics of the unorganized (traditional) and organized (nontraditional) retailing sectors of the Indian retail industry
- ► Grasp the role of foreign direct investment policies in establishing retail setups in India
- ► Understand the in-depth profile of the Indian consumers
- ► Recognize the factors that influence the apparel retailing in India
- ► Understand career opportunities in the Indian retail industry

As one of the oldest civilizations in the world, India has a strong culture that makes it a complex country in terms of understanding the market and consumers. India has taken a place of pride in international trade since at least the fourth century BCE, when the Mauryan emperors who unified the subcontinent built and maintained roads throughout the country to form trade routes. They minted coins for trade, which was done in a very

TABLE 5.1 Fast Facts about India	
Capital	New Delhi
Population	1.189 billion
Type of government	Federal Republic
GDP: purchasing power parity: in US$	$3.57 trillion
Export commodities	Petroleum products, precious stones, machinery, iron and steel, chemicals, vehicles, and apparel
Age structure	0–14 yrs: 30.5% 15–64 yrs: 64.3% 65 yrs plus: 5.2%
Religion	Hindu: 80.5% Muslim: 13.4% Christian: 2.3% Sikh: 1.9% Other: 1.8% Unspecified: 0.1%
Ethnicity	Indo-Aryan: 72% Dravidian: 25% Mongoloid and other: 3%

Source: CIAfactbook.gov

organized and corporate manner. During the first to eleventh centuries CE, India had 32.9 percent share of world gross domestic product (GDP), making it the world's greatest economy (Maddison, 2003). In the sixteenth century, Portuguese, Dutch, English, and French interests began to establish trade stations in India. The British East India Company was the most successful venture. By the middle of the nineteenth century, it controlled all of what is today India, Pakistan, and Bangladesh. In 1858, the British government took over. India's GDP plummeted from 24.4 percent in 1700 to 3.8 percent in 1952. India had been known for its wealth until it became a British colony. On August 15, 1947, India won its independence. The British influence on the country remains in the education system, infrastructure, and English-speaking population, all of which have facilitated international investment and brought employment to countless telephone customer service representatives.

India is the world's largest democracy and the tenth-largest economy in the world. The median age of this population is 25 years, which makes India a very young country (Table 5.1). What makes the country even more attractive is that these young Indian consumers like to spend money on shopping and the spending increased by almost 8 to 9 percent in the first decade of this century. Indian consumers are likely to grow four times in number by 2025 (Gadkari, 2009). To add to this, India has a GDP growth rate of 8 percent, and predictions are that the Indian economy will continue to grow to 90 percent of the U.S. economy by 2050. With credit increasingly available, the GDP growth rate is not expected to go down in the near future (Retail, 2009). With all these attributes and a bright future, India has emerged as a very lucrative market for retail investment. As a result, both domestic and international retailers are investing heavily into the retail sector (India, 2009).

India has the largest number of retail outlets in the world, with more than 15 million outlets compared to about 900,000 in the United States. Retail is one of the most important sectors of the Indian economy, contributing to 35 percent of GDP (Rao, 2006). The organized retail sector is in a rapid growth phase. Changing lifestyles and increasing income of Indian consumers have driven the development of large malls and the retail landscape in general. Today, there are approximately 552 malls in India. This retail expansion started in metropolitan cities. As larger metropolitan cities become saturated, retailers have begun targeting smaller cities for expansion.

THE RETAIL LANDSCAPE:
AS ATTRACTIVE AS IT CAN GET

Since the early 2000s, India has emerged as the world's third most attractive destination for apparel retailers. "We are extremely optimistic about the retail industry in India over the next 5 to 10 years. This sector is among the largest growth opportunities for Indian and international players," reported Shailja Dutt of Stellar Search, an India-based human resource provider (Retail sector, 2010). Apparel is the second most important retail category after food and groceries in India and is expected to grow at the rate of 12 to 15 percent per year.

The apparel industry is fragmented and dominated by a large number of mom-and-pop stores. Since 2000, the organized retail sector has gained momentum and is changing the face of the apparel retail industry in India. The retail industry faces many challenges, such as government regulations and increasing real estate costs (Retail, 2009). India is a complex market in many different ways. Its multicultural, multilingual, and multiethnic consumers make it a unique and interesting challenge as an emerging market for foreign retailers.

An understanding of Indian cities is fundamental in order for a retailer to establish the best possible areas in which to enter and grow their business. Economists categorize Indian cities into three tiers, based on factors such as infrastructure, skill availability, and quality of life (Table 5.2).

Tier I cities are major metropolitan areas with the best infrastructure. These cities have the biggest organized retail markets. This tier has a large concentrated segment of upper-class consumers. The cost of real estate is very high and so is the standard of living. These cities account for about 60 percent of the total real estate space and global consumers. Retailers interested in expansion start with Tier I cities, then slowly acquire real estate in other tiered cities (Images yearbook, 2009). As Tier I cities become saturated with organized retail formats, retailers move to the next tier

TABLE 5.2 India's Major Cities

Tier number	Cities included
Tier I	Bangalore, Mumbai, and New Delhi
Tier I-I	Hyderabad, Chennai, Pune, NOIDA, Gurgaon, and Navi Mumbai
Tier II	Kolkata, Mangalore, Ludhiana, Chandigarh/Mohali, and Bhopal
Tier III	Ahmedabad, Thiruvananthapuram, Coimbatore, Mysore, Nasik, Kochi, Nagpur, Jaipur, Indore, Shimla, Lucknow, Kanpur, Panaji, Srinigar, Patna, and Bhubaneshwar

Source: "Growth Potential: Tier II and Tier III Cities in India," India Reports, retrieved on March 1, 2011, from http://www.india-reports.com/Products/try/ IR-tier-2-3-011208-Try.pdf. Also INRnews.com.

cities. For luxury retailers, Tier I cities are the main markets followed by some cities of Tier I-I such as NOIDA and Gurgaon, where there are many upper-class people who would buy from high-end luxury stores. The consumers in different tiers differ based on income levels and expenditure due to standard of living in different tiers. For example, Tier I cities are home to large multinational corporations that pay more.

Tier I-I cities are very much like Tier I cities except that they fall a little behind in areas such as infrastructure development, concentration of population, and number of organized retail set-ups. Tier II and Tier III cities are slowly gaining importance as more and more companies set up their offices in these cities to take advantage of cheaper real estate prices. There is significant information technology (IT) and real estate construction activity. These cities are growing at a fast pace with increasing employment opportunities and increasing income levels. They are becoming important for retailers who are looking to expand beyond major metropolitan cities.

CONSUMERS: CONFLUENCE OF CULTURES

Every one of India's 28 states is different in terms of language or dialect, and some of them differ in terms of dress and food, making India an extraordinarily diverse country in terms of culture. For example, in the northern states, roti (a flat wheat bread) is eaten with vegetables; in the south, rice is the staple part of a meal. North Indians are known for their ostentatious clothing and displays of wealth, whereas south Indians have simpler tastes. North Indians have fairer skin tones and like to use a lot of makeup. South Indians are darker in complexion and like to use skin-lightening creams and generally tend to use less makeup. This diversity poses a big challenge for the retail industry.

Another big influence of Indian fashion is the movie industry in India, which produces a large number of movies each year (about 1,000 as compared to around 600 in Hollywood) in various languages. Although Bollywood (a word created by combining Bombay and Hollywood) is a major influence on fashion all over India, there are local movie industries that make movies in regional languages and dictate fashion in those regions. In addition, many budding designers across India are bringing an interesting dimension to the clothing and apparel needs of Indian consumers.

Buyers must also consider India's many seasonal variations. For example, the capital city of Delhi experiences winter between November and March, with temperatures ranging from 40 to 50 degrees F; on the other hand, Mumbai, the financial capital, does not really have a winter, with the lowest temperatures hovering around 70 degrees F. It is important for retailers to buy appropriate assortments for these two major cities. As the vice president of an international brand in India noted, "Zara launched in Delhi and Mumbai with the same winter merchandise. Who will buy trench coats in Mumbai? This is the most common mistake made by many international retailers."

Store layout and decor are critical for attracting Indian consumers. A browser visiting the store frequently likes to see changes in the layout; otherwise, he may get the impression that stock is not moving. Buyers ensure that the same item that has been in the store for a season is not carried again and that they replace it with a different design, style, and color.

India is also a culturally sensitive market. Converse once made shoes with pictures of a god on them. In India, to put a god on a dirty shoe is a sacrilege. This would not be acceptable to an Indian. In a similar instance, a software company created a map of India on their product showing the northern state of Kashmir as a disputed state between India and Pakistan. Although the rest of the world may consider Kashmir to be a disputed state, Indians do not. The company had to withdraw the product. A foreign retailer needs to understand the cultural sensitivities of the consumers before launching a product for the citizens of that country.

Retailers in most countries need to micro market their products for stores in different regions due to variations in weather, ethnicity, and major industries. In India, apparel retailers must also attend to cultural differences. The prevalent culture of a state dictates unique behavioral characteristics. There are even cultural differences between Tier I, Tier II, and Tier III cities within the same state. For example, in Tier I cities, there are more nuclear families as compared to other tiers (only husband and wife living with their children), whereas in Tier II and Tier III cities, one can still find extended families (where more than one family—usually two brothers along with their wives, children, and parents—live under one roof). People living in Tier 1 cities are more global consumers because they travel abroad, dress in Western clothing (a larger percentage than other tiers), and buy international brands. The consumers in Tier II and Tier III cities are more glocal consumers, expecting global quality at local prices and dressing more conservatively in Indian clothing (which may be

▲ **FIGURE 5.1** Big Bazaar is a department store chain on the lines of a Walmart supercenter. The stores sell groceries along with household items and clothing. The store chain is known for aggressive advertising for catering to the middle-class and lower-middle-class population. India Today Group/Getty Images.

due to the fact that they live in joint families and need to be more modest, as a mark of respect for the elders, compared to those living in nuclear families). This vast difference in the population makes it very difficult for retail chains to employ the same selling techniques across the country, as in the United States.

Despite these differences, there are some characteristics that Indian consumers share as a group (Bahadur, 2006). Indian consumers believe in saving rather than spending. Although this mind-set is changing among the younger generation, it is true for most Indians. They like to compare pricing in different stores before making any big purchase. Indians like to bargain. It gives them a feeling of having gotten a good deal. They believe that bigger stores are expensive. This aspect of their personality is also changing with organized retail becoming a regular part of their lives. Durability of the product is important. Even if the product is inexpensive, they expect it to last. Indian consumers don't take well to the concept of using something once and throwing it away.

Shopping is a social activity. Indian consumers like to shop with family or friends. With an increasing number of retail stores to choose from, the Indian consumer is becoming more and more demanding. They like attention while shopping. They want the sales staff to ask them if they need help because it makes them feel important. Although this may not be true with the younger generation living in Tier I cities, it is expected in smaller towns. Major shopping for clothing is done during the wedding season (May and December) and festival season (October and November). Festivals may be different for different regions of India (Sheth & Vittal, 2007).

One characteristic that sets Indian consumers apart from other Asian nations is that English is a commonly used language because of the British influence on Indian culture. The education system in most schools in India is in English, and it is also the common language of conversation in big cities. This makes communication with Indian consumers a lot easier for foreign retailers.

Some other factors that have been changing the customer profile of Indian consumers are (Bahadur, 2006):

- Increasing purchasing power of the young. India has the largest population of young people in the world, with 867 million people under the age of 45. According to the India Retail Report 2005 conducted by IMAGES-KSA Technopak India, there will be 550 million people under the age of 20 by 2015. Stores need to work on targeting this market by carrying products specifically made for this age group. This age group likes branded products, likes to shop, and likes to spend all of their disposable incomes. Hence, focusing on catering to this group may be a very profitable venture for retail stores.
- BPO boom. The Business Process Outsourcing (BPO) boom in India has given rise to a new segment of consumers: single, urban youth who work at call centers and spend the money they earn as they like, undeterred by family pressure to save. This group has a high disposable income and likes to improve their lifestyle and spend on leisure goods. They are brand

▲ FIGURE 5.2 Picture of Bollywood actress Aishwarya Rai in traditional as well as Western clothing. This picture depicts the prevalence of Indian traditional clothing in the current times in India. A. WireImage/ Venturelli/Getty Images .B. India Today Group/Getty Images.

conscious and love shopping at malls because they are pressed for time, parking is convenient, the interiors have a pleasing appearance, and shopping is easy. Shopping areas near BPO offices have done exceedingly better than other locations. Gurgaon, which is a suburb of New Delhi and a hub for many outsourcings offices, is an example of one such shopping area (Bharadwaj, Swaroop, & Vittal, 2005).

▲ **FIGURE 5.3** Indian Hindu woman with a bindi (a dot in the middle of the forehead). A red bindi is usually used by married women. Today, the bindi has also been influenced by fashion trends and is available in many different colors and designs. © Blend Images/Alamy.

► Women in workforce. The shopping habits of increasing numbers of women in the workforce have had a major impact on retail sales. These women are single and have no family responsibilities. Many domestic jewelry stores, like Kiah, Sia, and Tanishq, specifically target this group because they are the primary (or main) decision makers in their household and are interested in

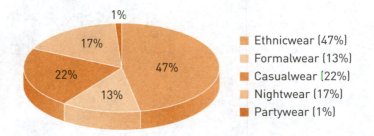

1%

17%

22%

47%

13%

- ■ Ethnicwear (47%)
- ■ Formalwear (13%)
- ■ Casualwear (22%)
- ■ Nightwear (17%)
- ■ Partywear (1%)

▲ **FIGURE 5.4** Indian women's wear market. This graphic illustrates the distribution of sales in different segments of women's apparel market in India. Illustration by Precision Graphics.

jewelry (Bijapurkar, 2007). This group likes to spend on accessories and beauty products, which has led to an increase in demand for products like watches, cosmetics, and perfumes.

WOMEN

Although Indian male consumers' apparel selection is significantly influenced by brand-related criteria, Indian female consumers do not care about brand names (Mohan & Gupta, 2007). Indian women generally prefer traditional dress, more so in Tier II and Tier III cities than Tier I cities. The slow shift in consumer adoption of Western apparel poses a challenge for international apparel brands and retailers seeking to gain market share in the women's wear segment. Indian ethnic garments and garments mixing ethnic and Western styling have dominated the ready-to-wear market for Indian women since the mid-1990s (Batra & Niehm, 2009).

Indian women select apparel by frequently visiting boutiques (Chattaraman, 2009). They like exclusivity and believe that smaller boutiques have better quality products. Many boutiques in India offer tailoring services. Women visit these boutiques to see their new design range, select the fabrics they like, and have clothes tailored. Many domestic retail chains offer fabric and tailoring services to meet this demand (Chattaraman, 2009). These stores

▲ FIGURE 5.5 Indian women in Indo-Western clothing. This type of clothing is very popular among the younger generation who wants to wear Western clothing but is still attached to the traditional Indian designs. © Visage/Alamy.

hire a tailor or sign a contract with an external tailoring service to fulfill the tailoring needs.

Most Indian women in their 40s and 50s still wear traditional Indian clothing to work, at home, and for social events. The younger generation (women in their 20s and 30s) usually prefers to wear Western clothing to work and out with friends but still wears traditional clothing to traditional and family-related social events (Batra & Niehm, 2009). Although this holds true for most states, professional women have begun demonstrating a greater preference for branded Western and Indo-Western apparel. International retailers who address their needs will eventually achieve greater profitability (Batra & Niehm, 2009).

MEN

Men's apparel constitutes 46 percent of the total ready-made apparel market in India, whereas women's apparel constitutes only 17 percent of this market (Cygnus Business Consulting and Research, 2004). Unlike Indian women, men in India prefer Western wear. As a result, men's clothing is the strongest category in most department stores, and they display a wide variety of domestic and international brands (Batra & Niehm, 2009). Among average-income male consumers, brand awareness is moderate, brand loyalty is low, and retailer loyalty is high.

Clothing reflects lifestyle and social status among India's affluent male population. This group of consumers frequently travels overseas and purchases international brands during their travels. There is a high level of awareness of international brands among this consumer group (Mohan & Gupta, 2007). Although this is an important segment for international retailers to target, these consumers prefer to make their purchases abroad. As Dhiren Desai, vice president of an international brand in India, says, "Due to high import duties in India, many international brands in India are more expensive than many (not all) other countries. Also, for the purchases made in Europe, the consumer gets VAT (value-added-tax) refund making it even cheaper."

BEAUTY INDUSTRY IN INDIA

Since ancient times, Indian women have used homemade products for their beauty regimen. Some popular beauty products of the past have been hair oils, kohl pencils, and bindis. But the availability of a large variety of branded products and increasing brand consciousness among the middle class have piqued women's interest in purchasing high-quality, branded beauty products. International retailers have had to modify their offerings to suit the regional requirements of Indian women. For example, in general South Indian women spend more on fairness creams and are more conservative than North Indian women in their choice of color cosmetics.

▲ **FIGURE 5.6** Fairness cream in a store. Store employee arranges beauty and whitening products, including Emami Ltd.'s (an Indian company) "Fair and Handsome" at a Big Bazaar outlet in Mumbai, India. Many cosmetic manufacturers are targeting Indians with fairness creams, pledging to make them more attractive and more successful by lightening their skin. Sales of whiteners increased 17 percent to 20.5 billion rupees ($432 million) from January to September 2010, according to research by the Häarlem, Netherlands-based Nielsen Co. Bloomberg via Getty Images.

The beauty industry in India is expected to grow 15 to 20 percent in the next few years (Ridge, 2008). To be a part of this growth, one requires an understanding of the needs of women in different parts of the country. There is lack of knowledge among Indian women regarding the wide range of beauty products offered by international retailers. For example, because Indian women have not traditionally used facial creams, under-eye creams, mascaras, sunscreen lotions, and face masks, they need to be educated about them.

Indian men living in Tier I and Tier II cities have also begun spending a considerable amount of time in grooming themselves.

Beauty salons that specifically cater to men are cropping up all over the country. Indian men are not shy about frequenting these places anymore due to a general change in attitude toward grooming (Bhattacharya, 2009). Many Indian brands that used to make beauty products for women have only now started making various products for men. The market offers products such as fairness creams, body creams, and hair color specially made for men. International retailers in the beauty industry have now begun to focus on this whole new set of consumers. The male grooming market is growing at a rate of 18 percent and according to predictions is expected to grow at 30 to 35 percent in the 2010s. It may be a very attractive sector for international retailers (Indian Cosmetic Sector Analysis, 2009).

CHILDREN

In the past, parents preferred to buy functional clothing for kids over branded clothing. Children's garments were usually purchased from small stores and from street shops, and only very high-status families bought branded garments. This trend is gradually changing and the market for branded kids' clothing is growing, as disposable incomes rise and foreign cultures influence the way people dress. Influenced by mass media and peer pressure, today's kids are more informed and self-conscious and like to have a say in their clothing purchases.

Children's apparel includes clothing for kids between 1 and 14 years of age. Jeans, shorts, and shirts are the evergreen pieces in kids' apparel. The market for kids' apparel in India exceeds $1.3 billion, of which around $3 million is branded kids' wear. The kids' wear market is growing at the rate of 10 percent per annum, which makes it one of the fastest-growing markets.

LUXURY RETAIL IN INDIA

International travel is increasing awareness of foreign brands among a growing upper-class population of India. The Indian luxury market includes such brands as Chanel, Burberry, Prada, Gucci, Bentley, Fendi, and BMW (India, 2009). When some luxury brands tried to enter the Indian market with previous season's merchandise, they failed. Indian consumers are well aware of what each brand offers. The Internet revolution, and the consequent demand for Indian brainpower, led to an economic boom that has created a whole new breed of wealthy, cosmopolitan Indians. Luxury buyers in India fall into three categories: the old rich, wealthy professionals, and first-generation entrepreneurs. The old rich buy luxury products to keep up their image; the wealthy professionals (CEOs and non-resident Indians) travel across the world and buy luxury products to show off their foreign travels; and the entrepreneurs buy luxury goods to show off their wealth. Luxury products are not new to Indian consumers who have been purchasing them during their frequent trips aboard, but having luxury stores in India is something new.

Indian consumers are sensitive to price, even in the luxury segment. They compare prices of products sold in India to those sold abroad before making purchases. "We want to bargain; we want to feel we have got a good deal," says Vikram Phadke, co-founder of the Indian retailer Evoluzione. Indian consumers feel uncomfortable making expensive purchases in India, surrounded by poverty. "Indian consumers have tremendous spending power, but also feel great shame in spending exorbitantly on luxury products in their home turf," says Charu Sachdev, head of the luxury retail wing of the Indian Sachdev Group. "But when in London, Paris, or Dubai, they will happily spend. Even NRIs (non-resident Indians) visiting their country of origin suddenly don't feel it is 'correct' to spend so much on a bag or dress," says Vikram Phadke: "He wants to buy, but does not want to be seen as buying" (Sridhar, 2010).

According to a study conducted in 2006 by the Mumbai-based O&M advertising, India is beginning to contribute in a big way to the global market for luxury products. This global market, estimated at approximately $69.4 billion in 2003, reached around $444 million in 2010, according to a study by Indian consulting company Technopak. The luxury retail business in India is expected to grow at 25

▲ **FIGURE 5.7** Emporio luxury mall in New Delhi. These malls are a recent phenomenon in India. They house many high-end international brands and have a large clientele in India. Photo by Mansi Patney.

percent per year from 2009 to 2024 (Luxury Unlimited, 2009). Many of these brands have operated boutiques in high-end hotels, owing to the lack of space for exclusive stores. But, with the opening of exclusive luxury malls, these brands now have space to display their products and reach their target market.

Indian consumers like to mix shopping for various product categories, such as luxury products such as designer handbags and other nonluxury items such as regular-priced clothing products. This aspect of Indian consumers makes it essential for luxury malls to have the right mix of stores. Malls in various parts of India that have not taken this factor into consideration suffer slow sales. To meet the demands of Indian consumers, some luxury brands are opening stand-alone stores in regular shopping areas. Luxury retail has tremendous potential in India and it will remain a growing market for years to come.

APPAREL RETAIL FORMATS: CHANGING ON A FAST TRACK

The diversity of retail formats in India is as prevalent as the diversity in its population. Even within the unorganized retail setting, there are many different formats. There are vendors who sell from carts, peddlers who carry baskets of products door to door, salespeople who host at-home parties, vendors who sell in the local weekly markets, and shopkeepers who own small shops with basic necessities. Some of these formats are unique to India (mainly the traditional formats), whereas others can be found in other developing nations as well. Retailers are changing their store formats based on market demands and the margins are shrinking due to fierce competition. There is a movement toward smaller organized retail formats for better control over operations.

In India, there are two categories of retail formats: traditional and modern (Mulky & Nargundkar, 2003). The format classification is based on size and location of the store, assortment of merchandise, type, and price of the merchandise offered, and the level of customer service.

TRADITIONAL RETAIL FORMATS

Traditional retail is the predominant setup in India. Research shows that this format is expected to retain 84 percent of retail market share at least until 2013. These formats are the ones that have been in existence for many centuries before modern organized retailing began in India. They do not have a defined structure and are family owned. The most common are mom-and-pop stores, street markets, and stores that carry multiple brands or nonbranded merchandise.

▶Mom-and-Pop Stores

Like mom-and-pop stores in the United States, these stores are family owned. The differentiating factors are that they are not only present in the main market areas but also in residential areas, and

they provide a high level of service. So far, the mom-and-pop-store formats have been able to adjust well to the increasing number of organized retail stores because they have been around for a long time and have customer loyalty on their side (Mom & Pop Stores, 2008). Because these stores are also set up near residential neighborhoods in both urban and rural areas, they are convenient. Mom-and-pop stores know their customers much better than any of the new entrants. Being small in size, they are able to make changes to their offerings at a much faster rate than any large retailer. They provide many desirable services such as home delivery, and credit to known customers. But, with the increasing price of real estate, eventually, the pressure might be too much for the mom-and-pop stores to handle. Another problem that this format may face is price-based competition. With their inability to order in bulk or negotiate based on the size of an order, and no law protecting them from quantity-based pricing, they may eventually be more expensive than traditional retailers. Apparel, textiles, beauty products, grocery, and many other varieties of products are sold through this format of stores. To keep up with the organized retailers taking over the market, some small retailers have been forming their own groups and hiring consulting firms to gain some competitive advantages. So, in the long run, even if this format is not able to survive in the large cities, they might still be able to have a market share in smaller Tier III cities and rural areas.

▶Street Markets

In this format vendors sit along the roadside and sell different products such as clothes, furnishings, flowers, vegetables, and other items. This method of selling is not only popular in rural areas but also in Tier I cities such as New Delhi and Mumbai. On "market days" (any chosen day of the week) when the mom-and-pop stores are closed, street markets are flooded with vendors selling a much wider range of products. These street markets are popular by the names of the day of the week they set up shop. For example, if the local mom-and-pop stores are closed on Mondays and the vendors set up their goods on that day, it is called "Monday market." Street-side vendors occupy space outside the closed storefronts. These types of markets are usually found near train stations, bus stations, or main market areas. The vendor lays a piece of fabric on the ground and displays his products on it.

The setup with different vendors resembles a bazaar with colorful banners to get the consumer's attention. Usually street vendors occupy the same spot from week to week so that their customers can find them easily. Some street vendors even pay a small amount of money to shop owners to reserve a place. They sell clothing and other goods at highly competitive prices and

▲ **FIGURE 5.9** Street market on a busy street in Mumbai. These markets are present in all cities in India. They sell locally made, inexpensive, and average-quality merchandise. Among the clothing sold are cheap imitations of the Bollywood fashion or other very basic designs. Photo by Jaya Halepete.

hence attract attention of their customers. The major problem with this method of selling is that, as cities take steps to expand roads and clear sidewalks, the street markets have less and less ground. Also, with very limited product offerings, they are not a threat to any other type of retailer. They do sell textile, apparel, and beauty products, but the offerings are mainly geared toward the lower to lower-middle-class populations.

▶Exclusive Multiple Brand/Nonbrand Stores

A store that carries multiple brands or nonbranded merchandise falls under this category. These stores are not always chains but are privately owned and exist all over the country, usually in the main market area. These stores are more popular in smaller cities where department stores have not yet entered the market. They have a loyal customer base. These stores usually specialize in one category of clothing, for example saris or salwar kameez, and carry a wide range of styles in that category. They understand the local market really well and carry products based on the taste of their local customers. Modern retail formats are a threat to this format of stores. But the ability to change their products easily with new fashions is a big advantage for this format.

These formats are becoming popular in the retail of beauty products. Stores such as the Health and Glow chain carry beauty products of various brands. Consumers prefer shopping at these smaller stores for high-level and personalized customer service. Sephora in the United States would be an example of this kind of format.

MODERN FORMATS

Organized retail formats are a complete contrast to the traditional formats. The emergence of these formats in tandem with large malls has completely transformed the Indian retailing environment. Although the modern retail format is present only in Tier I cities and some Tier II cities, such stores are expected to grow at a very fast pace across India through 2020. Malls comprise 90 percent of the total future retail development in India. The entry of modern retail formats has revolutionized overall consumer spending, making them a very important segment of the Indian retail industry.

▶ Supermarkets

This format is most prevalent in food retailing. Supermarkets attract consumers looking for convenience, quality, and cleanliness while shopping. The largest supermarket operator (in terms of market value) in India is Pantaloon Retail, which owns Food Bazaar (India, 2009). Apparel is not sold in these formats in India.

▶ Hypermarkets

In India's retail setup, food and groceries account for 76 percent of consumer expenditure. Hypermarkets typically stock both food and nonfood items (which include apparel and beauty products) at a 60 percent and 40 percent ratio respectively. Examples of such stores, which are similar to Walmart, are Big Bazaar (owned by Pantaloon Retail) and Star Indian Bazaar (owned by Tata Trent group). This format is becoming successful in India as a one-stop shop for time-pressed city dwellers. Retailers have managed to maintain lower pricing, which is also attractive to the consumers and works well for building customer loyalty (India, 2009).

▶ Department Stores

Department store formats carry multiple brands and multiple product categories including apparel, textile, and beauty products. Domestic retail chains carry a variety of traditional Indian and Western apparel to cater to the Indian consumers. Due to their large size and need for high customer traffic in order to be profitable, these stores are located in metropolitan cities. Retail chains have now started expanding and opening stores in Tier II and Tier III cities to capture the growing market (Sinha & Kar, 2007). Some examples of these stores are Pantaloon, Shopper's Stop (owned by K. Raheja Group), Globus (owned by R. Raheja Group), and Westside (owned by Trent Limited). Variety, novelty, and cosmopolitan ambience attract customers to these stores.

▶ Specialty Stores

This type of store format carries niche product categories, like Crate and Barrel in the United States. Besides home furnishings, categories include but are not limited to clothing, books, music, cosmetics, and medicine. Many retail chains have now established specialty stores that carry one of these categories. Single-branded stores, such as Levi's, Provogue, United Colors of Benetton, and Lee (India, 2009), have been in the Indian retail market since 1991.

▶ *Company Owned, Company Operated*

Many companies in India own and operate their stores, like the Gap and Old Navy in the United States. Such vertically integrated companies own the stores and manufacturing units, and run the stores instead of franchising or licensing their brands to other retailers. In addition to operating their own stores, they also sell their products through other retailers. Companies that produce fabric for men's formal clothing such as dress shirts and suits own these kinds of stores. These stores also sell custom-tailored clothing for customers who would like to select fabrics and have shirts and suits made. Some of the best examples of these stores in India are Reid and Taylor, Park Avenue, and Raymonds. These stores carry the entire range of fabrics produced by the company and tailor formal clothes based on the customer's requirements (Apparel Retail, 2004).

RETAIL OWNERSHIP: CHANGING WITH TIME

In both the traditional and modern retail sectors in India, most stores are family owned. Among the traditional retail formats, the stores are run by family members and then passed on to the next generation. Depending on the size of the stores, the sales staffs may be family members only or additional employees from outside the family.

The organized retail chains that first started in India were also family-run businesses. Many domestic retail chains are still family owned, such as Globus Stores and Ebony, but some, like Reliance and Pantaloon, have gone public, with stocks traded at the stock exchange in India. There is no clearly established or recognizable ownership trend, be it private limited, public limited, or family owned, in India's apparel retail market. However, various factors, such as government regulations, taxation policies, the need for funding from various sources, and the need for talent, may influence ownership patterns. International retailers have used various ownership formats, including joint venture and franchise.

FDI REGULATIONS:
STILL IN THE PROTECTIVE MODE

Investment made by foreign companies in India is governed by the government's 1999 Foreign Direct Investment (FDI) Policy and Foreign Exchange Management Act. This governing policy and act define all the rules and regulations to be followed by a foreign company interested in making an investment in India. The Indian national government, to encourage investment by foreign companies, made many changes to their foreign direct investment policies in 1998 and 1999. For the retail sector, India has the following regulations for FDI:

1. For franchisee and cash-and-carry wholesale formats, foreign direct investment can be 100 percent. This means that the foreign retailer can own and operate the company and does not need any Indian partner.
2. For single-brand stores, such as Gap or Ann Taylor, the government allows an investment of up to 51 percent, with its prior approval (India, 2009). To be approved, products should be sold under the same brand internationally and branded during manufacturing. Any additional product categories to be sold under the brand require separate government approval (India, 2009).
3. Multibrand store formats are not allowed.

The Indian government has regulations that encourage FDI. For example, foreign investors are entitled to take their earnings back to their home country, or repatriation, in case of a joint venture or any other method of investment with an Indian partner. They are not forced to reinvest the money in India. Foreign retailers are also allowed to repatriate their share of dividends, royalties, franchisee fees, and so on.

There is a lot of pressure from interested foreign investors and the locals (who want the foreign investors to bring in superior

TABLE 5.3 The Entry Structure for Some International Brands

Entry Strategy	Time Period		
	1980s or Earlier	1990s	Post-1999
Licensed	Louis Philippe, United Colors of Benetton and 012, Wrangler	Allen Solly, Arrow, Jockey, Lacoste, Lee, Nike, Van Heusen, Vanity Fair	Puma
Wholly Owned Subsidiary	Bata, Pepe Jeans	Levi's®	Hanes, Triumph
Joint Venture (Majority)		Adidas, Reebok	Diesel, Nautica, Sixty Group
Franchise or Distribution			Aldo, Burberry, Canali, Versace, Debenhams, Esprit, Gucci, Guess, Hugo Boss, Mango, Marks & Spencer, Mothercare, Tommy Hilfiger
Joint Venture (incl. Minority Stake)			Celio, Etam, Giordano

Note: The above table shows the structure used during entry, and not the structure that exists currently.

Source: "Global Fashion Brands: Tryst with India" (A Report by Third Eyesight)

http://thirdeyesight.in/blog/2009/05/09/international-brands-india-entry-strategies

© Third Eyesight, 2009

technology into India) on the Indian government to allow for FDI in multibrand store formats, which is still under review.

INTERNATIONAL BRANDS: STRUGGLING TO GET A FOOTHOLD

International retailers have chosen to enter the Indian market using various retail formats. Many single-branded international retailers such as Pizza Hut and Motherhood Maternity have entered India as franchise units, through **distributors** and manufacturers. Some other large international chains, such as Metro and Carrefour, have entered as cash-and-carry businesses. Still others are working with Indian companies on joint ventures, for example, Walmart is part of a joint venture called Best Price Modern Wholesale.

By 2008, the need for better control over the business made the franchise and distribution format far less popular, and the proportion of wholly owned or majority-owned subsidiaries increased (Table 5.3).

WHOLESALE CASH AND CARRY

Metro (Germany) started its operation as the first cash-and-carry business in India. Because FDI regulations allow 100 percent ownership for cash-and-carry business, international retailers are the sole owners of this type of format (India, 2009). In 2010, Carrefour opened its first store in the capital city of New Delhi with a cash-and-carry format. Only business owners are allowed to make purchases from a cash-and-carry format. The biggest advantage of this format is that the retailers are free to make decisions without worrying about mutual agreement between partners as in a joint venture. One of the disadvantages is that they lack expertise or consumer understanding that an Indian partner would bring.

MANUFACTURING AND LOCAL SOURCING

Companies that set up manufacturing units in India are allowed to sell their products in the country. Among apparel retailers, Tommy

Hilfiger, Levi's, and United Colors of Benetton have entered India this way. The government allows these companies to sell their products in India through their own stores, or franchising, local distributors, or existing domestic Indian retailers. The international retailer doesn't have to pay import duties on their products because they are manufactured in India, which means they can price their products competitively. But, they still need to understand the local consumer and provide the right merchandise mix.

FRANCHISING

Franchising is the easiest route by which to enter the Indian market because the international retailer does not need to invest in real estate and other store-related expenses. Most international retailers choose this format. Lacoste, Nike, Mango, and Marks and Spencer are among the retailers that operate in this format in India (India, 2009). Through this method, the international retailer does not need a large capital investment and gets to test the market; but the franchisee does not have a say in the kind of merchandise that should be sold and has to pay high duties on importing the apparel from the franchiser.

DISTRIBUTOR

Foreign retailers that set up distribution centers in India, including Swarovski and Hugo Boss, sell their products through domestic retailers. Distribution centers require less of an investment than opening actual stores. Also, local retailers understand the market.

JOINT VENTURES

Because single-brand international stores can enter India only via joint venture, this format is popular among international retailers interested in opening hypermarkets. Walmart joined forces with Bharati group of India to open stores on the subcontinent. But finding a reliable and long-term partner in India is not always easy. The biggest problem that one can face in a joint venture is that the partnership falls apart after considerable investment. But, for companies where the partnership does work, a joint venture can be very beneficial, as the local partner has a better understanding of the Indian consumer than the international retailer.

INFLUENCES ON APPAREL RETAILING: SAME OLD CONSUMERS, NEW DEMANDS

Since 2000, apparel retail has changed from a made-to-order market to a ready-to-wear market. Increasing use of standard sizing in organized apparel retail may be a big reason for this change, along with the new generation's demand for instant gratification. They want to wear a purchase without waiting for alterations. With increasing customer demand, retailers are improving their offerings in apparel as well as beauty products.

Apparel retailing in India underwent a major revolution in the century's first decade. New shopping avenues, the advent of organized shopping centers, and large shopping malls with food and entertainment under one roof have transformed Indian retail. The Indian consumer's embrace of this sea change is encouraging retailers to continue in the same direction.

MALL CULTURE

When Crossroads, the first mall of Mumbai, opened in 1999, it became a major tourist attraction in the city. Mall culture is something that an Indian consumer was not familiar with until the twenty-first century. Many Indians had never used an escalator, and shoppers suffered accidents as they struggled to get on and off the moving stairs. Today, Indian shoppers hop on and off escalators all the time at malls in every Tier I and many Tier II cities. Indian consumers are becoming accustomed to buying a large variety of products under one roof. Malls have become places to socialize and spend time with friends and family. Domestic retail chains, such as Pantaloons, Westside, Lifestyle, and Globus, are

▲ **FIGURE 5.10** Manish Malhotra with a Bollywood actress as a model at a fashion show. India's fashion week is gaining popularity with buyers from all over the world. India has its own fashion trends that most Indian consumers follow. AFP/Getty Images.

part of these malls and also present as standalone stores in some cities, unlike in the United States where stores are usually either only in the malls or in strip malls as stand-alone stores. The shoppers get an international shopping experience in such retail outlets with self-service shopping, air-conditioned stores, and wide-open shopping space (Ernst and Young Inc, 2007).

BOUTIQUES

Boutiques have become very popular and operate in malls as well as other shopping areas. These stores may be one of a kind or part of a chain. They sell exclusive, unique, or trendy products. The product range is vast, including apparel, jewelry, accessories, footwear, and so on. Satya Paul, Sheetal Design Studio, Ritu Kumar, Manish Malhotra, and Tarun Tahiliani are some top Indian designers that sell through their own boutiques. With an increase in disposable income among Indians, more and more people are buying designer wear (Ernst and Young Inc. 2007).

ART GALLERIES

Art galleries in many of India's Tier I cities display the works of independent designers who can't afford their own stores. The designer rents these galleries for a weekend, or the entire week depending on the budget of the designer. The products sold in art galleries are usually unique and cannot be found in regular stores. Many talented housewives develop designer outfits under their own private labels and then sell their lines in gallery exhibitions (Ernst and Young Inc., 2007).

ADVENT OF BRANDS

Brand name has been unimportant to a large percentage of Indians who have their clothes custom made for a long time. But, as the apparel retail market becomes more popular and associated with good quality, Indian consumers are becoming more and more brand conscious. The first company to sell shirts under a brand name in India was Liberty shirts in the 1950s. Peter England, Park Avenue, Charagh Din, Raymonds, and Arrow are some leading domestic brands. A growing demand for jeans sparked the branding process in the country. Lee, Levi's, Seven Jeans, and Pepe Jeans were the first international denim brands to enter India. Today, some well-established domestic denim brands, such as Flying

Machine, Killer, and Numero Uno, are competing fiercely with international brands. Branded apparel has captivated both the menswear and women's wear retail markets and is slowly capturing the children's market (Ernst and Young Inc., 2007).

FASHION WEEK

The Fashion Design Council of India (FDCI) had its first fashion week in India in 2000. India now has multiple fashion weeks in which designers from all over the country display their lines. These events attract buyers from all over the world. Extensive media coverage of these shows is increasing fashion consciousness among Indian consumers. Retail chains copy fashion-week trends to cater to customers who cannot afford the high-end clothing on display at these shows.

GETTING TO KNOW DOMESTIC COMPETITORS: A BOOMING DOMESTIC SECTOR

India has the largest unorganized retail market in the world. Traditionally a retail business in India was a small, family venture with the shop in the front and house in the back. Branded merchandise is becoming increasingly attractive to urban consumers with purchasing power. To compete with foreign brands, Indian retailers must realize the value of building their own stores as brands. It may help reinforce their market positioning, as brands communicate quality as well as value. A sustainable competitive advantage depends on combining products, image, and reputation into a coherent retail brand strategy.

The Indian retail scene is booming. A number of large corporate houses—Tata's, Raheja's, Piramals', Goenka's—have already made their foray into this arena, with beauty and health stores, supermarkets, self-service music stores, bookstores, everyday-low-price stores, computers and peripherals stores, office equipment stores, and home/building construction stores. The organized

▲ **FIGURE 5.11** Shoppers Stop website. This was the first retail chain in India and is a very popular chain even today. It has changed its pricing strategies several times, but today caters to middle- and upper-middle-class population. Courtesy of Globus.

players have attacked every retail category. Too many players in too short a time have crowded several categories without considering their core competencies or developing a well-thought-out branding strategy, and have crowded the market.

SHOPPERS STOP

This chain was started by K Raheja group of companies in 1991. Shopper's Stop has the advantage of being among the first retail chains established in India. It is known for its expertise and acumen specific to current practices in the retail industry. For example, Shoppers Stop initiated the accumulate-points-for-discounts program called "First citizen's club" where customers' purchases received points to redeem for merchandise of a certain value. In 2005, Shoppers Stop differentiated itself by including a bookstore and coffee shop in all its stores (Indian retail report, 2009). Although the company has changed its image multiple times, it is known for quality of service, product offerings, and a cosmopolitan shopping environment. It has partnered with some international companies such as Mother Care and Allied Industries of Australia to provide unique products to its customers. It also has private labels that provide merchandise at a lower price range to cater to a wider segment of customers.

WESTSIDE

Trent Ltd., a part of Tata group, owns Westside, which was started in 1998. The company acquired Littlewoods, a London-based retail chain, and renamed it Westside. Westside was India's first private-label-only store chain. It carries apparel for all segments, among other products such as footwear, cosmetics, household furnishings, and gifts, and has 49 department stores throughout the country. With its private label, the company offers unique products that draw repeat customers. In 2004, the company launched a hypermarket store format called Star Bazaar. They sell groceries, beauty products, consumer electronics, and household items at very affordable prices. The store also sells apparel. Trent Ltd. also has stake in Landmark, one of India's largest book and music retail chains (About Trent, 2010).

PANTALOON

The Future Group started Pantaloon in 1997. This group owns multiple retail formats, all of which have been highly successful and cater to a large segment of the population. Pantaloon is among the largest retail chain stores in India with 44 stores across the country. Pantaloon caters to customers who want good value for their money and are willing to pay extra for an improved lifestyle.

India's Future group has businesses in many different sectors such as consumer finance, capital, insurance, leisure and entertainment, brand development, and retail real estate development. The company has various retail chains selling different product categories such as Big Bazaar (similiar to Walmart), Food Bazaar (grocery store), eZone (similar to Best Buy), Central (a mall), and Home Town (a home goods store). The group's core value is "Indianness" with a philosophy of "Rewrite rules, Retain values" (About The Future Group, 2010).

LIFESTYLE

Landmark Group, a Dubai-based company, started this chain in 1999. Lifestyle has an extensive footwear department and carries a large selection of both Western and traditional women's and menswear. It carries high-quality children's clothing and toys. The store carries about 250 national and international brands under one roof. Its prices are affordable. In 2010 there were 21 Lifestyle stores in India (Lifestyle department stores, 2010).

GLOBUS

This retail chain was founded in 1998 by R. Raheja Group, which launched its first store in Indore, a Tier II city, in 1999. In 2010, they had 24 stores all over India and plan to have 100 stores by 2012. The store caters to Indian youth. It offers apparel for all segments, accessories, beauty products, and some leather products (Globus, 2010).

EBONY

This retail chain is a part of DS Group, which is involved in businesses that range from hospitality to infrastructure development (About the group, 2010). DS Group launched Ebony in New Delhi in

1994. This store chain offers a very high level of customer service. Its main goal is to provide a world-class shopping experience to the Indian consumer. It also has a private label that has been highly successful. In 2010, Ebony had eight stores across India, mainly in the northern part of the country (About the group, 2010). Its store in south India's Chennai closed down due to poor performance. The company does plan to open two to three stores in the southern part of the country.

HOW MATURE IS THE RETAIL INDUSTRY? A LONG WAY HOME

As domestic and international retailers flood the market, the Indian retail industry is rapidly expanding. Still, certain opportunities in apparel retail remain untapped. One of the major problems in the Indian apparel retail industry is the issue of standardized sizing. Retailers use their own size charts, so there is no consistency between a medium size at one store and the medium size at another. Consumers do not feel comfortable buying clothes without trying them on. Most retailers have a tailor on site that makes the alterations while the consumer shops. To avoid having to deal with alterations, some customers also prefer having clothing tailored as they can customize the garment to their needs. International retailers have an opportunity to streamline the shopping experience with the introduction of standardized sizing.

Online retailing for apparel is an untapped market in India. Internet shopping for apparel is not very popular in India due to sizing issues and insecurity over using credit cards. Consumers use store websites to browse new offerings, compare prices, and gather product information. With an increasing number of Internet users in India, many retail chains are now venturing into the online retail format. International retailers can use their expert knowledge and experience in this area to capture a spot in the apparel retail market.

Although the Indian retail market is growing at a rapid pace with many modern retail stores being set up in different parts of the country, the market is still not a mature one. There are issues related to consumer expectations (example: mom-and-pop stores' delivery of groceries), which modern retail formats do not meet. Many grocery stores do not have proper refrigeration systems, so one does not always find fresh vegetables. International retailers can study the market and make changes to fill in such gaps.

BUYING FOR APPAREL RETAIL STORES: BETTER COST AND QUALITY AT HOME

India is rich in raw materials and low-cost labor, both of which are prerequisites for a successful apparel manufacturing business (Textile Intelligence Report, 2006). The domestic textiles and apparel market in India is the fastest-growing market in the world (Ernst and Young, 2009). India has been an important source of apparel for retailers in Europe and the United States. With an increase in demand for apparel manufacturing in the domestic market, many of the manufacturing units that earlier made apparel only for export are shifting gears in order to cater to the domestic market. Exporters such as Gokaldas, Orient Craft, Royal Classic, Creative, and Shahi have either completely shifted to manufacturing for domestic brands or are considering doing so. India has many advantages that keep the domestic apparel manufacturers from looking outside. These are:

- ▶ Availability of raw materials and processing ability from fiber to apparel
- ▶ Availability of highly differentiated products with a setup for experimenting with new styles due to possibility of producing lesser quantities
- ▶ High level of flexibility with respect to order quantity and lead time for production
- ▶ A large, low-cost, and highly skilled labor population
- ▶ A large number of manufacturing units with high technology
- ▶ Removal of certain government restrictions of foreign investment in textile and apparel manufacturing

Domestic retailers are mainly looking to local apparel manufacturers to provide them with good quality apparel. However, some retailers are going to China to diversify their sourcing. Many international retailers that have set up shops in India want to increase their sourcing from India. For example, in 2009 Marks and Spencer made plans to source 70 percent of its apparel from India as opposed to its then 20 percent (Jain & Dutta, 2009). Although India seems to be the right place for companies with an Indian retail presence to source apparel from, low productivity in factories might be a challenge.

Indian manufacturers are known for producing clothes with the "Indian look," which is achieved through use of embroidery, mirrors, and sequins sewn on the clothing, tunic-style tops, and bright colors (a preference among most Indian women, although color choices may vary based on location). But the manufacturing setup is also capable of producing jeans, undergarments, tailored suits, formal shirts, and many other categories of clothing. Many domestic retailers are sourcing a large number of accessories from China, and apparel from Thailand and Mauritius. But a large number of retailers are having their private label apparel produced within the country. High import duties are another deterrent for retailers to import. On the other hand, to source within the country, a retailer needs to set up an office.

Another problem with importing is the major difference in customer needs for the same season around the world. For example, the fall lines of most international retailers have clothing in dark and dull colors such as grays and blacks. Fall is the beginning of festival season in India where everybody dresses in bright cheerful colors such as red, yellow, and orange. International brands that import clothing from their home countries in the northern hemisphere end up with offerings that are not suitable for the Indian market at that time. Hence, retailers that do have a large number of stores, or have major expansion plans, can consider setting up a local office and sourcing domestically so that they can produce special lines for the Indian market. Retailers that want to set up shop in India can easily do their sourcing domestically (Textile Intelligence Report, 2006).

RETAIL CAREERS: SKILLED PERSONNEL WANTED

Lack of skilled labor is a major problem in the Indian retail industry. To tackle this issue, many educational institutes are offering short-term programs to prepare individuals for careers in retailing. National Institute of Fashion Design (Delhi) and SNDT Women's University (Mumbai) offer undergraduate and graduate-level programs to prepare students for careers in buying and merchandising. Other private institutes, such as Pearl Academy of Fashion (New Delhi), offer diploma programs in merchandising, buying, and retailing. Many other institutes offer short-term certification courses for store management positions (Career in retail, 2009).

Formed in 2004, Retailers Association of India (RAI) is working with some of the top business schools in the country to offer a master's program in retail management. An educational qualification in retail or a related area would work to one's advantage for a career in retail. A large number of positions are available in the apparel retail business, in different areas such as logistics, store management, sales, marketing, store design, information technology, buying, and merchandising. With an increasing demand for qualified and experienced personnel and lack of talent, the retail industry in India offers job candidates much higher financial gains than its counterpart in the United States.

Retail companies in India are open to international students applying for internships. Many companies get foreign exchange students through student-run AIESEC (Association Internationale des Étudiants en Sciences Économiques et Commerciales, www.aiesec.org) international network. Local chapters of this network place students in internships in many different countries. The companies help students to obtain a temporary work permit and pay them during the internship period. The only positions that are lucrative for foreigners in India are upper-management positions because junior-level positions do not pay very well. Some websites that can be explored to find jobs in Indian retail are www.indiaretailjobs.com, www.naukri.com, and www.monster india.com.

FUTURE OF APPAREL RETAIL: LAND OF PROMISE

The rural sector is slowly becoming important for retailers, as it is half of the Indian retail market, amounting to $300 billion. With the increase in the per capita income of the rural Indian population by almost 50 percent in 2000 to 2010, rural areas are becoming significant markets for retailers. The retail sector is also providing employment to the rural population. Increased earnings among the rural population in turn are improving basic infrastructure, financial situations, and information services.

For every 1,000 Indian consumers, there are 11 retail stores. This statistic makes India the country with the highest shop density. In larger cities, this density is about 45 shops for 1,000 consumers. Retailers want to open more stores to cover the smaller cities quickly and gain first mover's advantage. But domestic and international retailers should be ready to face numerous challenges when trying to expand in India:

- ► Lack of proper infrastructure. It causes a major problem with transporting goods from one location to the other. Traffic volume far exceeds capacity. The government is working on building a network of highways, but it will take two to three years to have it in place (India, 2009).
- ► Supply chain issues. Not all Indian retailers have sophisticated technology such as bar coding, tablet-style personal computers, point-of-sale, and handheld systems. International retailers will have to bring their technology into the country to make the supply chain more efficient (India, 2009).
- ► Increasing cost of real estate. Many real estate agencies are developing malls and other retail space as demand increases. But the cost of retail space is rising apace. Most Indian retailers

prefer long-term leases. Lease rentals account for 7 to 8 percent of a retailer's revenue (India, 2009).

▶ Lack of skilled labor. Skilled labor is needed to manage stores at the front as well as back ends. Retailers must bring in trained personnel to manage their stores. Some domestic retailers have teamed up with management schools to train people for retail setups. Other retailers have established their own retail schools. And some retail chains contact local unemployment offices to find people, train them, and hire them to work as sales staff (India, 2009).

▶ Pilferage in stores. Indian retailers lose up to $1.13 billion a year to shoplifting, employee pilferage, and vendor fraud. Indian retailers use security cameras, thorough checking of sales staff, and security tags on expensive products, but a more sophisticated system needs to be implemented; for example, having security tags sewn into the garment as many American retailers do.

▶ Transportation. Trains and trucks form the major modes of transportation in India. The operators are members of unions, and every year before peak season, they go on strike with a set of demands. Retailers need to be prepared for delays and plan ahead.

▶ Uncertainty about the mall culture. A large number of malls are popular and crowded, but there are many malls in India with vacant store spaces due to high rents. With so many malls cropping up all over the country, each one may not be able to generate enough foot traffic in all of them to make all its stores profitable. So, it may be wise to wait and watch. On the other hand, there may be no space for new entrants in the future.

▶ Government policies. Corruption at every level of conducting a business makes dealing with the government a challenge because investors need to deal with several people and a lengthy process to get simple approvals for starting a business.

All these factors need to be considered while launching a store in India. The Indian retail industry is growing by leaps and bounds, and every retailer is in a rush to gain first mover's advantage; but retailers in India need to think first. They must ensure that they have the right square footage for the products they want to sell. A large store may be attractive, but it may not provide the required return on investment. In the race to have the maximum number of stores in the country, retailers should not fail to measure the performance of each store on a regular basis. Poorly performing stores need to be monitored and proper action must be taken to fix the issues. It takes time to establish stores and become a leader in the market. Many retailers in the United States (e.g., Walmart, Gap) and Europe (e.g., Carrefour) very well know the advantages of being slow but steady.

Although the Indian market may seem saturated with a large number of traditional and modern retail formats, there is enough scope for many more retailers to enter India. Some opportunities that international retailers can bank on are:

- ▶ Lack of modern retail setups. The unorganized sector still dominates Indian retail industry. As consumers become more demanding, modern retail facilities will attract them.
- ▶ Relaxation of FDI regulations. Although the pace may be slow, India is opening up to international retail investments. Franchising or joint venture might still be the best option considering the various restrictions on international investments.

Case Study 1

HÄAGEN-DAZS TEASER AD OFFENDS INDIANS

A badly phrased teaser ad by TBWA India to launch Häagen-Dazs ice cream in India has offended Indians and sparked a backlash by bloggers. The posters, hung near India's first Häagen-Dazs outlet opening in a Delhi mall, tried to strike a cosmopolitan note with a reference to the French Riviera and the words "Exclusive Preview for International Travellers. Access restricted only to holders of international passports."

In a blog post headlined "Sorry, Indians Not Allowed," a *Times of India* web editor said a friend was refused entry to the new ice cream store, and e-mailed him a photo of the ad, which the editor posted, calling the campaign "idiotic."

The post generated over 1,000 lively and mostly deeply offended comments, starting with one that said, "This is an insult of Indian nationals. . . . They should be barred from doing business in India." The next comment began: "The store should be shut down immediately," and subsequent commentors suggested that Häagen-Dazs should be fined or thrown out of the country, or both.

A SIGNIFICANT MISCOMMUNICATION

In a flurry of updates on the *Times of India* blog, Häagen-Dazs executives said that if anyone was barred from entering the store, it was only because it was too crowded, and apologized for the unfortunate wording of the teaser ad.

Anindo Mukherji, managing director of Häagen-Dazs parent General Mills in India, said in a lengthy statement: "The message was intended to suggest that you can enjoy, for instance, a taste of the French Riviera without traveling to France—by enjoying Häagen-Dazs. Unfortunately, the reference to the international-passport holder on the poster may have led to a significant miscommunication."

Meanwhile, the *Times of India* did an online news story that drew 330 comments, and posted a video interview with their own editor punctuated by written on-screen phrases like "Racism at home," "Scoop of controversy," and "Ice-cream maker denied Indians entry."

TBWA already handles Häagen-Dazs in ten countries in Europe and Asia, according to *Ad Age*'s annual Global Brands report, and did the India teaser campaign, although that relationship seems unlikely to continue. The two companies said in a statement: "That project has now ended. Häagen-Dazs will decide on their agency at the appropriate moment, as originally planned."

AN AFFRONT ON OUR PRIDE

As the debate rages in India, trade publisher Exchange4media, *Ad Age*'s partner in India, weighed in with comments from top industry executives:

"The whole campaign is issued with a clear idea of having fun," said KV Sridhar, Leo Burnett's creative director in India. "[But] we need to remember that India is very strong when it comes to social activists and NGOs, who like to make a small issue into a fire, and obviously that is supported by our very own media."

"Social media has changed everything," said Rahul Jauhari, national creative director, Pickle Lintas. "But brands are slow to catch on. What I am sure happened as a result of a silly oversight by the agency and the client got magnified in an instant. . . . In today's times, it is even more critical to be conscious of what your brand is saying, because today every consumer is a voice that will be heard, in favor or against what the brand does. . . . One wrong tweet can lead to a PR nightmare."

Source: Laurel Wentz, "Häagen-Dazs Teaser Ad Offends Indians," *Advertising Age.* Retrieved on December 15, 2010, from http://adage.com/globalnews/ article?article_id=141246

Discussion Questions

1. Do you agree with the quote "The store should be shut down immediately"? Does this seem to be a plausible solution to the problem? Why or why not?

2. "The whole campaign is issued with a clear idea of having fun." If the intention of the ad campaign was fun, where did the company go wrong?

3. Imagine yourself to be the advertisement head of the company, keeping in mind the social and cultural factors that shape Indian consumer behavior. How would you go about designing an ad campaign for its launch in India?

4. What are the most important things to be learned from this case study in relation to advertising and nationality?

Case Study 2

IT HAPPENS ONLY IN INDIA: A UNIQUE APPROACH TO RETAIL BRANDING

The retail sector in India is highly fragmented, with the organized segment being a very nascent minority; focus on brand building seems to be critical in this regard. Sir Terry Leahy, CEO of Tesco, said in a recent interview, "In a world with infinite information and complex choices, consumers will increasingly navigate by trust" (Leahy, 2007). This trust will largely be an offshoot of the confidence that shoppers tend to repose in individual as well as corporate brands. In his essay "Branding in South East Asia," Kim Faulkner observes that "New Asian brands are emerging, which, while drawing inspiration from the largesse of international brands, are trying to carve their own niche. These brands are trying to capitalize on the indigenous Asian cultures by recognizing that internationalism does not mean trying to be Western in Asia" (Faulkner, 2006).

The idea of incorporating the local customs in the DNA of the brands is not confined to marketing gimmicks but has become an integral component of the operational structure and format of successful Indian retail brands. *Subhiksha*, a South India–based discount retail chain, has structured its brand around the concept of the Indian housewife's conviction of getting the best value for her money. So *Subhiksha* has designed its promotional campaign with the slogan "Saving is my right!"

The Indian socio-economic fabric is a collage of variegated customs, climates, languages, and economic makeup. Successful brands trying to establish a relationship with the Indian consumers have not shown any sensitivity toward these heterogeneous contexts. Enterprises like Big Bazaar, a low-cost hypermarket owned by Future Group, is one of the other retailers that has successfully adapted and designed its stores according to the Indian way of shopping while keeping in mind the geopolitical nuances. The Indian retailer has to innovate in order to create new demand and capture the existing one. Retail brands in India have realized this and are gearing up to meet with this challenge.

There has been an attempt to reflect the cultural consciousness and economic tendencies behind the shopping orientations of their customers. Big Bazaar has managed to do this quite successfully. In his autobiography *It Happened in India*, Biyani-owner of Future Group writes, "Our store in *Sangli* (a small township 400 kms. southeast of Mumbai) is a bit different from what you would see at say High Street Phoenix in Mumbai. . . . It isn't air-conditioned; instead there are air coolers installed inside the store. Also there are as many shoppers there on weekdays as on weekends. Unlike office going people in big cities, people in smaller towns do not restrict their shopping to weekends. The store factors in the local taste, preference and culture, and in that way not two Big Bazaar outlets look the same." For instance, in the Gujarat-based Big Bazaars outlets, edible oils are sold loose because that is how the region has shopped for oils all along before the advent of modern retail. This is probably the reason why the store has become synonymous with the idea of utility shopping in India.

As brand guru, David Ogilvy rightly said, "Any damn fool can put on a deal, but it takes *genius, faith, and perseverance* to create a brand." And it appears as if the Indian retailers have put their imagination to work and are gearing up to consolidate their mindshare before the Walmarts of the world make their presence felt.

Source: Chaturvedi, Preeti, "It Happens Only in India: A unique approach to retail branding," BrandChannel, Brandpapers. Retrieved on December 15, 2010, from http://www.brandchannel.com/papers_review.asp?sp_id=1307]

Discussion Questions

1. Sir Terry Leahy, CEO of Tesco, said in a recent interview, "In a world with infinite information and complex choices, consumers will increasingly navigate by trust." What are some of the other factors that might help consumers to make a decision?

2. Is consumerism being looked at in the right light by some of the retailers that are quoted in the study?

3. Branding is becoming a recognized discipline—but it still needs to be understood as an integrated process. What is your advice to the foreign retailers trying to venture in the country?

REFERENCES

A.T. Kearney (2006). Global retail development index report. *Emerging market priorities for global retailers.* Retrieved August 6, 2007, from http://www.atkearney.com/shared_res/pdf/GRDI_2006.pdf

A.T. Kearney (2006). *Global retail development index.* Retrieved August 16, 2007, from http://www.atkearney.com/main.taf?p=5,3,1,141,1

About The Future Group (2010). Retrieved October 29, 2010, from http://pantaloon.futurebazaar.com/page.jsp?page=aboutus&catalog=futurebazaar

About Trent (2010). Retrieved October 29, 2010, from http://www.mywestside.com/aboutus.aspx

Agarwal, P., Dhir, A. & Sachdeva, P. (2008). *Building sustainable businesses in the growing domestic market.* Retrieved November 21, 2009, from www.technopak.com

Apparel retail: Labeling the Indian Market (2004). Retrieved November 15, 2009, from http://www.ibef.org/artdisplay.aspx?cat_id=375&art_id=4705

Anonymous (2008). Building Sustainable Business in the Growing Domestic Market. Retrieved October 4, 2009, from http://www.businesswireindia.com/attachments/Fashion_White_Paper.pdf

Anonymous (2009). *Indian Cosmetic Sector Analysis.* Retrieved November 13, 2009, from http://www.marketresearch.com/product/display.asp?productid=2268159

Arnould, E.J. (1995). West Africa distribution channels, environmental duress, relationship management, and implications for western marketing. In Sherry, J.F. Jr.(Eds.), *Contemporary Marketing and Consumer Behavior* (pp. 119–127).London: Sage Publishers.

Bahadur, S. (2006). *Retail scene in India.* Retrieved November 15, 2009, from www.chillibreeze.com

Batra, M. & Niehm. L. S. (2009). An opportunity analysis framework for apparel retailing in India. *Clothing and Textiles Research Journal Online.*

Retrieved March 17, 2009, from http://ctr.sagepub.com/cgi/rapidpdf/0887302X08327360v1.pdf

Bharadwaj, V., Swaroop, M. & Vittal, I. (2005). Winning the Indian consumers. *The McKinsey Quarterly*, 6, 66–71.

Bhattacharya, P. (2009, Feburary 2). *India Quarterly: Indian Beauty Market Roundup*. Message posted from issue of *GCI Magazine*. Retrieved Dec. 1, 2009, from http://www.gcimagazine.com/marketstrends/regions/bric/38826982.html

Bhatnagar, M. (2008, March, 6). *Organized retail in India gathers momentum*. Retrieved August 1, 2008, message posted to http://www.domain-b.com/industry/Retail/20080306_retail.html

Bijapurkar, R. (2007). *Winning the Indian market: Understanding the transformation of consumer India* (1st ed.). Singapore: Saik Wah Press.

Biyani, K. (2007, April). The Promised Land for Retailers, *Images Retail*, 6(4), p. 37.

Careers in Retail Management (2009). Retrieved November 15, 2009, from http://www.docstoc.com/docs/7810371/careers-retail-management

Chattaraman, V. (2009). *The Indian Consumer*. Retrieved June 3, 2009, from http://www.udel.edu/fiber/issue4/world/indianconsumer.html

Chauhan, S. (2006). *Foreign direct investment in retail: bane or boon*. Retrieved November 7, 2007, from http://ssrn.com/abstract=912625

Cygnus Business Consulting and Research (2004). *Executive summary of apparel retailing in India*. Retrieved March 6, 2008, from http://www.cygnusindia.com/Industry%20Insight-apparel%20Retailing%20in%20India-Executive%20Summary%20&%20TOC-March%202004_.pdf

Datamonitor (2008). Menswear in India: Industry profile. *Datamonitor Industry Profile*, 1–25.

Dhanabhakyam, M. & Shanthi, A. (n.d). *Indian retail industry—its growth, challenges and opportunities*. Retrieved October 10, 2009, from http://footwearsinfolinethree.tripod.com/indian_retail_industry_its_growth_challenges_and_opportunities.pdf

Dickinson, H. (2005). *India is emerging as real opportunity*. Retrieved November 9, 2007, from http://webebscohost.com/ehost/detail?vid=5&hid=107&sid=5027321

Dominic, K. (2007, August, 3). *Indian retail: an overview.* Retrieved November 14, 2007, from http://www.networkmagazineindia.com/200703/coverstory01.shtml

Ernst & Young Inc. (2007), *The great Indian retail story.* Retrieved October 4, 2007, from http://www.ey.com/global/download.nsf/ India/Retail_TheGreat_Indian_Retail_Story/$file/TheGreat_Indian_Retail_Story.pdf

Faulkner, K. (2006) "Branding in South East Asia," from Brands and Branding, *The Economist*, London, pp. 203–204.

Gadkari, S. (2009). *Indian retail industry 2009.* Retrieved October 4, 2009, from http://www.scribd.com/doc/22694630/India-Retail-Industry-analysis

Globus (2010). Retrieved October 20, 2010, from http://www.globus.in/v2/about_globus.asp

Goyal, P. (2007).The most significant factors to consider while launching a new apparel brand in India. Retrieved October 4, 2009, from http://www.fibre2fashion.com/industry-article/9/809/the-most-significant-factors-to-consider-while-launching-a-new-apparel-brand-in-india1.asp

Images yearbook 2009: The business of fashion (2009). Images multimedia pvt. Ltd., New Delhi, India (2009). Retrieved November 15, 2009, from http://www.pwc.com/en_GX/gx/retail-consumer/pdf/india.pdf

India in Business: Retailing overview (2009). Retrieved on August 25, 2009, from http://www.indiainbusiness.nic.in/industry-infrastructure/service-sectors/retailing.htm

India: Background (2010). Retrieved on November 1, 2010, from https://www.cia.gov/library/publications/the-world-factbook/geos/in.html

India's Textile and Apparel Industry: Opportunities for Sourcing and Collaboration (2006). Retrieved November 5, 2009, from www.researchandmarkets.com for *Textiles Intelligence.*

Indians prefer to discover and converse (2007, April 11). *The Hindu.* Retrieved September 6, 2007, from http://www.thehindubusinessline.com/2007/04/11/stories/2007041104190500.htm

India third most attractive market for apparel retailers (2008, June 2). *The Economics Times.* Retrieved July 22, 2008, from http://www.economictimes.indiatimes.com/News/News_By_Industry/Cons_ProductsgarmentsTextiles/India_third_most_attractive_market_for_apparel_retailers/articleshow/3094123.cms

Jain, C. & Dutta, D. (2009). Explore beyond the obvious: India's position in the global textile and clothing trade. Retrieved December 7, 2009, from http://www.udel.edu/fiber/issue4/world/explore.html

Leahy, T. (2007, April). "Retail and the World Economy," from *images Retail*, 6(4), 44.

Lifestyle department stores (2010). Retrieved on October 29, 2010, from http://www.landmarkgroupme.com/retail/landmark-brands/lifestyle-department-stores/

Luxury Unlimited (2009). Retrieved on December 7, 2009, from http://india-now.org/download/luxury_june06.pdf

Madison, A. (2003). The World Economy: Historical Statistics, OECD, Paris.

Mohan, R. & Gupta, C. (2007). Consumer preference patterns in apparel retailing in India. *Proceedings of the Fourth Asia Pacific Retail Conference,* Bangkok, Thailand. Retrieved March 17, 2009, from http://citeseerx.ist.psu.edu/viewdoc/download?doi=10.1.1.120.6508&rep=rep1&type=pdf#page=223

Mom & Pop stores will retail 84% of the pie until 2013 (2008). Retrieved November 20, 2009, from http://www.india-reports.com/retail-weekly/08May1-6.aspx

Mulky, A. & Nargundkar, R. (2003). Modernisation in Indian Retailing: Managerial and Policy Perspectives" in *Udyog Pragati*, 27(2), no. 2, 1–8, April–June 2003. Prayag, A. (2007, April 11).

Rao, K. (2006, June 1), "Retail: India—a window opens", *Foreign Direct Investment*, pp. 1.

Retail (2009). Retrieved November 10, 2009, from http://www.ibef.org/industry/retail.aspx

"Retail format changing to suit market requirements." Retrieved August 25, 2009, from http://www.indianrealtynews.com/retail-market/retail-format-changing-to-suit-market-requirements.html

Retail sector sees a bright future (2010, September 6). Retrieved November 1, 2010, from http://www.expressindia.com/latest-news/Retail-sector-sees-a-bright-future/677935/

Ridge, M. (2008). Beauty worldwide watch: India. Retrieved October 12, 2009, from http://www.wwd.com/beauty-industry-news/beauty-world-wide-watch-india-1853335/print

Sinha, P. K. & Kar, S. K. (2007). *An insight into growth of new retail formats in India*. Retrieved November 15, 2009, from www.iimahd.ernet.in/download.php?downloadid=448

Sheth, K. & Vittal, I. (2007). *How half the world shops: Brazil, China, and India*. Retrieved November 15, 2009, from http://www.mckinseyquarterly.com/Americas/How_half_the_world_shops_Apparel_in_Brazil_China_and_India_2075

Sridhar, L. (2010, October 20). Different strokes, the luxury consumer in India today is difficult to stereotype. Retrieved October 20, 2010, from http://www.businessworld.in/bw/storyContent/2009_09_18_Different_Strokes.html

Stephen, M. (2009, October 23). *India Luxury retail booming in the midst of a global economic slowdown*. Message posted on http://www.articlesbase.com/small-business-articles/indian-luxury-retail-booming-in-the-midst-of-a-global-economic-slowdown-1371693.html

RUSSIA

6

Andrey Gabisov

Jaya Halepete

Mansi Patney

OBJECTIVES

After reading this chapter, you will

- ▶ Know the unique characteristics of Russian consumers
- ▶ Understand the Russian retail industry and its challenges
- ▶ Grasp the regulations for foreign direct investment in Russia
- ▶ Know the various entry formats chosen by foreign retailers

In 1991, Russia opened a new chapter in its history of more than a thousand years when the breakup of the 74-year-old USSR made it an independent republic. Russia was an isolated country by the end of the cold war and communism. Today, the Russian market continues to deal with: logistical issues, infrastructure problems (including delays at ports due to congestion), high custom fees and taxes, poor quality of products, red tape, and corruption. Nevertheless, economic reforms and an abundance of natural resources have helped Russia to return to its rightful place on the world stage (Table 6.1). Russia possesses the world's largest reserves of gas, oil, coal, and

TABLE 6.1 Fast Facts about Russia

Capital	Moscow
Population	138.7 million
Type of government	Federation
GDP: purchasing power parity: in US$	$2.1 trillion
Age structure	0–14 yrs: 14.8%
	15–64 yrs: 71.5%
	65 yrs plus: 13.7%
Religion	Russian Orthodox: 15–20%
	Muslim: 10–15%
	Other Christian: 2%
	Unspecified or None: 63–73%
Ethnicity	Russian: 79.8%
	Tatar: 3.8%
	Ukrainian: 2%
	Bashkir: 1.2%
	Chuvash: 1.1%
	Unspecified or none: 12.1%

Source: CIAfactbook.gov

other minerals and energy resources, and it ranks among the highest exporters of natural gas, oil, and steel. However, due to its over-reliance on commodity exports, Russia is vulnerable to changing commodity prices all over the world. The government is trying to develop diverse sectors of the economy, such as technology and retail, to reduce Russia's dependency on exports.

Since 2008, a drop in the price of oil has hurt the Russian economy, but it still remains an attractive country for investment. According to American consulting firm A.T. Kearney, "Russia remains Europe's largest consumer market, with rising disposable incomes and an expanding middle class, and it offers massive growth opportunities for retailers with a long-term approach." The average per capita income is increasing, so consumers are spending more. Rising wages, increasing standards of living, and changing consumer habits, along with growth in the retail sector, are changing the face of Russian retail. The Russian market is highly fragmented. For example, the top five food retailers' sales account for only 7 percent of total sales, leaving room for large retail chains to enter the market, grow, and take the lead. It is not very expensive to acquire domestic companies, due to their low valuation.

The first quarter of 2010 saw a growth of about 57 percent in the Russian clothing market, spurred by an increase in customer demand, the entry of international retailers (such as Italian luxury fashion house Dolce & Gabbana and Japanese casualwear designer Uniqlo), and increase in sales of brands such as Zara and H&M. Many luxury retailers that exited the market during the recession of 2008 gradually returned. Russia as a retail market is regaining its popularity among international retailers.

THE RETAIL LANDSCAPE: WESTERN IS GOOD

Retail has been one of the fastest-growing markets in the Russian Federation. When the Soviet era ended, many Russians started small businesses in retail. Huge economic growth followed an economic crisis in 1998, in which the Russian economy was overwhelmed by massive debt, low energy prices, and a host of other political and economic issues. The Russian ruble dropped three times more than the United States dollar, wiping out many Russian companies, especially those with low levels of management and "Red Directors," CEOs with only Soviet experience who failed to acknowledge the laws of the capitalist market, such as the need for marketing. Significant changes have occurred since 1998. The Soviet legacy has given way to new ideas and more professional management. Vladimir Putin ushered in accompanying economic and political changes when he became president in 2000. Under his government the system didn't become fairer and less corrupt, but it

▲ **FIGURE 6.1** Pedestrians pass by a luxury fashion store on Nevsky Prospekt Street, St. Petersburg, Russia. © Yadid Levy/Alamy.

definitely became more stable and clear, which business requires. The retail industry has become more modern, and many foreign investors have entered the market.

In the mid-1990s, standards of living dropped significantly, and people had no money to buy basic consumer goods. There was no middle class, except for a small segment in Moscow, the capital and most populous city. A segment of extremely rich people became wealthy through shady deals. This wealthy class had no idea what products were good or bad. After three quarters of a century of communist living, they were ready to consume everything from abroad and price was not a concern. Companies such as the premium multibrand apparel chain Bosco di Ciliegi and JamilCo, a retail chain that sells exclusive-right premium brands such as Burberry, Escada, and Sonia Rykiel, and middle-segment brands such as Timberland started their businesses during this period. They are industry leaders today.

Most future retailers and brands came from Russian distribution companies that were working with European brands. For example, Bosco Sport, which outfits the Russian Olympic team, is owned by Bosco di Ciliegi, which distributes many foreign premium brands. The Russian retailer Finn Flare was originally set up in Finland and has grown to more than 50 stores in Helsinki, Moscow, Saint Petersburg, and Astana. Its franchising network consists of about 130 stores across Russia and Kazakhstan. In 1969 Finn Flare hired a new export manager named Raimo Aaltonen, who would go on to develop the business to the highest standards. In 1991 he bought the business. During the same year a young Russian entrepreneur named Ksenia Ryasova started her own business in Russia. She sold apparel from Vietnam, where she had lived for three years, and then started her own multibrand retail chain, "People in New." In 1996

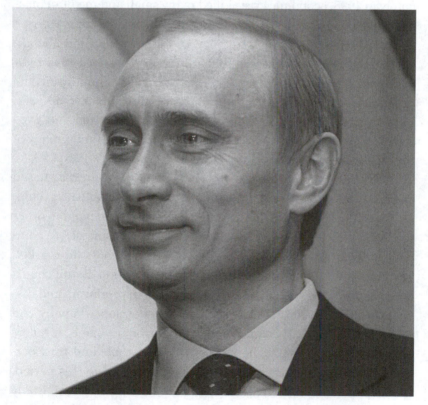

▲ FIGURE 6.2 Vladimir Putin President of Russia, April 2000. Allstar Picture Library/Alamy

she met Raimo Aaltonen and signed an exclusive distribution agreement for the Finn Flare brand in Russia. According to the agreement, she could produce her own apparel designs under the Finn Flare brand and mix them with the assortment that was coming from Finland. The People in New brand had to be terminated because of the overwhelming success of Finn Flare. The Russian Finn Flare distributor became a huge name in Russia, and in 2006 Ksenia bought Finn Flare and became its president.

The success of Finn Flare revealed Russian consumers' preference for Western goods and Western brands. In the 1990s Russian manufacturers could not deliver either quality or stable production, but Russian distributing companies were growing rapidly. Unfortunately in 1998, economic crisis killed many small and medium businesses. As many small companies went bankrupt, the time was ripe for introducing new formats and new business technologies. Retailers that survived the first wave of bankruptcies changed their marketing strategies. They began catering to middle- and low-income consumers. Imports of cheaper products from Asia picked up pace. Russian manufacturers had to rethink their production and were forced to create lower-priced products. Due to lack of funds, many of the largest players could not invest in the retail sector.

By 2000, retailers began to enjoy economic growth. Retail chains developed. Strong retail chains that had established themselves in Moscow and St. Petersburg now looked to expand in other regions. Small stores began consolidating their businesses to compete with large retailers. Foreign investors entered the market, bringing new technology and increased competition. Retail chains became powerful and began dictating terms to producers and distributors. From 2005 to 2008, retail chains developed rapidly and their management became more professional. Large retailers enjoyed steady growth. The market became stable and transparent. The manufacturing industry was reborn. During this period, the level of competition was the highest among retailers. Many retailers began expanding, and with money to spend, retailers began diversifying their businesses.

Since the end of 2008 competition among retailers has intensified. Political stability and economic growth in Russia prompted many foreign retailers to invest in the market. Some Russian retailers entered the middle-income segment. Due to the increasing number of retailers, the demand for real estate grew. Real estate in Moscow and St. Petersburg is very expensive, which hindered further expansion. During the world financial crisis of 2009, many retailers left the market. Now there was availability of store space in malls, but it became hard to get financing and even harder to get consumers. Nevertheless, some mass-market foreign retailers (such as H&M) decided to enter the market. They had resources, cheap products, and little competition. Existing retail outlets and stores lacked cash to cover expenses. Small- and medium-sized businesses suffered from this more than big retail chains. They were not ready to face new competition. Big apparel companies such as those in other industries changed their business models to focus on low-income segments of the market. But apparel in Russia is still priced higher than in many other countries, which affects consumption.

Many industries in Russia are updates of Soviet organization, but retail is an exception. Entrepreneurs have introduced not only quality products from all over the world but also all modern trading technologies, workplaces, and formats, thus creating a very different retail market.

CONSUMERS: DEPRIVED NO MORE

Russian consumers have shed their "sleeping bear" image, now spending more than other European consumers. Russian consumers are similar to consumers in the developed economies, but the level of importance given to various shopping attributes is different. Russian consumers pay more attention to communicating status and the need for uniqueness than consumers of developed nations (Karpova, Nelson-Hodges, & Tullar, 2007). In the past, Russians were satisfied with cheap imitations. But now, the new consumer mantra is "Quality is worth the money." For a long time they did not have many options in shopping for clothes due to a lack of established branded stores. These consumers were also not willing to overpay for apparel and were looking for better quality and a range of products. In 2007, foreign retailers entered the market to meet the demands of Russian consumers.

Consumers in large cities and regions beyond vary drastically. Retailers interested in expanding in different regions of Russia need to understand these variations and cater to distinct needs. For example, in St. Petersburg women like Scandinavian style with less bijouterie and not very bright colors, whereas in Kazan women like bright colors and sparkling bijouterie.

Russian consumers spend twice as much on apparel as Europeans and Americans. About 28 percent of their income goes for apparel purchases (Advertology, 2008). The majority of these purchases are made to update their wardrobes (Fashioner, 2009). Although it is difficult to generalize consumer behavior for all the cities in Russia, it is true for many regions with prominent retail chains. Fast fashion (clothes suitable for only one season as the fashion changes rapidly) is very popular in major cities, but casual and sportswear is the most popular category in many regions. A market for eveningwear has developed only in Moscow and St. Petersburg.

Russian consumers mainly like to shop at large malls, followed by small stores and smaller malls, and an even smaller group buys from street vendors (Fashioner, 2009). The high cost of real estate and corruption make apparel in Russia very expensive. But premium-segment consumers are willing to pay a lot more for apparel than their counterparts in other European countries. Paying more money for a product is in itself a status symbol (Levinskij & Zhegulev, 2010). Russians are brand conscious and willing to pay more for branded apparel than nonbranded apparel and prefer foreign brands for durable goods. Many Russian consumers who were raised in the Soviet era desperately want to own Western brands, which were very scarce in their youth. This proclivity toward spending more to show status is one of the reasons why almost 71 percent of Russians do not have any savings at all (FDU, 2010).

In 1998, people spent more than half of their incomes on food, but that expenditure is now being replaced by spending on goods and services, recreation, and education, among others, mainly because of the increase in disposable income and the desire to emulate the Western lifestyle. Almost 15 percent of Russian shoppers like to experiment with new brands on a regular basis, and this number is even higher (22 percent) among 16- to 24-year-olds. Brand name is very important for Russian consumers, and they associate high quality with foreign apparel (Russia, 2004/2005).

MEN

In 2006, men's clothing and footwear represented only around 20 percent of the products available, and the lack of specialized stores for men came to the attention of leading retailers. For example, in 2006, the underwear retail chain Dikaya Orkhideya launched specialized stores selling men's underwear under the VI Legion brand.

Who is the Russian male consumer? Russian men generally come to the store with an idea of what they want and what they need. They very rarely come to the store to buy something just for fun. Mostly they don't get any pleasure from shopping. That's why they like quick and professional service. Fashion authority for them is a shop assistant, girlfriend, or wife. If teenagers check magazines for new trends, the older generation may not. Interestingly, men spend less money on apparel than women and also consume less. For example, in 2009 only 41.2 percent of men bought themselves something new (compared to 58.8 percent from all women).

The small male population accounts for a lower level of men's apparel consumption than women's. However, men's income is expected to increase as part of post-recession economic growth. In addition, a new generation is growing up. The 21- to 30-year-old group are children of modern culture with its keen attention to fashion. An impressive change of behavior patterns should result in more frequent consumption. It gives industry analysts reason to forecast that, notwithstanding the financial crisis, men's clothes and footwear retailers will grow faster than women's.

WOMEN

Aliona N. Andreyeva, an associate professor who specializes in research on marketing of luxury goods and fashion marketing, describes Russian women this way: "The variety of fashionable images and modern fashionable women in Russia is amazing! All palette of style, all colors are present in the modern Russian fashion: from international trendsetters to unique Russian national authenticity. Ability to change depending on a situation or context, as it seems to be is a unique feature of Russian women. It is not important whether there was this context at the time of Ivan the Terrible, Peter the Great, or Joseph Stalin. Russian women always possessed the unique ability to survive, love, and be fashionable."

Russians have a very specific nature. They differ from Europeans or Americans as much as for example as Japanese do. Twentieth-century English anthropologist Geoffrey Gorer and others have characterized Russian women with actions and feelings that are difficult to understand. Russians can combine together humility and impudence, cruelty and goodness, heathenism and orthodox religion. Russians are known to run to extremes. A similar behavioral pattern still applies to apparel buying behavior. On the one hand, Russian women like to imitate Western ways, and their tastes are becoming more and more cosmopolitan. On the other hand, however, they display a distinctly Russian bent toward unpredictability. Russian women value the opinions of others very much, but they value the opinions of their men secondarily. They rate the opinions of other women and their girlfriends first. Russia is a huge country with many different nationalities and religions. It means that consumer behavior can vary a lot. But in most cases these rules apply.

Most women can't afford to be only homemakers in Russia. They have to work and still fill traditional roles (Russian women in America, 2009). Women make up 46.9 percent of the employed population in Russia. Women are the majority in public health service (85 percent), education (81 percent), credit and finance (78 percent), and information and accounting services (75 percent), but only 22 percent of the labor force in the construction industry.

▲ **FIGURE 6.3** Modern Russian woman dressed for a fashion show.
Getty Images/Vittorio Zunino Celotto.

Russian women like to dress well and tend to invest a lot in their wardrobes, including shoes. Working women who have husbands to support them have more money to spend. A young woman between the ages of 20 and 25 spends two-thirds of the funds available to her on apparel and accessories. Young women also make their boyfriends buy apparel for them. Married Russian women with children and single mothers have a negligible amount to spend. Women younger than 22 shop at street vendors and buy inexpensive apparel imported from China, South Korea, and Turkey. These younger women do not have any preference for brands.

Unfortunately, income never improves for many Russian women, who continue to shop at the street vendors and nonprestigious shopping centers throughout their lives. Young single women earning well may shop for brands in the malls. Women over the age of 27 are considered "older." They tend to dress more conservatively. They wear knee-length skirts or longer, show less cleavage, and dress in suits. Although older women don't seem as provocative as the young women, even they wear outstanding clothes, transparent tops, and short dresses (but very rarely, just to show off) (Interesting facts, 2009).

Russian women like to buy jewelry, especially rings and necklaces. Brand reputation and craftsmanship are crucial (Style & Design, n.d.). The drab Soviet era is long gone, and today's Russian female consumers are fashionable, quality-conscious, and brand aware. Rather than buying simply because of the label or for the prestige of the brand, Russian consumers are increasingly looking for better designs, fabrics, and workmanship. Russian designer Valentin Yudashkin says, "In Russia, women always aspired to look and dress beautiful. Nowadays when everyone has more of an opportunity (to dress up), it is designers' duty to help women in that."

Although Russians have a deep-seated penchant for luxury clothes and jewelry, there is a fast-growing trend toward the casual (Russian passion for fashion, 2009). This trend, coupled with the "trading down" (buying less expensive clothing) and "back to basics" (buying more basic clothing such that more and mix and match combinations are possible) approaches adopted by Russian

▲ **FIGURE 6.4** Chanel creative director Karl Lagerfeld appears at the fashion show of Chanel's Paris-Moscow ready-to-wear collection at the Maly Theater, 2009. © ITAR-TASS Photo Agency/Alam.

buyers, may bolster clothing sales in Russia during bad economic times. Russian women, who comprise the major fashion customers, no longer slip on skyscraper-high heels to go shopping and are opting for a softer, less flashy look. As Russian consumers adopt a more casual lifestyle, business attire is giving way to comfortable clothes at the office. Many retailers believe that athletic clothing is poised to grow; there is a rising interest in sports and a greater awareness among Russian consumers of healthy lifestyles (Russian passion for fashion, 2009).

CHILDREN

Children constitute about 20 percent of Russia's 142 million people. With the middle class growing in Russia, the demand for better-quality and imported clothing for children is on the rise. The demand for good-quality apparel exceeds its supply. About 10 percent of higher-income Russian consumers shop for their children at malls and boutiques. They prefer to buy only imported clothing. About 30 percent of Russians cannot afford even inexpensive locally made products, and they buy cheaper Chinese imports at open-air markets (Parshukova, 2004).

BEAUTY INDUSTRY IN RUSSIA

Russia is the fourth-fastest-growing beauty and toiletries market in the world (Blagov, 2007). About 30 percent of Russians spend $90 per month on beauty products. The most profitable sector among all personal care lines is skincare. Maybelline, MaxFactor, and L'Oreal are the top brands in mass beauty products. But, for facial and body care, Kalina, a local brand, is the top seller. Russian consumers believe that a domestic product is best suited for Russian skin. This belief, however, does not apply to luxury brand cosmetics. Some of the niche luxury brands, such as Editions de Parfums and Frederic Malle, have been well received in Russia. International luxury brands have a sizable market in Russia.

More than seven decades of communism and its emphasis on function have left Russian women craving beautiful clothes and looks. Plastic surgery, skincare treatments, and other services that foreigners took for granted were only available for the Soviet elite. But there was a huge demand from the mass market after communism collapsed. The beauty industry has grown at the rate of 20 percent annually since 2000, with a slight slowdown around 2005. The Russian consumer is also showing greater interest in men's products along with natural products. Brands such as Givenchy for men are being heavily marketed to capture men's growing interest in beauty products.

▶ Beauty Industry and Women

From 1997 to 1999, almost 40 percent of beauty products were sold through kiosks, open markets, or department stores. Today, specialty beauty stores, direct sales, and pharmacies are the most popular places for buying beauty products. Hypermarkets, the Internet, and drugstores are other popular shopping formats for beauty products. Consumer demand for higher-quality products along with a better shopping experience spurred the development of new formats. Russian women prefer shopping where they can get help from skilled staff and makeup experts. L'Etoile (one of the main distribution channels of cosmetics, enjoying 40 percent of the Russian market) and Ile de Beaute are the top two beauty retailers in Russia. Still, Russia is far from being a saturated market (Grishchenko, 2009).

Both mass-market (like Avon or Lumene) and niche brands (like MAC) are working on getting the attention of Russian consumers. Although the beauty segment is in its infancy, it is likely to become more popular in the 2010s. Intensive advertising helps consumers learn about a brand, which generates profits for it. Russian consumers who experience niche brands for the first time during foreign travel look for them when they get back home. The beauty industry should be a very attractive product segment for international retailers interested in entering the Russian market.

Retailers face certain challenges in this segment. It is very difficult to find distributors who can deal with logistics issues such as lack of good roads and warehouses, the high price of fuel, and low level of infrastructure. Changes in import regulations (for example, uncertainty over a customs clearance regulation in 2010 when Russia, Belorussia, and Kazakhstan united in a Custom Union) can also create problems. So it is essential that foreign investors do their homework and plan their entry strategy carefully in order to succeed in the Russian market.

▶ Beauty Industry and Men

The men's cosmetic industry is becoming very important and is growing rapidly in Russia. The current growth is about 15 percent annually for the next ten years, which is anticipated by the results of 2005 that summed up to $195.4. Men between the ages of 30 and 50 show a high level of interest in beauty products. The most popular brands are Clarins men, Lancôme, and Biotherm homme (Russian beauty products, 2010).

Skincare has become part of the daily routine of a large segment of Russian men. Initially women were the primary purchasers of cosmetics for their men, but now men buy beauty products for themselves. They visit stores to purchase cosmetics and are becoming active in learning about new products and trying them. They make purchases of cosmetics in specialized stores and beauty salons. Men use shower gels, deodorants, aftershave lotions, hand and foot creams, facial scrubs, and cleansing gels (Cosmetics in Russia, 2009). With the growing interest of Russian men, cosmetics are beginning to become a worthwhile market for foreign retailers.

LUXURY RETAIL IN RUSSIA

Moscow is considered one of Europe's most fashionable cities. Luxury fashion products are sold in many different formats including boutiques and are mainly dominated by foreign brands. Many international luxury brands, such as Louis Vuitton, Cartier, Prada, Chanel, Hermès, and Tiffany, have established themselves in this market.

Demand for luxury products, however, has dropped since 2009. One of the reasons for this is the drop of income forced by the global financial crisis. Stores have to offer a discount of 70 percent (which otherwise would sell even though they were priced higher in Russia than other countries) to match the price point of the same luxury brand products that are sold in Paris, Milan, and other European capitals. Russian consumers were not willing to pay the high prices for a product that was available for less in neighboring countries. With discounts as high as these, it takes Russian storeowners five to seven years to break even (Luxury brands, 2010). In addition to this obstacle, the cost of operation in Russia is prohibitive because of high rents for retail properties (Machnicka, 2008). Most luxury brand consumers in Russia prefer to shop in other European countries because of the price difference. With the reduced demand for luxury products, many international retailers have put their expansion plans on hold and are trying to improve their existing stores instead.

▲ **FIGURE 6.5** Customer picks clothing at the boutique of fashion designer Sultanna Frantsuzova. These specialty stores sell exclusive high-margin products. © ITAR-TASS Photo Agency/Alamy.

Luxury brand stores are mainly located in the malls of the regional capitals. The development of this segment depends completely on the Russian economy. An increase in demand for luxury products as a result of an improved economy can help the luxury market to grow. Foreign luxury retailers may need to watch and wait before making any further investments in Russian luxury retail.

APPAREL RETAIL FORMATS: A NEW WAVE

The development of retail trade in Russia led to the introduction of new formats. In the 1990s, private shops and stores served nearby residential areas. A small store served an entire street. But now everything is different. Trade centers occupy thousands of square feet. As in many developed countries, stores have become places not just for shopping but also for leisure activities. Store size has increased not only because of the growing number of products but also the growing number of services. A typical supermarket now includes a snack bar, laundry, and many other services. Consumers can rest assured that all their needs will be met when they go to the store.

Today, there are many different store formats in Russia. They differ in size, pricing strategy, assortment offered, and services offered. Most of the retail formats present in other emerging markets are present in the Russian retail market. Apparel retail appears in many popular formats, such as small multibrand outlets, stock centers, and supermarkets. Archaic Soviet-era formats with many counters and only one separate cash desk coexist with modern formats using modern technology and management strategies.

TRADITIONAL AND MODERN FORMATS

Russia's traditional retail formats (street vendors) still capture a major share of sales in different categories of products in most emerging markets. Modern formats are popular yet have a smaller share in overall sales in the country.

▶ Street vendors

Street vendors sell the most volume of all the apparel sold in Russia. Traditionally they occupy either big markets in the city (they usually are situated in suburban areas in highly developed cities like Moscow or St. Petersburg) or small markets near subway stations or railway stations. The shops may be covered by a roof but most often they are tents or kiosks. Street vendors bring goods from China and usually try to avoid customs. Cheap rent and cheap logistics help them offer goods at very low prices. Usually illegal Chinese immigrants or immigrants from ex-Soviet republics (Armenia, Georgia, etc.) run these markets.

Moscow's Cherkizovsky was the biggest market in Europe until police shut it down in 2009. Over 60,000 immigrants from China worked there, along with people from Russia, Korea, Vietnam, and the former Soviet republics. This market sold illegal

▲ **FIGURE 6.6** Street vendor in St. Petersburg. A large volume of all the clothing sold in Russia is sold through this format. They are located in busy areas, pay a very low rent, and sell clothing mainly imported from China. © Peter Forsberg /Alamy.

▲ **FIGURE 6.7** GUM department store mall in Red Square, Moscow. GUM is actually a shopping mall. The trapezoidal building features an interesting combination of elements of Russian medieval architecture and a modern steel framework and glass roof. At the end of the Soviet era, GUM was partially, then fully, privatized, and it passed through a number of owners before it ended up in the hands of the supermarket chain. As a private shopping mall, it was renamed in such a fashion that it could maintain its old abbreviation and still be called GUM. GUM is now an abbreviation for "Main Department Store." It is a popular tourist destination for those visiting Moscow. © Bill Heinsohn/Alamy.

goods and had a turnover of about $21 billion per year. Along with clothing, one could buy drugs and weapons in this infamous market. The police confiscated goods worth $2 billion. The government is now planning to close all street markets by 2012 and convert them into organized markets. This will help increase apparel production in Russia, and reduce competition from cheap imports from China.

▶ *Department Stores*

Department stores in Russia offer a wide range of goods including clothing, furniture, and food. Stores that carry multiple brands pay particular attention to the depth of assortment. The service level is very high, as are the prices. Both old and new retail chains operate in this format. Chains built before the founding of the Soviet Union are known for their beautiful interiors. Some of these stores are popular tourist sites, for example, Moscow's Gostiny Dvor (one of the most famous department stores in Russia; in the Soviet Union it was called "TSUM"). Some department stores carry their own brands of clothing along with international brands. Offering a wide variety of merchandise makes the store more profitable. Stores created since 2000 have a clear positioning and marketing strategy. Finnish department store chain Stockman is a good example of well-operating management. Stockman shops sell a wide variety of products. The assortment is broad, but not very deep. Prices are from low to medium. Sometimes they sell products under their own brands just to increase the depth of assortment. These shops are decorated, with different sections of goods. They occupy a floor or two, and offer self-service.

GUM, which is another example, is one of the oldest and most beautiful stores in Russia. This department store is a major tourist attraction in Moscow. Since the seventeenth century traders have met at this site. At the end of the nineteenth century, Moscow merchant's guild decided to build a big store on it where every merchant could find a place and the customers would receive the best shopping experience. On December 2, 1893, Russian emperor Alexander III officially opened the new department store. It quickly became famous for its beauty and size. It became even more popular during the Soviet period, when it became a tourist attraction as a symbol of Soviet trade. In 1990, GUM, which was government property, was bought out by some businessmen. During the 1990s it changed owners several times and, finally, in 2004 the Russian retailer Bosco di Ciliegi bought out a majority share. Before this deal Bosco di Ciliegi was already renting a significant amount of square footage in the store. This deal helped them get control of the store and renovate it. Bosco di Ciliegi decided to make the store friendly for visitors. The personnel became more professional, and customer service improved. Today GUM houses many high-end boutiques along with independent brands. Bosco di Ciliegi has also opened several cafes and premium food stores in the building.

▶Specialty Stores

These are one of the most popular apparel retail formats in Russia. These stores offer a limited range of products and focus on a target audience selected by strict and rigid marketing decisions. Most of these shops are small in size. They sell expensive products with high margins only for this target audience.

▶Supermarkets, Hypermarkets, Superstores, and Wholesale Clubs

Russian supermarkets usually occupy between 5,400 to 22,000 square feet (500–2000 square meters) of area and are located in the city. Development of these formats is the main strategy for the biggest food retailers. Supermarkets usually offer a wide assortment with lower prices than other stores. The low prices are attributed to the fact that they have larger sales volume. Superstores are bigger—about 86,000 square feet (8,000 square meters)—and are located on the outskirts of the city. Retail chains Patterson (Russian retail chain owned by X5 Retail Group), and Perekrestok (retail chain owned by X5 Retail Group) (June 2010) use a supermarket format. X5 Retail Group likes to play with different formats. This company owns several of the biggest Russian retail brands in different segments. The company was created in 2006 after the merger of two big retailers—discounter Pyaterechka and middle-segment supermarket chain Perekrestok. After the merger, X5 Retail started a very aggressive expansion program. They buy more and more competitors like Patterson. But mostly the brands disappear after the merger and the assets are moved to one of the leading brands Pyaterochka or Perekrestok.

In big cities like Moscow or St. Petersburg it is hard to find space for big stores, so there are more hypermarkets. Prices in hypermarkets are much lower than in supermarkets, but the supermarket has a more convenient location. Superstores and hypermarkets usually build big retail chains, such as Krasnodar-based Magnit, the food retail chain with the most stores (3,464 stores as of June 2010), or O'key, a food retail chain from St. Petersburg, with 52 stores in Moscow and St. Petersburg. Another very popular format is the **wholesale club**, which offers a limited assortment of food, household products, clothes, and the like. To make purchases one has to be a member of the wholesale club, like Costco or Sam's Club in the United States.

▶Discount Stores

Discount stores are widely spread all over Russia. Most large food retail chains use this format to fight for market share. Discounters operate on the principle of self-service and sell mainly food products at very low prices. The range of goods is very low and usually doesn't include apparel. The biggest discounters are retail chains such as Pyaterochka, a discount food retail chain established in 1999 and owned by X5 Retail Group, with more than 1500 stores across Russia, and Dixie, a discount food retail chain with 552 stores across Russia.

▶Factory Stores

Factory stores are shops owned by producers and situated near the factory. Sometimes they sell last season's products or factory seconds.

▶ Online Retailing

People in big cities use not only traditional formats but also relatively new virtual stores (**online retailing**). Many of them are developing rapidly and will soon have visible market share. But Russia's undeveloped postal service has slowed the format's development considerably. In 2010, eBay entered the Russian market and immediately the postal service collapsed. Moscow's center for international post was overloaded with work. Postal services blamed customs and customs blamed the postal system. But in the end it was consumers who suffered.

By 2010, trade via the Internet was one of the fastest-growing formats. Plenty of virtual apparel stores, such as boutique.ru, sell goods brought from either China or Europe, or goods they bought from retail chains at a discount. Some producers and retail chains have opened their own web stores. And some, such as Nike, offer exclusive online merchandise that cannot be found in traditional stores.

▶ Catalog Retailing

In the 1990s a very common way for Russians to purchase European goods was through **catalog retailing**. One of the most popular was a German catalog called "Otto," but there were plenty of others. In stores selling from catalogs the only problem was again the postal services. Big companies tried to avoid it by offering distribution to an office in the city, which took care of distribution. It helps the client to avoid all the bureaucracy and risks of Russian post by leaving it to the retailer. Buyers could place their orders either by mail or in the office of the company. The product could be delivered to the customer either at home or in the office with a warehouse.

▶ Vending Machines

Vending machines are not as developed in Russia as they are in the United States or Japan. But there are some very interesting examples of this format in Russia. Russia's biggest fruit importer,

JFC, has its own brand of bananas, called Bonanza. To popularize its brand, the company put up vending machines that sell bananas (a common practice in Japan). The goal of this campaign was not so much to make a profit as to market their product. The vending machine was a medium for advertising.

STORE OWNERSHIP: PRIVATE OR PUBLIC?

The domestic retail chains in Russia have primarily been privately owned businesses. But since 2000, many retailers have gone public to help finance their retail activities. They need additional financing to grow their businesses to compete with foreign investors. Only a handful of retailers have been able to go public. The requirement of transparency of accounts and regulatory requirements deter most companies from attempting to go public.

FDI REGULATIONS:
CORRUPTION IS THE DETERRENT

Russia offers a stable investment environment. The inflow of foreign direct investment in Russia has been increasing since 2000. The domestic market's increasing demands and consumers' increasing disposable income make Russia a premier emerging market for investment. The government is encouraging this investment by abolishing most of the constraints on foreign businesses and easing some of the regulations. Steps to encourage further investment include increased tax relief and decreased administrative barriers. The Russian government is also investing in infrastructure to promote foreign investment (Gerendasi, 2009).

There are no restrictions on the type of format in which a foreign retailer may enter the Russian retail industry. A foreign retailer can own land and open a store in Russia without any basic restrictions. The foreign retailer is expected to abide by anti-monopoly legislation and not engage in unfair competition or restrictive business practices. For example, a foreign retailer (as well as Russian) cannot cooperate with other retailers in order to fix the price of any product or force distributors to pay an entrance fee (payment for the right to work with the retailer) for their products (Nikiforov, 2005).

The government plans to implement several measures to decrease corruption and make the process of establishing new business much easier. These plans are designed to boost foreign retailers' interest by making it easy to enter the Russian market. As a case in point the Russian government plans to optimize its tax system and create preferential treatment for investors that will develop innovative technologies. These innovations are not limited to information technology (IT) and telecommunications but also extend to textile production.

INTERNATIONAL BRANDS: RISKY BUSINESS

The Russian market is very complicated when it comes to store management. The main question that all foreign retailers have to answer is: "Is it better to operate our own retail chain in Russia or to perform as wholesaler?" In apparel retail, not many companies operate their own chains. Zara and H&M have independent store chains because they prefer to have complete control. Most companies perform as wholesalers or distributors. Nike and many other premium fashion brands follow this business model (finding a local Russian partner for a brand is much easier if the brand is popular in its parent country). They sign agreements with Russian companies and sell them fixed volumes of their goods. That way, the foreign chains minimize the risks but have stable distribution. The risk of an unreliable partner is much lower than the risk of operating independently. Franchise stores are another format that foreign retailers often choose. This format again reduces having to deal with various problems associated with doing independent business in Russia.

Business models in Russia are increasingly becoming oriented toward decreased costs. Owners have started thinking more about efficiency. But the market won't continue to grow without help from the government.

INFLUENCES ON APPAREL RETAILING:
ENTER AT YOUR OWN EXPENSE

Many different factors influence the apparel retail industry in Russia. Most of these factors apply to retailing in general.

NEW MALLS

New malls are being constructed in Russia at a fast tempo. Russia was the leading European country by new malls commissioned in 2010. On the other hand, Russia's major cities still lack space for shopping areas, mostly because federal and regional legislation makes acquiring land extremely difficult. Russia is the biggest country in the world with huge territory and abundance of people. The low level of retail development gives potential investors huge possibilities for new business development.

HIGH COST OF INVESTMENT

The cost of capital in Russia is high, and running a retail business is difficult under these circumstances. To survive in this kind of environment, retailers use semilegal financial schemes by evading certain taxes (Russian retail, 2005). But this factor can be compensated for by rapid growth of business. The growth of the Russian economy is highly dependent on oil and gas prices. In the short term, they are not going to fall. It means that the growth of the Russian economy will continue and Russians will have more money to spend.

BUREAUCRACY

There is a complex bureaucracy in Russia. This results in a lot of red tape for importing goods and buying real estate in the country. Import regulations and customs lack transparency. Another problem is undeveloped legislation. Some laws are very complicated and extremely hard to follow. The regulations in Russia differ by region. This conflicts with retailers' interest in cost effectiveness by using a centralized supply chain. Investors should consider employing local talent in the companies because they may better understand the legal requirements.

IMPORTS INCREASE COST OF PRODUCTS

The majority of the clothing sold in Russia is imported and is very expensive owing to the high cost of importing. Logistics expense increases the manufacturer's price by 12 percent, and the customs clearance step increases this price by a whopping 40 percent (if the customs clearance is done officially, which is very rare). Store markup is 300 to 500 percent to cover all the overhead expenses, such as rent, personnel, electricity, credit payouts, taxes, and transactional costs connected with communicating with the government.

POOR INFRASTRUCTURE

Lack of proper infrastructure in the country causes transportation problems. The roads are in poor condition, and traffic is heavy. A lack of electricity and poor communication lines also create major problems for retailers.

GETTING TO KNOW DOMESTIC COMPETITORS: PRICE MATTERS

Foreign investors interested in the Russian market should look at some of these highly successful domestic retail chains.

Sela wear and accessories: Sela corporation was founded in Russia in 1991. It is a vertically integrated company operating more than 443 stores across the country. It is also present in some other countries, including Ukraine, China, Estonia, and Israel. Sela sells mass-market apparel for kids, teens, women, and men. It operates in a small store format with a limited assortment. The clothing is made in China. The capability to produce inexpensive clothes under qualified management helped this company achieve great success in Russia. It has a sourcing office in China that looks for factories across the People's Republic of China (PRC) to carry out its production. The company now also has some of its production in Russia. Sela is one of the leading apparel retail chains in Russia that continues to grow in its regular store format along with franchise operations.

OGGI (OODJI): OGGI has been in existence since 1998, with its first store opening in 1999 in St. Petersburg. This retail chain has 252 stores in Russia and also has a presence in some other nations. It is a mass-market apparel retail chain selling apparel and accessories for women. They plan to expand worldwide and have rebranded themselves as OODJI in 2010. The name change was because it was easier to pronounce OODJI in various languages, and the company believed that the new name had a better appeal.

Gloria Jeans and Gee Jay: This company has existed since 1988 and now has about 250 stores in Russia. It is a vertically integrated company selling mass-market apparel for teenagers, kids, and young adults. Gloria Jeans is the biggest apparel producer in Russia.

Incity: This company was created as a mass-market brand for urban women in the age group of 18 to 35. They carry classic lines, casual lines, and jeans. The company was founded in 2005. In 2010 they had 228 stores all across Russia. Their pricing strategy, which includes putting low-priced products on sale and other promotional techniques, makes their products low cost.

Savage: Since its founding in 2000, Savage has provided mass-market apparel for urban men and women in the age range of 25 to 35 years. They have about 160 stores in Russia and are also present in Ukraine and Kazakhstan. They are expanding using the franchising model.

HOW MATURE IS THE RETAIL INDUSTRY?
LONG ROAD HOME

The Russian market is far from mature. In 2010, stores satisfied the needs of about 60 percent of the population, a figure that reveals room for more retailers in the country. A large retail network in Russia has about 15 stores on average, compared to 1,000 stores in the United States. The Russian market is by no means saturated.

Foreign retailers are introducing more sophisticated formats. The low valuation of domestic chains makes it easy for foreign retailers to acquire them. In 2009 and 2010, the French food retail chain Carrefour and Walmart reconsidered the market for potential acquisitions. Domestic retailers in Russia use mergers and acquisitions as the main instrument for expansion. A good example of domestic acquisition is Eldorado, one of Russia's leading electronic retail chains. Established in 2004, Eldorado was originally a regional retail operator with its first outlets in Samara and Kazan. It moved into the Moscow retail market by acquiring three shops of the small electronic retailer Mikrodin in 1998, and nine Electrical World shops (another small electronic retailer) in 2002, making Eldorado one of the biggest players in the capital. Similarly, in 2003 the food retail chain Kopeika rolled out about $30 million to acquire Prodmag, a Moscow-based network of discount shops. In 2010, Russia's most active retailer in mergers and acquisitions was the X5 Retail Group, which has consolidated many competitive retail chains. It now owns Kopeika, which will be terminated.

Since 2009, rents and the cost of construction materials have dropped significantly, opening up a window of opportunity for foreign retailers. The growing GDP of the country, a growing middle class with higher disposable income and a desire to spend money, and lack of good-quality products make Russia a very alluring market for foreign investors.

BUYING FOR APPAREL RETAIL STORES: IMPORTING IS IN

After the financial crisis of 1998, the price of imports in Russia skyrocketed by almost 300 percent. This increase created a niche for domestic Russian manufacturers and producers of raw materials, thereby increasing domestic production. The stabilization of Russian currency has returned prices to pre-crisis levels, so products can be imported into Russia again. The domestic industry faces several issues, such as shortage of raw material, obsolete production equipment, and lack of funds. Because of these problems, domestic producers cannot compete with imported products in either price or quality. Therefore, products such as fashion items, knits, and synthetic fabrics are largely imported from various countries into Russia.

The low volume of textile production in Russia is another challenge for domestic clothing manufacturers. Almost all textiles come from abroad. Most apparel is imported from China (35 percent), Turkey (12 percent), Germany (8 percent), and Italy (6 percent) (Advertology, 2008). Customs clearance creates additional costs, and in the end production in Russia becomes very expensive. In 2009 Russian clothing producers introduced initiatives to help their industry. They asked the government to create Special Economic Zones for producers, which will lower taxes for Russian apparel producers. They also want the government to allow them to import textiles without customs payments.

Buyers for small retail chains and outlet stores (excluding premium brand stores) buy apparel from outlet representatives. They buy goods either in stores that offer them discounts, or in discount outlets. Most of last season's apparel is bought in Milan. Buyers visit Milan once a season and buy large quantities of clothing on sale. Then all the goods are shipped to Russia by air. After customs clearance in St. Petersburg or Moscow, the goods arrive at the store. Some products get to Russia illegally and are fake. They are brought mostly from Italy and Turkey.

Large retail chains import apparel into Russia from Italy, Turkey, China, and Germany. Russia covers more area than any other country and straddles the Ural mountain range that divides Europe and Asia. Most goods come to western Russia by ship from Guangzhou, China. Large amounts of apparel are brought to eastern Russia via the Trans-Siberian Railway or trucks from China.

RETAIL CAREERS: FOREIGNERS NOT WELCOME

Retail is one of the fastest-growing and dynamic segments in the Russian economy. It offers a rare opportunity to quickly build a successful, high-paying career. Many retailers pay for higher education because they want their employees to be highly qualified. Retailing is one of the most competitive job markets, and top companies understand that people are key assets.

Store personnel or sales associate is one of the positions most in demand in the Russian retail industry. There is also a very high demand for middle management and senior managers because of the rapid growth and expansion of retail chains. Only educated professionals can manage complex store formats such as department stores. Unfortunately, such personnel are still lacking, even in big cities like Moscow and St. Petersburg. People do not have the required educational backgrounds. Even if they have good experience, it is not enough for working in a modern retail chain. Managers in accounting, logistics, and finance are always welcome and can easily find work as long as they have a good education and work experience.

Traditionally, students start their careers working part-time in a store. Most merchandisers and promoters are students. These are good part-time jobs because they give students a foothold in a big company. Sales assistants are also in demand. After graduation, most students go directly to offices and do not work in stores. Starting out as low-level assistants, they can advance over time to become heads of divisions. These positions are not restricted to business graduates. After a couple of years as a merchandiser, an employee can join a corporate education program to gain the knowledge that is needed to obtain a management-level job. Food retailers have the hardest competition and the highest-growing rate in the industry. They invest in their employees, as they need to have good people working for them.

To build a successful career in retailing requires a good educational background. Professional education for the retail industry is not very well developed in Russia. Several good business schools and universities prepare students as marketers and specialists in finance, accounting, and logistics. In addition, some institutes teach courses that prepare students to be assortment managers. But in general the education level is low and qualified students are lacking. Most companies are looking for employees with an education in economics and good knowledge of foreign languages. Some websites where one can look to find jobs in the Russian retail industry are www.job.ru, www.hh.ru, and www.rabota.mail.ru.

Development of the retail industry has forced many retail chains to rethink their management strategies. Big chains need professionals in top-management positions in order to secure stable growth and business development. The lack of professionals in Russia has led to a demand for foreigners as managers. Unfortunately the Russian government is not very welcoming of foreign workers. The paperwork to obtain a work permit and visa can take anywhere from 12 to 24 months to process. The process is complicated not only for the employee but for the employer as well, who has to deal with employee registration and tax calculations. These obstacles are one of the main reasons that foreign talent steers clear of Russia. A law under discussion in 2010 would allow foreigners to stay longer in the country and obtain all permissions much quicker. A work permit would take only a month. Unfortunately, it would be available only for highly skilled professionals who must prove their exceptional skills. But the new regulations would be the first step toward leniency. There are still many things that need to be improved before the world's top managers will consider Russia as a good place to work. The main problem is still the quality of life, which is not very high in Russia. Corruption, the absence of infrastructure for foreigners, and the lack of English-speaking — people make Russia unattractive to foreign employees. Both government and citizens understand the need to make Russia more comfortable and safe for foreigners, especially with the Winter Olympic Games coming to Sochi in 2014. The country is changing and Russians are keen to shed their country's unfriendly image.

FUTURE OF APPAREL RETAIL: OPPORTUNITY KNOCKS AGAIN

Apparel retail in Russia is a very complicated business. One faces many obstacles in this market. The biggest problem is finding a place for the store. When you find a location, there are the hurdles of high rent, bureaucratic red tape, and corruption. Even in big cities like Moscow, Yekaterinburg, St. Petersburg, and Kazan, where there are rather large numbers of trade outlets, rents are high. According to *Forbes* magazine (Russia), retailers spend up to 30 percent of their proceeds on rent (Levinskij & Zhegulev, 2010), which is twice the rent in other European cities. The number of trade outlets is still lower than in Europe or the United States. For example, Moscow, Russia's most developed city, has fewer trade outlets for every 1,000 citizens than Madrid, Stockholm, or even Prague (Levinskij & Zhegulev, 2010). But despite the pitfalls, many foreign retailers operate successfully in Russia. For example, the French retail chain Auchan is one of the most successful food retail chains in Russia. They had second place by income per square feet in 2009, and in 2010 they were one of the top three retailers by total income, alongside Russian retail monsters X5 Retail Group and Magnit. Key elements of their success are good store locations and low expenses. Their success strategy seems simple, but it is in fact a hard-won achievement because food retail is one of the most technological and complicated businesses.

The cost of credit in Russia is very high. Foreign companies have an advantage over Russian retailers because they can find investments outside of Russia much more easily than Russian companies. Credit rates in Europe and the United States are significantly lower than in Russia. This difference can give foreign companies a huge competitive advantage especially now that the market has shrunk.

The market situation is very advantageous for foreign retailers. Many local retailers have gone bankrupt since the 2008 economic downturn, so there are more opportunities to acquire existing retail chains and obtain good retail properties, which are a scarce commodity in Russia. In addition the market began to grow and in 2010 was expected to regain precrisis sales levels soon.

On the other hand, there are some difficulties. A foreign retailer needs to be aware of the high transactional cost connected with communicating with the government. Starting at the Russian border, retailers have to find their way through the complicated Russian law. Russian officials are not keen to help the businesses. After customs, the next issue may arise with tax officials. It is not always possible to negotiate officially. Even the courts don't help much. In the end, a retailer faces a dilemma: either close the business or find ways around the regulations. Even big multinationals like IKEA face tax problems. All these costs increase the risk that net income will be very low, about 10 percent. These hindrances affect competition in the market and the way foreign retailers enter the Russian market. The government is taking steps to fight corruption and force banks to lower credit rates. If these measures are implemented, they will have positive effects on the apparel retail industry and make the Russian retail market a lot more attractive to international investors.

In sum, some of the challenges that a foreign retailer needs to keep in mind before considering investing in Russia are:

- Lack of space with adequate infrastructure, parking facilities, and so on
- High rent for properties and competition for prime real estate
- Different types of customers in big cities as compared to outer regions
- Complicated regulations and high cost of imports
- Prevalent corruption
- Lack of trained and experienced retail professionals

Case Study 1

CARREFOUR ABANDONS
RUSSIAN FOOD RETAIL MARKET

The French international hypermarket chain Carrefour came to the Russian market in 2009 following other foreign-owned retailers such as the German-owned hypermarket chain Metro Cash & Carry, which opened its first store in Russia in 2001, followed by French rival Auchan in 2002.

Carrefour opened its first store in Russia in June 2009 in Moscow. A second store opened in Krasnodar in September, and its third outlet was scheduled to begin operations in Lipetsk before the end of the year 2009. In 2009, the company also signed a lease to open its fourth location in the River Mall in Moscow, where it intended to launch a store in 2011. In 2009, Carrefour operated 15,600 stores in 35 countries worldwide. Carrefour is the largest hypermarket chain in the world in terms of size, the second-largest retail group in the world in terms of revenue, and third largest in profit after Walmart and Tesco.

On October 15, 2009, after only four months in the Russian market, Carrefour announced plans to sell off its holdings in Russia. The company cited several factors behind its decision, such as inadequate growth and acquisition opportunities in the short and medium term that would have enabled the company to become the leading retailer in Russia. But there are likely to be other factors at play in Carrefour's decision to pull out of such a potentially lucrative market. Industry observers believe the main reason is that Carrefour failed to acquire the grocery chain Seventh Continent (with 140 stores in Russia) after negotiations were suspended.

Another factor in Carrefour's exit from Russia could be that despite the strong growth potential in the Russian food retail market, the obstacles to market entry were too great, including a complicated legislative framework and government bureaucracy. Corruption also persists at both regional and local levels, further hindering business development.

Carrefour announced that its three Russian stores would remain open until the company found a buyer. Press reports indicate that Carrefour is making proposals to various Russian retailers to find a franchising partner, which it has done in Africa, the Middle East, and Japan. The company would offer domestic retailers to develop a chain of stores under the brand name Carrefour. However, most retail players are satisfied with their own brands. Finding a franchising partner is attractive to Carrefour because it gives them the opportunity to return to the market in the future. Currently only the Victoria Retail Group (more than 210 stores in Russia) has shown interest in franchising under the Carrefour umbrella.

Although Russia undoubtedly remains a risky market, the long-term gains from successful market entry could be abundant. Indeed, Carrefour may come back to this country after necessary market reforms and when the country becomes more open to international retailers.

Source: USDA Foreign Agricultural Service Global Agricultural Initiative Report, prepared by Olga Kolchevnikova. Retrieved on December 15, 2010, from http://www.apeda.com/TradeJunction/Report/NOV_2009/CarrefoureAbandonsRussianFoodRetailMarket_MoscowATO_RussianFederation.pdf

Discussion Questions

1. Why do you think Carrefour went wrong in Russia?
2. What about Russia is important to consider before entering the market?
3. Do you think Carrefour could have avoided this mistake?

Case Study 2

BUSINESS IN RUSSIA: RETAIL'S ROCKY ROAD

Pundits leapt on French retailer Carrefour's decision to pull out of Russia last autumn as more evidence of "foreigners fleeing Russia." The company had opened its doors in the midst of the international financial storm that made many Russian consumers stay indoors until the weather improved. But lost in the flood of bad news was the fact that Carrefour's rival, fellow French supermarket chain Auchan, was not only staying but has continued to expand.

Carrefour was not alone in its retreat. In 2007, Edeka Zentrale AG closed its Marktkauf hypermarket, whereas Turkish company Ramenka spent most of the last couple of years gradually closing its chain of Ramstore hypermarkets and supermarkets. However, other international players are thriving: cornflakes, after all, do not enjoy the same geopolitical significance as oil and gas.

Auchan has been the most active of the burgeoning number of foreign companies hoping to cash in on Russia's 142-million-strong consumer market. It nipped in to buy Ramenka's hypermarkets and continues to expand its operations in Russia (just as it has next door in China).

Rapidly earning a strong reputation in emerging markets, the privately held retailer from Lille entered Russia early and is now one of the most popular anchors among property developers, according to Jacob Grapengiesser from East Capital, a fund manager concentrating on Eastern Europe and a significant holder of shares in Magnit, the country's second-largest grocery retailer.

Auchan has 38 stores in Russia and plans to open 6 new hypermarkets in 2010. Jean-Pierre Germain, CEO of Auchan Russia, said the company is willing to "adapt to different markets in different regions of Russia." As an illustration, a rollout of Raduga stores—a new, low-cost outlet—has begun in smaller cities with populations of fewer than half a million people. The company suggests it could open up to 100 of these stores this year.

According to Natasha Zagvozdina from investment bank Renaissance Capital, the French company is joined in the list of the country's top five grocery retailers by Germany's Metro, which has been expanding aggressively across the region, alongside three Russian operators; foreign retailers are now the third- and fourth-largest retailers in the Russian market.

It's also the size and early development of Russia that makes the prize so tempting; Grapengiesser predicts that "[modern grocery chains] will continue to grow for many years." In fact, despite continuing to capture business from outdoor markets and other independent operators, grocery chains still enjoy less than a 40 percent share of food sales across Russia, according to Zagvozdina. "The consolidation opportunity in Russia is absolutely huge," she states, a view backed by the claim of Lev Khasis (CEO of the leading grocery retailer X5) that over the next decade his company hopes to double revenue every three years.

Magnit's deputy CEO Oleg Goncharnov told Russia Now: "Today the Russian retail sector has a turnover of $200 billion a year. We are the second-largest player, but we only have a 3 percent market share. There is an enormous potential and Russia is one of the most dynamically developing retail markets in the world."

Not only did Magnit leave its expansion plans for 2009 unchanged, it even saw revenues increase that year by a third, easily beating 2008 (a record year for the company) and despite Russia's overall economic decline of just under 9 percent. But there is a lot of work still to do. The size of Russia, its poor transport infrastructure, and an absence of experienced third-party logistics operators make supply and distribution key. Those activist investors believed to have pressured Carrefour? Try convincing them to live with five years of losses while distribution networks are built.

This leaves acquisition the only realistic route these days for new entrants according to Marat Ibragimov, an analyst in Citibank's Moscow office, but while no one is counting out a large deal in the coming years, it looks unlikely in 2010. X5 and Magnit have seen their share prices lead the recovery on the stock markets as their lower-priced formats have benefited from dropping disposable income levels, making an acquisition frighteningly expensive, especially looking at the fragmentation of the market.

Auchan is not the only retailer with ambitious plans after seeing its position strengthened in the last year or two then. Magnit, for instance, with the aid of a successful second public offering at the end of October (which raised $365 million) plans to plow $1 billion into opening up to 580 new stores in 2010 (to add to the 3,228 it already operates, the vast majority smaller stores outside the major cities), as well as strengthening its logistics infrastructure. Russia's food retail business was already the fastest growing in Europe, but whereas most Western European countries are going backwards, the Russian market is expected to go up a gear from the end of this year.

Source: "Business in Russia: Retail's rocky road," Rossiyskaya Gazeta (Russia). Retrieved on December 15, 2010, from http://www.telegraph.co.uk/sponsored/russianow/business/7256781/Business-in-Russia-Retails-rocky-road.html

Discussion Questions

1. Auchan has 38 stores in Russia, and plans to open 6 new hypermarkets in 2010. Jean-Pierre Germain, CEO of Auchan Russia, said the company is willing to "adapt to different markets in different regions of Russia." What are your thoughts on Auchan's adaptation piece?

2. What are some of the risks involved with acquisitions in a developing economy?

REFERENCES

Andreyeva, Alyona. Designer brand in fashion business. Saint-Petersburg State University Publishing, p. 256.

Anonymous. Average spending on menswear. RBC. Retrieved August 31, 2009, from http://marketing.rbc.ru/news_research/31/08/2009/ 562949970677727.shtml?&investigations=1

Anonymous. Biggest Russian retail chains rating. Opt Union. Retrieved April 9, 2007, from http://www.opt-union.ru/publications.php?id=46

Anonymous. Children apparel retailers want to compete with street vendors. 3A-marketing. Retrieved December 3, 2007, from http://www.3a-marketing.ru/news/1196667990

Anonymous. Clothes by need. Fashioner. Retrieved November 13, 2009, from http://www.fashioner.ru/index.php?path=node/3/news/read/1292

Anonymous. Food retail chains in Russia, 2008 (demo version). RBC, 2008, p. 29.

Anonymous. Russian Apparel market growth. *Advertology*. Retrieved July 13, 2008, from http://advertology.ru/article63623.htm

Anonymous. In Jeans. Sostav. Retrieved March 6, 2008, from http://www.sostav.ru/news/2008/03/06/issl2/

Anonymous. What for do the Russians spare. FDU: Personal Finance. Retrieved March 3, 2010, from http://www.fdu.ru/investment/ news0006401B20/default.asp

Belyanina, Jana. (2009, October 13). "Europe and China Attack Russian Apparel Market." *Geopolitica*. Retrieved October 13, 2009, from http://geopolitica.ru/Articles/773/

Blagov, S. (2007, May 14–20). To Russia, with love. ICIS Chemical Business Americas, p. 24.

Cosmetics in Russia (2009, April 8). Retrieved May 23, 2010, from http://www. cosmeticsinrussia.com/showart.phtm?reg=full&type=f&num=2039

Federal Service of Government Statistics (2009). Retrieved May 21, 2009, from http://www.gks.ru/bgd/regl/b09_13/Main.htm

Gerendasi, P. (2009). Doing business in Russia. Retrieved May 21, 2010, from http://www.pwc.com/ru/en/doing-business-in-russia/assets/doing-business-in-russia-2009.pdf

Grishchenko, G. (2009, September). Facing challenges, Russian beauty industry maintains potential. Retrieved January 15, 2010, from http://www.gcimagazine.com/marketstrends/regions/bric/57017582.html

Golubev, Pavel. Baltic Status, March 2009. Interesting facts about Russian women and women rights in Russia. (2009, August 14). Retrieved May 17, 2010, from http://www.waytorussia.net/WhatIsRussia/Women/Facts.html

Karpova, E., Nelson-Hodges, N. & Tullar, W. (2007). Making sense of the market: An exploration of apparel consumption practices of the Russian consumer. *Journal of Fashion Marketing and Management,* 11(1), 106–121.

Loshakova, Darya. (2009). Market of cheap apparel will grow. Sostav, No. 2 (670). Retrieved February 27, 2009, from http://www.sostav.ru/articles/2009/02/27/ko3/

Levinskij, A., Zhegulev, I. & Red, P. (2010). *Forbes* Russia, January pp. 92–98.

Luxury brands no longer in demand in Russia (2010, March 16). Retrieved May 21, 2010, from http://english.pravda.ru/business/companies/112598-0/

Machnicka, M. (2008, January). Russian clothing and footwear market: Much room for foreign retailers. Retrieved January 15, 2010, from http://www.pmrpublications.com/press_room/en_Russian-clothing-and-footwear-market_-much-room-for-foreign-retailers.shtml

Ministry of Economic Development of Russia (2009). About Social-Economic Development of Russia in 2009. Retrieved February 3, 2010, from http://www.economy.gov.ru/minec/activity/sections/macro/monitoring/doc20100203_01

Nikiforov, I. (2005). The commercial laws of the Russian Federation. Part 4. Foreign direct investment. Retrieved May 21, 2010, from http://www.epam.ru/index.php?id=22&id2=400&l=eng

Parshukova, M. (2004). The market for children's apparel in Russia. Apparel and Textiles. Retrieved May 21, 2010, from http://www.musavirlikler.gov.tr/upload/RF/The%20Market%20for%20Children.doc

Russian beauty products (2010). Retrieved May 21, 2010, from
http://www.beautytipshub.com/russian-beauty/russian-beauty-
products.html

Russian retail industry: Structure and growth forecasts (2005). Retrieved on
January 15, 2010, from http://www.russiajournal.com/node/19099

Russian passion for fashion (2009, March). Retrieved May 25, 2010, from
http://www.hktdc.com/info/mi/a/tq/en/1X000AWA/1/HKTDC-Trade-
Quarterly/Russian-passion-for-fashion.htm

Russian women in America (2009, June 14). Retrieved May 24, 2010, from
http://www.russianwomendating.us/2009/06/russian-women-in-
america.html

Shienok, D. (2010) Middle class is out of clothes. Retailer. Retrieved February
27, 2010, from http://www.retailer.ru/item/id/16146/

Style & Design: Global Luxury Survey (n.d). Retrieved May 30, 2010, from
http://205.188.238.181/time/specials/2007/article/
0,28804,1659346_1659333_1659199,00.html

TURKEY

7

Serkan Yalcin

OBJECTIVES

After reading this chapter, you will

- ▶ Understand characteristics of apparel retailing in Turkey
- ▶ Comprehend traditional and contemporary retail establishments in the Turkish apparel industry
- ▶ Know international apparel retailers in Turkey and foreign investment policy in Turkey
- ▶ Understand factors affecting retailing in the Turkish apparel industry
- ▶ Grasp characteristics of apparel consumers in Turkey
- ▶ Know career retailing in the Turkish apparel industry

In 1923 the Turkish Republic was established upon the remnants of the Ottoman Empire, with a visionary named Ataturk at its helm. After the end of the stagnant Ottoman empire, Ataturk helped Turkey to recover many aspects of Turkish life, including the alphabet, government structure, and dress. He helped to lay the foundation for an economy that is booming today, with a cumulative GDP increase of 122 percent over 2006–2010. Twenty-first-century Turkey is the fourth-largest labor force among 27 European countries. Turkey has a large population of qualified, cost-effective, and motivated people; this population also means a

TABLE 7.1 Fast Facts about Turkey	
Capital	Ankara
Population	78.79 million
Type of government	Republican Parliamentary Democracy
GDP: purchasing power parity: in US$	$874.5 billion
Age structure	0-14 yrs: 27.2%
	15-64 yrs: 66.7%
	65 yrs plus: 6.1%
Religion	Muslim: 99.8%
	Other: 0.2%
Ethnicity	Turkish: 70-75%
	Kurdish: 18%
	Minorities: 7–12%

Source: CIAfactbook.gov

large consumer base, especially in terms of increasing purchasing power (Table 7.1). Foreign companies often find the Turkish labor force to be educated, skillful, and effective. In an interview published on newsroom.cisco.com on September 26, 2006, Paul Mountford, Cisco's senior vice president responsible for emerging markets, stated, "Central and Eastern Europe (CEE) are exciting areas of the world. Specifically in Turkey, the largest of the CEE countries, we are seeing an increase in foreign direct investment that has been spurred by the vibrant people, excellent trade networks, strategic location, and start of European Union accession talks." Many foreign companies also consider these characteristics of the Turkish population as favorable to do business in Turkey.

As the Ottomans knew as they built their empire 700 years ago, Turkey's strategic location in the world makes it a hub country suitable for regional headquarters. Turkey is located between Europe,

Central Asia, and the Middle East. Turkey has close ties with the European Union. It has been in the European customs union since 1996 and a European accession country since October 2005. The customs union increased trade liberalization between Turkey and the European Union. Such liberalization opens more doors to European retailers in the Turkish market, especially when they want to bring their products with them instead of producing in Turkey. A liberal investment climate in Turkey has made it attractive to international retailers, which has resulted in large foreign direct investment by multinationals. Turkey is also well ahead of all competitors among the Organization for Economic Cooperation and Development (OECD) countries in terms of average business startup time (Invest in Turkey, 2009a); it takes about six days to set up a company in Turkey.

Foreign companies benefit from many features of the Turkish economy. In particular, Turkey's young population and strategic location are big draws for foreign companies that choose the country as a site for both production and sales. Foreign companies prefer to operate in Turkey to get the benefit of its large consumer base. In addition, many multinational companies choose Turkey as their regional headquarters to manage their operations in the Middle East, Africa, the Balkans, and the independent states of the former Soviet Union. For example, BASF chose Istanbul as their business center for Turkey, the Middle East, and North Africa. BASF is now Turkey's largest foreign-held appliance firm and has managed its Middle East and Caucasus sales, marketing, and post-sale services from Turkey since 1999. Turkey's geographic location has evidently made it a very attractive market for many international retailers.

Attractive as Turkey's location is to foreign investors, they must keep in mind the country's mixed national and business culture. Understanding consumer behavior and business practices requires an understanding of Turkey's unique blend of European and Asian cultures and business practices. Islamic values mean a great deal to many people as well as to some companies. Such values affect the apparel purchases of a considerable number of women. However, such values are not as important to the Turkish government as they are in some Arabic countries. Successful foreign investors understand Turkey's unique characteristics.

THE RETAIL LANDSCAPE: A PROMISING MARKET

The retailing sector in Turkey saw $160 billion in total sales (of which $60 billion is organized retail) in 2008 and is the economy's fourth-largest sector. Forecasters expected the retailing sector to grow to a sales volume of $199 billion by 2010. The Turkish retailing sector is the seventh largest in Europe and the tenth largest in the world. Less than half of the retailing is organized, and the rest of it is done through informal formats. Many new shopping centers are being built in Turkey, which will increase the percentage of the organized retail format along with an increase in people employed in the retail sector. By the end of 2010, there were about 350 shopping centers in Turkey. But a segment of the Turkish population does not like shopping at the organized shopping channels, perceiving that the products they sell are more expensive than at informal retail setups. People still feel the need for small grocery stores, once and still the most popular retail outlet (for many people) for groceries due to convenience and the habit of shopping in this format (Euromonitor, 2009). Taken together, these factors reveal a dynamic and growing economy attractive not only for new domestic entrepreneurs but also foreign investors.

Since the 1980s, international activity in the Turkish retail industry has been on the rise. Some companies, such as Proctor & Gamble, have been present in Turkey for more than a decade with Istanbul serving as their headquarters for operations in Turkey, the Caucasus, the Central Asian Republics, and Israel. Benetton, Turkey's first international ready-to-wear company, has been operating in the country since 1985 and has made Turkey a springboard for doing business in Turkmenistan, Georgia, Uzbekistan, Tajikistan, Kyrgyzstan, and the Middle East. Zeynep Selgur, the managing director of Benetton, has indicated that Benetton in Turkey is in a key geographical location and has a young, disciplined, professional corporate team to make the country a regional base.

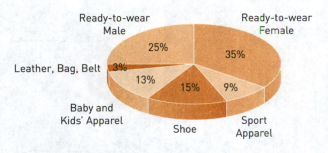

Ready-to-wear
Male
25%

Ready-to-wear
Female
35%

Leather, Bag, Belt 3%

13%

15%

9%

Baby and
Kids' Apparel

Shoe

Sport
Apparel

▲ FIGURE 7.1 Sales in apparel segments in Turkey. Illustration by Precision Graphics.

Foreign retailers began entering the Turkish market itself through joint ventures or licensing agreements. The largest cities offered considerable opportunities to foreign investors to attract their attention and enter the retail market. In Turkey, the textile industry is one of the largest and earliest-established industries. The apparel industry was established during the 1950s and initially served only the domestic market. It did not grow much until the 1970s. With new export-oriented economic policies in 1980 and related investments, the textile and the apparel industry began to develop and have increased in international competitiveness (State Planning Organization, 2004). Among the strengths of the Turkish textile and apparel industry are domestic cotton production, proximity to the European Union market, skillful labor, investment in infrastructure and telecommunication systems, and a large domestic market. In 2005, the apparel sector had a share of 11 percent in terms of total retail sales (1.63 billion U.S. dollar [USD]), 48 percent in terms of total number of retail outlets, and 19 percent in terms of retail employment (Machnicka, 2009). The following graph shows the sales percentages of different apparel segments.

CONSUMERS: A MIX
OF OLD AND NEW TRADITIONS

Ataturk's 1925 Hat Law and the 1934 Clothing Law tried to change the way people dressed to give people a Western look. These laws restricted the wearing of religious clothes for people in charge of

▲ **FIGURE 7.2** Image of people in clothes before Ataturk, the Turkish leader. (left) Image of people in clothes after Ataturk. (right) Change in regulations with regard to clothing changed the way people dressed. (left) Courtesy of Library of Congress and (right) Time & Life Pictures/Getty Images/Margaret Bourke-White.

religious duties outside their praying places and banned laypeople from wearing them, especially a kind of hat and coat favored by men.

It led the way toward Western modes of dress. Since then, advertisements, movies, television shows, and other media have influenced Turkish consumers' preference for apparel. In addition, Turkish immigrant workers all over the continent bring European fashions home when they return for the summer.

In Turkey, regional differences also create distinct consumer preferences. People dress more conservatively outside big cities and more fashionably in big cities and some tourist destinations. An advertisement for Mavi Jeans shows teenagers in weird or sexy clothes. When surprised parents tell their children that such clothes are not appropriate, they retort, "We are in Istanbul," meaning that it is OK to wear such clothes in a big city.

The media's effect on clothing is enormous in Turkey. More and more liberal lifestyles are emphasized in movies, serials, commercials,

▲ **FIGURE 7.3** Mavi Jeans advertisement. This brand of jeans is very popular but has been considered controversial due to use of models that are scantily dressed. Courtesy of Mavi.

and magazines. Americans are often surprised by the sexual content of TV programs in Turkey, which they perceive of as an Islamic, and therefore conservative, country. In fact, Turkey's government is secular. Although Muslims are in the majority, religion does not have any impact on the government or the media, unlike many other Islamic countries surrounding Turkey.

Turkey is a developing country with a per capita GDP of around $11,000 compared to $47,000 in the US, $37,000 in the UK, and $31,000 in Italy (CIA, World Fact Book, 2009b). Although high-end luxury apparel retailers are present, especially in malls and streets in wealthy neighborhoods, the number of consumers for expensive luxury is not as high as developed countries'. In addition, international and domestic producers beside foreign luxury retailers offer relatively cheap and high-quality products. The women produce the highest level of apparel sales, so international retailers need to understand them well.

WOMEN

Purchases by female consumers over 28 years old constitute more than one third of all apparel sales, making this the largest segment in apparel retail sales. Young and middle-aged people, women of all ages, and those with higher education tend to spend more on apparel products. About 60 percent of people who visit shopping centers are below 30 years of age (HTP Arastirma ve Danismanlik and Retailing Institute, 2003). Older female consumers generally prefer to shop in apparel stores conveniently located near their homes. Women dress according to where they live. In general, in large, developed cities such as Istanbul, Ankara, and Izmir, women wear more revealing or sexy clothes, whereas in small, undeveloped cities and in surrounding villages, they dress more conservatively.

Because Turkish consumers are mostly Muslim, many Turkish women prefer to wear clothes (at least outside their homes) that cover their bodies. Muslim women are not allowed to show their body parts (except face, hands, and feet) to men other than their

▲ **FIGURE 7.4** Some but not all Turkish women choose to wear the Islamic head covering, or hijab. Getty Images/Yoray Liberman.

husbands and immediate male family members. Families some-times force their daughters to cover their bodies, but there are no such restrictions among Turkish female consumers who do not prac-tice Islam. However, women who do practice Islam sometimes do not cover their bodies due to their job requirements or depending on where they live. Unlike some Arabic countries, Turkey does not have laws that require all women to cover themselves when they go out.

It is very hard to calculate the number or ratio of female con-sumers living by Islamic principles. Muslim women in small cities and neighboring villages generally follow Islamic covering style. Even in big cities, the number of such female consumers is not low. When American and European retailers introduce their collections to the Turkish market, they miss this segment, especially in their spring and summer collections. Large and small domestic retailers dominate this segment. Especially since the turn of the century, more and more Turkish apparel companies are focusing on clothing for the faithful. International retailers Tekbir, Aydan, and Dicle are targeting upper- and middle-class female consumers who prefer Islamic dressing (such as wearing *hijab,* not-too-tight clothing, fabric that is not see-through, and not showing the body is any way). International retailers would be wise not to miss this female segment.

Among other female segments, especially young and middle-aged women, there is more fashion or brand consciousness, and they welcome products from international retailers selling clothing, bags, accessories, fragrances, and other cosmetic products. Among young Turkish female consumers, brand consciousness is high. Market analysis and some top Turkish stylists indicate that young Turkish female consumers (aged 15–22) prefer casual but famous brands during the day but present themselves as older by wearing sexy clothes in the evening. Cemil Ipekci, a famous Turkish designer, claims that such young female consumers have a Turkish understanding of the West in that they tend to dress like mature women and try to copy famous models. He adds, however, that there is no such tendency among their European and American counterparts. Mr. Ipekci also indicates that as in many Eastern countries, Turkish consumers are biased toward Western products, which they perceive of as high quality (Haber Turk, 2006). Therefore, brand name is very important for such young consumers. However, the intensity of brand bias decreases, if not disappears, among mature female consumers.

MEN

Sales of menswear constitute the second-largest segment (25 percent) with respect to total apparel sales. As in the women's segment, young men's brand consciousness is higher than older men's (HTP Arastirma ve Danismanlik and Retailing Institute, 2003). There is not much difference between the way Turkish men and Western men dress. Religious Muslim men tend not to wear shorts that fall above the knee, sleeveless T-shirts, relatively tight pants, or other tight clothes.

Younger male consumers prefer casual but branded products. Whereas more formal clothes and accessories such as jackets, suits, high-quality shirts, pants, shoes, and watches are among some favorite products worn by Turkish male consumers, in villages and small cities, middle-aged and older male consumers usually wear casual pants, not denim, and shirts. In many villages, especially in the eastern part of Turkey, both men and women tend to wear baggy pants (*salvar* in Turkish), which are comfortable for doing farm work.

BEAUTY INDUSTRY IN TURKEY

An improving standard of living and an increasing young, employed population, along with growing interest in looking young and attractive, has led to a greater demand for beauty products in Turkey. Among all the beauty products, hair care has the largest share of the cosmetics and personal care products industry in Turkey. Men's grooming products, lip and eye makeup, antiperspirants, perfumes, and cologne are other important product categories for the Turkish market. About 38.3 percent of Turkish consumers buy personal care and cosmetic products once a month. Mostly women (with a 40.8 percent of share) shop for personal care and cosmetics for the household. Outlets along the streets are a more popular venue for shopping for personal care and cosmetic products than shopping centers. Young and middle-aged people, women (49.6 percent), and highly educated people tend to spend more on such products and are the ones who shop at shopping centers.

The use of beauty products among men is more widespread among the young and middle-aged, as well as men with a certain income level. Deodorants are major male beauty products, whereas the male shower and facial beauty products segments are small compared to European countries. Although the male beauty products segment is growing, it is still far behind compared to Western European countries. Many Turkish men limit their beauty concept to shaving products. So, Turkish brands such as Arko focus on shaving segments (Turkish Council of Shopping Centers and Retailers, 2009). As for fragrances, one can easily find any brand in Turkey. Young and middle-aged men with higher income levels are the most likely users of those fragrances.

CHILDREN

Turkey has relatively higher birth rates than many European countries and thus a larger market for children's clothing. More and more stores selling only children's clothes are setting up shop. In the past, stores generally had a kids' section along with youth and adult sections. Today, there are lots of stores targeting kids, including LC Waikiki (Turkey), Bucuruk (Turkey), Benetton 0-12 (Italy), Mother Care (The UK), Wenice Kids (Turkey), B&G Store (The UK), Nubebe (Turkey), Panco (Turkey), Zara Kids (Spain), Accessorize (The UK), Claire's (The US), Chicco (Italy), and Diesel Kids (Italy). However, these retailers serve only middle- and upper-income-level consumers. Many other domestic producers target low- and middle-income-level consumers. In general, families with low education levels and low income, especially in small cities and villages, have more babies and small kids. Such families cannot afford expensive branded clothing for their children. It is normal for many families to buy baby and kid clothes in local weekly bazaars, not even in normal inexpensive stores. So, both income level and family structure play important roles in the choice for baby and kids apparel.

LUXURY RETAIL IN TURKEY

Turkey has an extremely wealthy middle and upper-middle class. Turkey is also among the top 20 countries in the world based on income of individuals in USD. Consumers in Turkey are also known to spend freely when the economy allows for it. They also save and so have money to spend on luxury products. Uniqueness is a very important attribute for a luxury consumer in Turkey and limited-edition products sell very well in this market. Turkey has some new malls that have opened in the last five to six years, for example Kanyon mall, which houses many luxury brands such as Harvey Nichols (British company), Lacoste (French), and so on.

Counterfeit luxury brand products are the biggest issue for luxury retailers in Turkey. The copies are impeccable and look very much like the original. The leather industry being very well developed in Turkey, counterfeit goods are easy to produce and sell in the market. The stores that sell these products get away with bribing the officials who may stop them from selling the fakes (Amed, 2008).

APPAREL RETAIL FORMATS: FROM BAZAAR TO ISTINYE PARK

Among the key organizations in the apparel sector are the Turkish Clothing Manufacturers Association, Turkish Fashion and Apparel Federation, to which many local apparel associations belong, and Istanbul Textile and Apparel Exporters Association. The format of the Turkish apparel retail industry has four major retail establishments: malls or shopping centers; apparel shops (outlets generally on busy streets); apparel in supermarkets, hypermarkets, or megamarkets; and local bazaars organized weekly.

TRADITIONAL RETAIL FORMATS

Turkey has put its own spin on the same traditional formats that exist in many other countries.

▶*Apparel Shops (Outlets)*

Compared to the American apparel retail market, Turkey has substantially more sales through apparel stores located on busy streets and in local bazaars. Apparel stores on streets are not generally as sophisticated as their counterparts in shopping centers. However, it is possible to find high-quality and unique apparel in such stores. Istanbul's Bagdat Street and Nisantasi (a small neighborhood popular for apparel shopping) in Istanbul include high-quality and luxury outlets.

▶*Local Bazaars*

Apparel retailing in Turkey also includes retailers in **local bazaars**, in which fruit, vegetables, grocery items, shoes, and textiles are

▲ **FIGURE 7.5** Grand Bazaar (Kapali Carsi), located in Istanbul, is the largest enclosed market in the world with about 5,000 shops selling jewelry, ceramics, carpets, and spices, among other items. This is an example of a traditional market in Turkey. © David Pearson/Alamy.

also sold. Such bazaars, established along various streets, are very informal and not common in developed countries. Sellers get permission from local authorities to set up sales stands. Payments in such bazaars are generally in the form of cash with no receipts given to the buyer. Sellers are individuals rather than companies. Sellers get products from various producers or they themselves produce or grow products (as in a farmer's market). The Turkish Council of Shopping Centers and Retailers estimates that around 4,000 local bazaars are organized weekly (2009). However, the apparel sold in these bazaars is not of high quality. A beloved organized local bazaar was Sali Pazari, which was organized every Tuesday and Friday in the Kadikoy neighborhood of Istanbul city. It ceased to exist in 2008 due to modernization efforts. There will be a more organized market instead. This bazaar well represented

local bazaars in Turkey. The clothes sold in this market were considered to be the cheapest in town. Shoppers could find not only apparel but also furniture, jewelry, and antiques. Many neighborhoods have their own weekly (generally on different days in different neighborhoods) bazaars, where people go on foot with their own small shopping carts and have the opportunity to buy many different things. In particular, grocery items are fresh and of much better quality than those sold in stores.

MODERN RETAIL FORMATS

These are formats that are usually seen in all developed nations.

▶ Supermarkets, Hypermarkets, Megamarkets

Until the late 1980s, shops—whether grocery, jewelry, apparel, or other kinds of retail—were generally located on the first or ground floor of buildings where people lived. It was normal for a person, especially a mother, to call for grocery items (bread, cheese, newspaper, etc.) from her balcony to be delivered in a basket hanging from a rope on the balcony down to the grocery store. Grocery shopping does not get more timely or convenient. The number of such small retail stores is on the decline, and many people miss them. Such small stores are being replaced by big stores (called supermarkets, hypermarkets, or megamarkets). Some such stores aren't convenient in terms of location but make up for it in low prices and product category convenience, as many products can be found in such big markets. As automobile ownership increases in Turkey, more and more people tend to choose such big markets.

Since the early 1990s, such big stores have trended more and more toward selling their own brands (also called store brand, private-label brand, or home brand) in many product categories, including apparel. Migros pioneered selling products with its own brand (Migros). Other stores and chains such as Metro (Germany), Gima (Turkey), Tansas (Turkey), Kipa (Turkey), Ismar (Turkey), Continent (Turkey), and Carrefour (France) also sell many products under their names. Tansas, Turkey's second-largest retail chain, uses approximately 30 subcontractors to produce products under its own brand, which account for 23 percent of its total sales. Similarly, Gima sells more than 150 private label brands, accounting for more than 20 percent of its total sales. Initially, small manufacturers produced such private-label products. Because demand for branded products has increased, companies producing their own brands have also begun to produce for such stores. Sutas is producing milk for Tansas and Camlica is producing soda for Gima. These stores are able to offer competitive prices for such private-label brands because they are able to cut considerable costs regarding advertising, transportation, and distribution, and use producers' surplus (Savasci, 2003).

▶ Malls/Shopping Centers

Together with increases in industrialization and modernization, more and more malls or shopping centers have opened, especially in big cities. Istanbul, the trade capital of Turkey, hosts the highest

▲ FIGURE 7.7 Cevahir Mall, Istanbul. This mall has a mix of various international and domestic brands, movie theaters, an amusement park, food court, bowling alley, restaurants, and ten floors including parking. This is one of the largest and most modern malls in Turkey. Photo by Serkan Yalcin.

number (61 in 2010) of shopping centers. In addition to Istanbul, more and more shopping centers are opening in other big cities such as Ankara, Izmir, Bursa, and Antalya (Savasci, 2003). Such shopping centers, similar to their counterparts in Europe and the United States, host a number of retailers from local Turkish apparel companies (such as Vakko, Beymen, and Damat) to the world's well-known brands (such as Cacharel, Dockers, LaCoste, Tommy Hilfiger, Paul & Shark, Gant, and Marks & Spencer).

Shopping centers can be classified into four (Lambert, 2006) in terms of rentable space:

1. Very big (80,000 square meters (861,120 square feet) and above). Examples include Istanbul Cevahir, Istinye Park, and Ankaramall.

2. Big (40,000–79,999 square meters) (430,560–861,119 square feet). Examples include M1 Tepe Alisveris Merkezi, Galleria Alisveris Merkezi, Profilo Alisveris Merkezi, and Tepe Nautilus.
3. Medium-sized (20,000–39,999 square meters) (215,280–430,559 square feet). Examples include Akmerkez, Capitol, Karum, Kanyon, XL Mall As Merke, Metrocity, and Armada.
4. Small (5,000–19,999 square meters) (53,820–214,279 square feet): Examples include Whiteworld, CarrefourSA-Haramidere, Orion, Arcadium, Tesco Kipa, and Mega Center.

Opened in 2005, Cevahir Mall, the largest shopping center in Europe, is on the European side of Istanbul and offers 117,972 square meters (1,269,850 square feet) of retail space to rent and includes 330 stores. Ankamall is located in Ankara, the capital of Turkey, and opened in 2006. It offers 106,480 square meters (1,146,150 square feet) of retail space to rent and includes 302 stores. In 2007, the upscale Istinye Park opened in Istanbul. It includes 291 stores and offers 85,250 meter squares (917,631 square feet) of retail space to rent. Generally, very big, big, and medium-sized shopping centers are modern shopping malls. Because they are located in well-heeled parts of town, Akmerkez and Istinye Park include many more expensive brands than other malls. However, one can find very luxurious and expensive brands together with other normal and inexpensive brands in many malls in Turkey.

▸ Department Stores

Major department stores in Turkey are as follows: Begendik, Beymen, Boyner, Mudo, Vakko, and YKM (Yeni Karamursel Magazasi) (www.mymerhaba.com).

Begendik is located in Ankara and consists of departments for all a consumer's needs from textile to cosmetics and kitchenware, except alcoholic drinks. The prices are mostly for the middle class but the selections are really good.

Beymen provides its customers with stylish but wearable clothing, shoes, and accessories for everyone in the family under their own exceptionally high-quality locally manufactured brand name as well as a selection of world-renowned brands such as Donna Karan, Dice Kayek, and Sonia Rykiel among others. Beymen also has a sleek yet comfy range of home decor items as well. Beyond the quality of their goods, Beymen is known for providing extraordinary service. Beymen also has a brand of both casual and elegant clothing for children and the younger sportier crowd called "BM Club."

Boyner Holding, one of the leading holdings and the owner of Beymen, opened Boyner (former Carsi), which stands by its motto "Buy quality for less" and to produce goods under the name Altimod as a sister to Altinyildiz brand, which is a high-quality name in Turkey. Boyner has since become a well-known department store with branches in almost all shopping malls. In addition to clothing, it has departments for sports, kitchen, home decoration, glassware, fashionable bags and shoes, as well as internationally known brands of cosmetics. Mudo is one of Turkey's best fashion companies. Mudo goods are stylish, and include a range of both professional and casual men's and women's clothing, as well as children's fashion and a selection of attractive rustic home decor.

Vakko: "Fashion is Vakko" has long been the motto of this ultra-chic Turkish style house. Vakko's beginnings were modest. It began in 1934 when Mr. Vitali Hakko started a small millinery called Şen Şapka (Merry Hat). As the business expanded the name was changed to Vakko, and the company began to produce haute couture scarves of Turkish silk, cotton, and wool. When the first Vakko store was opened at Beyoğlu, Istanbul, in 1964, it was the biggest store that had ever been built there to date and made Vakko the biggest brand-name phenomenon on the Turkish clothing scene. Vakko has continued to develop its wares by creating a line of home decor, clothing line for men, perfumes V de Vakko (for men), Katia (for women), and Piu Piu (for children). The Vakko Company also opened Vakkorama stores that cater to younger tastes and is home to Power FM, a radio station that focuses on international pop music. One of the traditional gifts that Turks give to one another is a box of chocolates or candies wrapped in style. If you want to impress a Turk, choose from Vakko's wide assortment of chocolates, which always have that perfect finishing touch of class, which is the trademark of Vakko's packaging.

YKM is one of the oldest department stores in Ankara. Its principle is to meet the needs of all the members of a family. With its own credit card YKM provides installment payments to its customers without interest.

▶ Specialty Stores

There are lots of small specialty stores selling specific apparel items such as scarves, sports apparel, leather apparel, and so on. One famous specialty store in Turkey is Derimod, which has produced leather apparel since the 1970s.

STORE OWNERSHIP: FAMILIES RUN THE SHOW

Over 50 thousand companies operate in the Turkish textile and apparel industry. More than 90 percent of these companies are family owned, and more than 80 percent are small and medium-sized enterprises employing 250 and less employees (Eraslan, Bakan, and Kuyucu, 2008). Children take over these businesses when their parents retire. This family dominance is prevalent even in very large firms in Turkey. Koc Holding, a Fortune 500 company, was established and managed by textile magnate Vehbi Koc, then managed between 1984 and 2003 by his son Rahmi Koc, and then his grandson Mustafa Koc, the current chairman of the board of directors. Vehbi Koc (1901–1996) was a brilliant entrepreneur. Through his partnership with Ford, General Electric, and Mobil prior to the 1950s, and his other business ventures afterwards, he quickly developed his company and became one of the largest groups in Turkey.

LC Waikiki, operating under Tema Holding, has been the market leader in the apparel industry since 2006, with over 250 stores throughout Turkey. Among other large Turkish apparel retailers are Beymen, Vakko, and Mavi Jeans. Beymen was established in 1971 and now is a part of Boyner Holding. Beymen has 33 stores throughout Turkey. Vakko was established in 1934 and is now an upscale apparel company in Turkey. Mavi Jeans was established in Istanbul in 1991 and has been the market leader in the denim sector since 1996.

FDI REGULATIONS: WIDE OPEN

In 1954, the Turkish government passed the Foreign Capital Incentives Law, which outlined restrictions on and conditions for foreign investments in Turkey. A new foreign direct investment law enacted in 2003 canceled this law and its restrictions, and made Turkey one of the most liberal (with respect to foreign direct investment) OECD countries. The key features of this law are (The Undersecretariat of Treasury, 2009):

- Foreign investors are free to make foreign direct investments and are to be treated the same as domestic investors. Thus, foreign companies will not be restricted in terms of ownership, income, management rights, and the like. This freedom levels the playing field for foreign companies in competition with domestic companies, and ensures their full ownership. In addition, foreign investors do not face pre-entry or pre-establishment screening requirements anymore nor do they need to notify the Undersecretariat of the Treasury of Turkey. They just need to follow regular company establishment procedures like domestic Turkish firms.
- Foreign direct investments cannot be expropriated or nationalized. Nationalization is the fact that host country governments take over companies. As this law prevents nationalization, expropriation is not an issue in Turkey.
- The new law removed any financial restrictions related to foreign investment. Foreign investors can freely transfer net profits, dividends, proceeds from the sale or liquidation of all or any part of an investment, compensation payments, amounts arising from license, management, and similar agreements, and reimbursements and interest payments arising from foreign loans through banks or special institutions.

- ▶ Foreign companies may freely acquire (in lieu of rent) real estate.
- ▶ For the settlement of disputes arising from investment agreements subject to private law and investment disputes arising from public service concessions contracts and conditions concluded with foreign investors, foreign investors can apply either to the authorized local courts or to national or international arbitration or other means of dispute settlement, provided that the conditions in the related regulations are fulfilled and the parties agree thereon. That is, in case of any dispute or lawsuit, foreign investors have the right of dispute settlement in local courts or international arbitration agencies.

The bottom line of this law is that foreign companies are treated equally and are subject to the same regulations as domestic Turkish firms. Turkey also has double taxation prevention treaties with 71 countries. A double taxation treaty means that a foreign company will not be taxed twice on the same income by both its home government (country A) and host country (country B) government. If there is no such a treaty between two countries, then country A would tax the company's income generated in the foreign market as the company belongs to or registered in the home country, and the host country B would also tax this company for generating profit in country B. So, this company would have to pay income tax (on the same income, the one generated in the foreign country) twice, which would make international operations less profitable and less attractive. To prevent this double taxation and ease the tax burden, countries sign double taxation prevention treaties. Foreign investors are encouraged to read the Investors' Guide for Turkey published by the Investment Support and Promotion Agency of the Republic of Turkey Prime Ministry.

INTERNATIONAL BRANDS: STRATEGIC LOCATION IS THE KEY

There is no restriction on entry for multibrand or single-brand international retailers. International apparel retailers target men's, women's, and children's segments, but their presence in the women's wear segment is the most visible, both in the malls and on the high streets. The women's apparel segment accounts for 35 percent of all apparel sales in Turkey. Many international apparel retailers (such as Bottega Veneta, Gant, Ermenegildo Zegna, Nine West, Paul & Shark, Marks & Spencer) serve middle- and upper-class customers. Despite the world financial crisis, Prada opened two stores in Istanbul in 2009.

In addition to multinationals in the clothing industry, multinationals in the beauty, personal care, and cosmetic industries also operate in Turkey. Many large cosmetics and personal care companies (such as Procter & Gamble, Henkel, Colgate Palmolive, and Unilever) have production and marketing centers in Turkey and operate through either licensing or joint venture. Unilever, taking advantage of Turkey's strategic location, also manages its Central Asian, Caucasian, and Balkans operations from Turkey (Invest in Turkey 2009a; Yilmaz 2007). In the Turkish market, domestic companies, such as Evyap (seller of soaps, hand gel, and shower gel under many different brand names, such as Duru, Fax, Activex, and Ava), offer stiff competition.

Turkish consumers are generally brand-conscious consumers in many product categories, such as clothing, cars, fragrance, and shoes. In the 1980s, when foreign trade policies changed and import substitution policies were abandoned, many foreign brands entered the Turkish market. Turkish consumers were much more obsessed with foreign brands in the 1980s and early 1990s than they are now. For example, in the 1980s and early 1990s, many young men and women just had to have a pair of Levi's. Although many foreign brands are still in demand and regarded as superior, the emergence of many domestic producers and nationalistic advertisements has increased the popularity of domestic brands. Fragrance is perhaps the exception, because famous brands are always in high demand despite much higher prices in Turkey than in Europe or the United States, owing to import costs and the fact that average personal income is two to four times higher in the West.

ENTRY FORMATS BEING CHOSEN BY INTERNATIONAL BRANDS

International retailers choose different entry formats to enter different countries based on their expansion plans and the regulations for foreign direct investment in the country. Common formats in Turkey are export, subcontracting, joint venture, licensing, and distribution.

►Export

An international retailer may choose the export mode to enter the Turkish market. The choice of export results from the decision of the exporter not to engage in direct investment, such as local production, in Turkey. Although Turkey offers many advantages for many companies regarding local production, such as availability of resources, labor, and favorable foreign investment laws, some companies may have better production choices (locations) and prefer exporting over local production. The main advantage for such companies in adopting the export mode would be to avoid high investment costs that associate with local production. If such retailers have efficient production bases, they produce in these locations and export to their sales markets from their production location. However, export may not be a good option to enter Turkey because export generally associates with low profits. Also, export does not allow foreign companies to be knowledgeable about further opportunities in Turkey because their involvement level is low. At the end of the day, export choice is related to the retailers' strategic orientation and commitment level toward Turkey. Unilever and Colgate/Palmolive both produce in and export to Turkey, whereas Procter & Gamble mostly exports to Turkey. L'Oreal, Wella, and J&J also mostly export to Turkey.

►From Subcontracting to Joint Venture

Some Turkish apparel producers have long served international apparel companies as subcontractors. Others have operated through licensing. However, to increase their effectiveness, international apparel retailers have preferred the joint venture format to benefit from their Turkish partner's knowledge of the domestic market. For example, in 2005 Benetton signed a licensing agreement with the Boyner Group to initiate its Turkish operation. Boyner Group manages all commercial activities of the United Colors of Benetton, Sisley, Playlife, and Killer Loop brands in Turkey (Benetton, 2005).

▸Licensing

Other international brands have not committed as much as Benetton, preferring the franchising entry format. For example, Fiba Holding purchased franchising rights from Marks & Spencer and GAP and thus has the right to open and manage Marks & Spencer and GAP stores in Turkey.

▸Distributor

Some international retailers have entered the Turkish market through distributorship agreements. For example, Jones Apparel Group (the designer and marketer of Jones New York, Nine West, Anne Klein, Gloria Vanderbilt, Kasper, Bandolino, Easy Spirit, and Evan-Picone, among others) entered Turkey through a distributorship agreement with Park Bravo, which purchased distributorship of Nine West in 1997. The Canadian premier lingerie retailer La Senza also chose this format when it entered the Turkish market in 2005 through Park Bravo.

INFLUENCES ON APPAREL RETAILING: MORE CONSUMERS AND BETTER PRODUCTS

Turkey's retail sector saw 11 percent growth in 2008. The apparel retailing sector is in its growth stage, and developers are turning their attention to other cities as opportunities for new schemes become more limited in Istanbul. In fact, the capital city, Ankara, and a number of secondary cities—Izmir, Bursa, Antalya—already have significant representation in terms of shopping centers. Still, almost half of Turkey's provinces do not have any modern-concept shopping centers (Machnicka, 2009).

FASHION-CONSCIOUS CONSUMERS WITH MONEY

Young, fashion-oriented Turkish consumers spend remarkable amounts of money on designer goods and clothes. Together with increases in GDP, more and more consumers will be able to afford such products. In addition, research reports highlight Turkey among the top markets for retail and consumer investment (PWC & AMPD, 2007). Income distribution is not evenly balanced in Turkey; however, the size of the affluent minority and upper-middle class is comparable to the entire size of some small European countries (PWC and AMPD 2007; Kocak 2006). Moreover, the British market analysis firm, Euromonitor, classifies Turkey among the fastest-growing consumer markets in Europe (Euromonitor, 2009). Not only are rapid economic expansion and higher standards of living enabling Turkish consumers to purchase higher-value products but a consumer survey conducted by IBS also indicates that Turkish consumers are becoming more brand-oriented and seek to purchase international brands.

ESTABLISHED DOMESTIC RETAIL SECTOR

Turkey's retail sector offers vast opportunities because the country is relatively underdeveloped, has a large population, and has new plans for shopping schemes. However, incumbent domestic companies that have already adopted modern retailing logic mean that foreign brands may not easily establish themselves. Foreign retailers will no doubt face intense competition from such domestic retailers, including in apparel as Turkish apparel companies establish their own brands rather than serve as sole subcontractors. Forecasters anticipate that Turkey will have a lively and very dynamic retail sector (Machnicka, 2009).

The apparel retail sector has grown in line with the rapid growth of the general retail sector in Turkey. Two major facts affect the growth in apparel retail: increasing investments by foreign

▲ **FIGURE 7.8** Models display outfits by Turkish designer Oezlem Sueer at a 2004 fashion show in Duesseldorf. AFP/Getty Images/ Patrik Stollarz.

retailers, and increasing openings of malls, shopping centers, and other retail outlets because many Turkish textile producers switched to apparel retailing during the financial crisis. The crisis forced companies to merge or switch to retailing due to decreasing profit margins in apparel production.

BRAND-BASED COMPETITION

Brand awareness has grown to the point that price competition and the sale of basic textile goods will not contribute much to the sector's development. In response to the demand for brands, the Turkish apparel industry has launched a nationalist branding campaign. "Turquality" was introduced in January 2004 jointly by the Under Secretariat of Foreign Trade, the Turkish Exporter's Association, and the Istanbul Association of Textile and Apparel Exporters. Turquality unites the words "Turk" and "quality" in an effort to highlight the quality of Turkish products and services and upgrade the international perception of products made in Turkey. The project also aims to provide a stimulus for the textile industry to upgrade its technology and reposition itself in the international market as producers of higher-end, quality apparel. Turquality is a complex mix of marketing, quality upgrading, and strategic positioning (Kocak, 2006).

Brand-based competition is most intense in the sports and denim sectors. In sports apparel, Adidas, Nike, Kinetix, and Puma are among the leading retailers, whereas Levi's, Lee, Mavi Jeans, Rodi, and Leke lead in denim. Effective marketing campaigns, advertising, and orientation toward a target market are among some key success factors in apparel retailing. However, the availability of a vast number of brands in the sector prevents brand loyalty because consumers often switch brands. Brands that advocate a particular lifestyle or personality (such as Mavi Jeans) are able to increase their shares (HTP Arastirma ve Danismanlik and Retailing Institute, 2003). The chairman of Benetton underlined the favorableness of the Turkish population for its youth, increasing income, and fashion wisdom. Statistics show that 17 percent of the Turkish population is aged between 19 and 27 and this age segment has a 26 percent share of total apparel purchases in Turkey; also this group is more responsive to fashion trends.

GETTING TO KNOW DOMESTIC COMPETITORS: RISING FROM THE CRISIS

The Turkish textile sector heavily felt the effects of the global financial crisis of 2008/2009. Many factories and subcontractors closed their doors and went bankrupt. Such textile firms generally chose one of the three options: engage in a merger, switch to apparel retailing, or invest in other sectors. Many choose to become apparel retailers by creating their own brands. In addition, foreign retailers coming to the market have helped to substantially increase the level of competition.

Some examples of textile firms that switched to apparel retail include (Eraslan, et al., 2008):

- ► Fabric producer Ozon Group, under the brand name Defacto
- ► Thirty-six-year-old leather producer Desa
- ► Fabric producer Tohum Holding, with 30 stores
- ► Textile producer Tedi, by opening 57 stores in one year
- ► Oz-El Groups, the world's third-largest textile accessories producer, under the A'Plus brand

In addition, other textile manufacturers have collaborated on forays into retail. Seventy-eight textile producers worked together to create MOL, retail outlets that sell quality products at prices so cheap they beat East Asian imports.

Such collaboration is not widespread. As many as 15,000 different brands in the apparel sector indicate a preference for individualism among apparel producers. Such unknown small apparel producers and retailers compete intensely. The Italian model, which some Turkish economists propose to increase the competitiveness of both the textile and apparel sector, argues that small companies should create big and powerful companies. In addition, major specialized production facilities should replace many small production facilities, which are inefficient in their use of assets. With specialized production and collaboration among producers, such textile and apparel producers may increase their competitiveness (Eraslan et al., 2008).

There is also the Asian effect on the competition. Turkey, like China, is a giant in the export of textile and apparel products. They are direct competitors. Products imported from various Asian countries and especially those from China have had some market share in the Turkish clothing and footwear markets. The quality of such products is not high, but with competitive prices they can find many Turkish buyers. This competition is perhaps more intense in the European Union market because Turkey is a key apparel exporter to the European Union. Turkey has a customs union agreement with the European Union, indicating that Turkey needs to abide by EU customs rules. Although this agreement has opened some doors to Turkish textile and apparel producers benefiting from common customs, it also brought some disadvantages. For example, the European Union removed customs barriers (especially quotas) with China in 2005, leading to considerable increases in Chinese exports to the European Union. These increases also affected Turkey, which had to adopt this customs removal as well according to the customs union agreement. When the domestic market became vulnerable to a flood of Chinese products, Turkey applied the protection rule of the customs union agreement. To restrict the market penetration of Chinese manufacturers, the Turkish government launched a procedure that required them to apply for certification. Thus, Turkey was able to minimize the effects of Chinese textile and apparel exports. Whereas some Turkish textile and apparel companies preferred the cheap Chinese products, others raised concerns about the sustainability of quality of these products.

The textile and apparel sector focused on production and export for decades before reorienting itself toward organized, brand-based retail chains in the apparel sector. Domestic chains such as Collezione, LC Waikiki, Ipekyol, Vakko, and Sarar together with international chains such as Benetton, Bata, LaCoste, Nine West, Zara, Mango, Adidas, and Nike have well established themselves based on brand or experience in the Turkish market. New chains such as Boyner (formerly Carsi) and YKM are trying to obtain market share through transformation of their positioning, brand conceptualization, and advertising campaigns.

For international retailers willing to enter the Turkish market, these four formats are recommended:

1. If their brand is well known, international retailers can capitalize on this through sole ownership. Prada, which opened two stores in fashionable Istanbul neighborhoods in 2009, is a good example.
2. If a brand does not provide very high leverage in competition, a joint venture with a well-positioned Turkish firm would be a good option for entry. Even well-known brands choose this option because the apparel sector is very sensitive to cultural and religious differences, which are considerable between Turkey and Western countries.
3. Purchase an established brand in the Turkish market.
4. Enter the market and then try to gradually increase brand awareness. This may take time, and there are many established brands in the market. For unknown brands, this may be very hard to achieve.

BUYING FOR APPAREL RETAIL STORES: LOOK NO FURTHER, IT'S ALL AT HOME

The Turkish apparel industry makes sourcing easy for retailers in many ways: richness in materials (Turkey is the world's sixth-largest cotton producer and also an important producer of man-made fibers); nearness to major markets (especially the European Union); the ability to respond quickly to orders; qualified labor; the presence of apparel-related industries; the capacity to create fashionable, well-designed, and innovative products; participation in a customs union agreement with the European Union; and free trade agreements with many countries (State Planning Organization, 2004).

There are more than 50,000 companies in the Turkish textile and apparel industry. About 95 percent of these companies are family owned, 85 percent of these companies are small and medium-sized enterprises, and 25 percent of these companies engage in export. Technology-oriented production is realized only by big firms. In the Turkish textile and apparel sector, there are two kinds of manufacturing companies: the ones that set standards in the sector by producing high-quality thread, yarn, and wovens, and the ones producing ready-made, no-brand clothing using domestic and imported fabrics. These second category producers sell their no-brand apparel to retailers through intermediaries. No-brand apparel makes up a large portion of domestic apparel production and export. In addition, there are wholesalers and retailers that are not producers.

Foreign apparel is marketed in Turkey through foreign sourcing firms and distributors, which organize sales and marketing programs according to consumer base or demand characteristics. Many international apparel and textile firms have procurement and contact offices and retail outlets in Istanbul, which they use as the procurement center for their European and Asian outlets. In addition to Istanbul, cities such as Izmir, Bursa, Ankara, Denizli, Gaziantep, Kayseri, Tekirdag, and Adana are major apparel sourcing sites.

International retailers either export their apparel products to Turkey or use domestic subcontractors or companies if they are in a joint venture or licensing agreement. For example, Benetton has many subcontractors in both Italy and Turkey. Levi's has production facilities in Turkey and Levi's Turkey is also exporting to many countries in the Middle East, the Caucasus, and Central Asia. Turkey is a main production location for Adidas, which established its

Turkish division in 1999. In 2010, Adidas Turkey exported to 45 countries. Yesim Tekstil, a large Turkish textile and apparel firm located in Bursa city, produces for Nike, Gap, Banana Republic, Old Navy, Zara, Pull & Bear, Massimo Dutti, Esprit, Hugo Boss, Lands' End, Tchibo, and Schlafgut. For international apparel retailers, the Turkish market has proved to be a good location for both production and retail.

Apparel chains operating in Turkey have no problems with sourcing. Thousands of domestic producers and imports provide apparel to both domestic and foreign apparel retailers. There are companies that are vertically integrated (production and sales). There are sole producers and sole retailers as well; wholesalers and other intermediaries build bridges between these sole producers and sole retailers.

RETAIL CAREERS: NEED MORE TALENT

The growth of the Turkish retail sector demands qualified labor. Unfortunately, the supply of qualified sales representatives for the increasing number of shopping centers and stores is far behind the demand. Retailing in Turkey is not seen as a career but just temporary work. Educational programs in retailing are very limited. Anadolu University and Kocaeli University offer retailing certificates and college degrees, and some vocational high schools offer courses in retailing. Some companies (such as Mudo, Teknosa, and Hatemoglu) educate their employees themselves and are able to decrease labor turnover in their retail outlets to a certain extent. However, managers and college professors agree that there is a huge demand for qualified employees in the retail sector in Turkey (Konuk, 2008).

In Turkey, the Ministry of Labor and Social Security is the government agency dealing with the work permits that foreigners need to work in Turkey. The agency organizes work permits under three categories: work permit for a definite period, work permit for an indefinite period, and independent work permit.

DEFINITE PERIOD

Unless there are other provisions in the bilateral or multilateral agreements to which Turkey is a party, permission to work is valid for a maximum of one year. After one year, the permit may be extended up to three years, on condition of working for the same company and in the same job. At the end of that three-year period, the work permit may be extended for a maximum of three years to work in the same profession with any employer. The work permit may also be granted to the spouse of any foreigner who has come to Turkey to work, as well as the children under the foreigner's care, under the condition that they have legally resided with the foreigner without interruption for at least five years.

INDEFINITE PERIOD

Unless there are other provisions in the bilateral or multilateral contracts to which Turkey is a party, foreigners who have resided in Turkey legally and continuously for at least eight years, or who have worked in Turkey for six years, may be granted a work permit without terms.

INDEPENDENT WORK PERMIT

The Ministry of Labor and Social Security may grant an independent work permit to foreigners who want to work independently on the conditions that they have resided in Turkey legally and uninterruptedly for at least five years and that their work will have a positive effect on national employment and economic development (Ministry of Labor and Social Security, 2009).

Some useful web resources on Turkish retail jobs are: www.elemanara.com (Turkish), www.cvtr.net (Turkish), www.eleman.net (Turkish), and www.kariyer.net (Turkish). Some industry websites are www.perakende.org, www.ampd.org. (Turkish), www.perakendehaber.org, and www.perakende.tv.

TABLE 7.2 Selected Foreign Clothing, Footwear, and Accessories Retailers in Turkey in 2009

Chain	Owner/Franchisee	Store Count as of March 2009
Benetton	Benetton/Boyner	120
Levi's	Levi's	85
Bata	Bata/Derimod	50
Lacoste	Lacoste	43
Marks & Spencer	Marks & Spencer/Fiba Holding	37
Mango	MNG	37
Nine West	Jones Apparel Group/Park Bravo	35
Zara	Inditex	25
Claire's	Apollo Management/Alshaya Group	24
Dockers	Levi's	22
La Senza	La Senza/Park Bravo	20
Billabong	Billabong	17
Gap	Gap Inc/Fiba Holding	14
Pull and Bear	Inditex	13
Bershka	Inditex	13
Stradivarius	Inditex	13
C&A	C&A	12

Source: Machnicka (2009)

THE FUTURE OF APPAREL RETAIL: AN OPPORTUNITY CALLING

Being a very large sector, the textile and apparel sector plays an important role in the Turkish economy and generates huge employment (Table 7.2). The financial crisis of 2008/2009 adversely affected the sector, especially the production side. The Turkish government provided some help: Manufacturers with 30 employees or more benefit from 50 percent energy support (government subsidizes their fuel bills), exemptions from value added tax (VAT) and customs duties, interest rate subsidies, discounts on social security payments, and so on. This package of incentives that supports the whole of the clothing and footwear industry in terms of production, export, and domestic sales, will be available through 2012. Clothing and footwear are both among the last sectors to be affected by economic crises because they provide essential items for everyday life. Both sectors are, therefore, strongly expected to recover more quickly than many others within Turkey (Euromonitor, 2009).

Four distinct trends emerge from the examination of publications, speeches, and sector reports related to the Turkish apparel sector:

1. More and more investments by foreign apparel retailers
2. Establishment of new shopping centers, not only in big cities but also in others
3. Tendency on the part of domestic textile firms to become apparel retailers
4. Growing brand awareness and creation of brands and quality products (for example, the Turquality campaign)

As the Turkish economy becomes more stable and the government enacts favorable foreign investment laws, foreign investors become more willing to operate in the Turkish market. So, competition from foreign investors is expected to increase in the apparel retailing sector. An increasing number of stores or retail outlets by the incumbent apparel firms and the establishment of new shopping centers are indications of retail growth in general and apparel retailing growth in particular. The conversion of domestic textile companies into apparel retailers will no doubt intensify the competition in international apparel retailing, especially as more and more Turkish apparel brands make their debuts in international markets in the spotlight of the Turquality campaign.

Growth in apparel retail requires success in creating a brand. Turkish apparel firms have not been as successful in this as their foreign counterparts. The transfer of foreign knowledge through experience would be valuable to them. Malgorzata Machnicka, retail analyst at PMR, indicates that large European retailers have difficulty surviving in Turkey. The joint venture is a preferred means of entry into the Turkish market. Joint ventures offer an excellent opportunity for shared knowledge (Machnicka, 2009).

International brands or retailers began to enter the Turkish market during the 1980s, mostly through licensing agreements or joint ventures. In the apparel sector, these included such stores as Benetton in 1986, Mothercare in 1988, Levi's in 1989, and LC Waikiki in 1991 (Ar & Saydan, 2004).

Case Study 1

LC WAIKIKI: THE MOST LOVABLE BRAND

LC Waikiki, the leader in the Turkish clothing industry, is a good example of the establishment and growth of a Turkish apparel firm. LC Waikiki was originally a French apparel firm established in 1985 by George Amoual, the French designer and his partner. In 1988, LC Waikiki was searching for a subcontractor to meet its increasing demand. LC Waikiki signed a subcontractor contract with Taha Textile, and later became Taha Group, a branch of Tema Holding, the current owner of LC Waikiki. Taha Group was then the subcontractor of many big companies. Taha Group established Tema Textile to operate in the retail sector and introduced LC Waikiki products to Turkish consumers in 1991 (LC Waikiki, 2009).

LC Waikiki entered the Turkish ready-made clothing market with a line of childrenswear and later added adult clothing to its range of products. Within a short time, LC Waikiki expanded its product line to include collections designed for infants, children, youth, and adults. Tema Textile purchased the LC Waikiki brand in 1997. The number of retail outlets increased from 21 in the early days to 250 in 2009. After the purchase, the company introduced many other sub-brands. By combining superior product quality and reasonable pricing policies with wise investments, LC Waikiki has quickly become a leader in the apparel market in Turkey. It continues to reinforce its position through ongoing investments, the provision of uniform service and product quality throughout the country, and the importance it attaches to its customers. In 2009, the company set its sights on being among the three largest brands in Europe by 2020 (LC Waikiki, 2009).

LC Waikiki has had the growth problem or rather vision. The following actions have been taken. First, the company focused on further developing its identity by opening contemporary stores that have a Western look just like typical stores seen in the U.S. malls. Then, the company established Zirve Architect, an affiliate, to develop store concepts for Tema Group and Taha Clothing. They also opened procurement offices in China, Bangladesh, and Egypt. Other collections and brands (such as Southblue and XSIDE) were also introduced. Southblue targeted adult male and female consumers desiring elegant clothes, whereas XSIDE targeted younger consumers desiring casual apparel. However, Tema Group did not limit itself to production and sales of only its own brands. Rather, Tema Group also tried to increase its growth and competitiveness through production for the world's leading brands such as Marks & Spencer, Top Shop, Decathlon, and Tommy Hilfiger among others (LC Waikiki, 2009).

Today, Tema Group produces apparel sold in LC Waikiki stores through both domestic and global supply chain systems. The performance of the company is very significant. The company achieved sales growth rates of 45 percent and 46 percent in 2007 and 2008, respectively. With its 250 stores in 51 cities of Turkey, it serves millions of consumers. In 2003, the company ranked 185 on the Capital 500 list, a Turkish company ranking similar to the Fortune 500. By 2008 it had moved ahead to 73. The company is the leader in the ready-made retailing category in terms of turnover and profitability. It also holds the title of the most lovable brand in the clothing category according to the survey of Lovemarks of Turkey (LC Waikiki, 2009).

The case of LC Waikiki (Tema Group, Taha Holding) exemplifies a successful business strategy through brand development and global supply chain establishment. The company initially was the subcontractor of LC Waikiki and later purchased the brands. The company may use a similar strategy to further grow in international markets because it currently produces for other brands as well. Such a carefully planned growth strategy may also suit other companies.

Discussion Questions

1. Tema Holding long produced for LC Waikiki before purchasing it. Is long experience in an industry and especially in the apparel

industry a must for success? Would new apparel companies or brands have little chance for success?

2. Is acquisition a good way to grow in the apparel industry? What factors should be considered before acquisition decisions?

3. LC Waikiki initially sold children's clothing and then expanded to other segments as well. How can an apparel firm assess whether its brand will be liked by other segments as well?

Case Study 2

MAVI JEANS: MADE IN MAVILAND

Mavi Jeans is another success story in the Turkish apparel industry. Mavi Jeans was established in Istanbul in 1991 and has been the market leader in the denim sector since 1996. Mr. Sait Akalilar, the name behind Mavi, had years of experience producing for international brands. Mavi Jeans, then called Erak, started denim production in 1984 and produced for Lee, Mustang, Wrangler, His, Otto Versand, Eddie Bauer, Calvin Klein, Old Navy, and Canoe. The company basically used this experience and added a Mediterranean flavor together with good market positioning and to create Mavi Jeans, which became the first Turkish apparel brand to expand to international markets. Its establishment in 1991 was followed by its national advertisement in 1993, its first export in 1994 to European countries, and its first export to the U.S. and Canadian markets in 1996. Afterwards, German, North African, Middle Eastern, and Eastern European exports followed. In addition to showrooms in Los Angeles, Vancouver, New York, Dallas, and Frankfurt, many other world cities were opened. One of the largest shops in New York City's Union Square belongs to Mavi Jeans. Some celebrities (Cher, Chelsea Clinton, Geri Halliwell, and some MTV people) have been seen in Mavi Jeans. Some successful advertisement themes of the company have been "It's too much (i.e., we did a lot of things)," "Made in MaviLand," and "We've gone too far (i.e., we passed our rivals)" (Mavi Jeans 2009; Kocak 2006; Articlebase 2009).

Mavi Jeans' performance and popularity over the years has been significant. In 2000, Mavi Jeans ranked 128 in the list of top 500 companies in Turkey and 77 in the following year. Many surveys indicated that Mavi Jeans brand comes second in popularity after Coca-Cola. Popular magazines (such as *Time*) have devoted pages to Mavi Jeans; the American magazine *Cosmogirl* calls jeans manufactured by Mavi the sexiest jeans in the world. Mavi Jeans was included among the best 16 jeans in the Style and Design issue of *Time* magazine in 2006 (Articlebase, 2009).

Mavi Jeans' success comes from its philosophy of building a brand around its customers while incorporating details true to the brand's Mediterranean spirit, which is lively, cheerful, and colorful. The perfect fit notion is the key point of Mavi's marketing strategy. Perfect fit refers to the fit not only to the bodies of its customers but also their lifestyles and budgets. The company states that like the individuals who wear them, each pair of Mavi jeans has a distinct personality. Over the years Mavi has grown from just selling great-fitting jeans to offering an entire lifestyle collection (Mavi Jeans 2009; Kocak 2006).

Mavi Jeans followed a different approach for growth from many others. Generally, companies initially do extensive feasibility studies, market research, and advertising campaigns. However, Mavi Jeans tried to capture the hearts and minds of consumers. The company tried to understand what men and women want to wear according to tastes and preferences. In addition, Mavi Jeans produced jeans accustomed to the Turkish consumers' body characteristics. This effort led to increases in the number of different-sized denims. The company followed the same philosophy while entering the U.S. market, which the company indicated demands classical, comfortable, as well as fashionable denim. Like in the Turkish market, in foreign markets extensive advertisement campaigns began not at the time of initial market entry but afterwards. In overseas markets, Mavi Jeans initially opened small stores selling consumer and fashion-friendly denims and opened large stores later (Kocak 2006; Articlebase 2009).

Success in both domestic and international markets is not easy. Mavi Jeans' initial success is related to understanding and positioning its products according to customers' needs through its perfect fit notion. The company seems to have understood the meaning of today's global market notion instead of domestic market notion. The company followed a careful internationalization strategy, investing in many key markets and increasing its visibility worldwide. Therefore, rather than entering price competition, the company was able to create its unique positioning through differentiation in both domestic and international markets. The company later began big advertisement campaigns to further increase its visibility.

One can learn about unique positioning through Mavi Jeans' example. Understanding true needs, preferences, and tastes of consumers has been the key in the success story of Mavi Jeans.

Discussion Questions

1. Suppose that you wanted to operate in the denim sector. You see that there are firmly established brands in the sector. You do not want to engage in price-cut wars becauses you want to position yourself as an upscale retailer. What would you do to create a unique position for your denim?

2. How reasonable do you find Mavi Jeans' rather unconventional advertising strategy, with respect to timing? Why?

3. Why do you think Mavi Jeans' notion of positioning through "perfect fit" and "the Mediterranean spirit" was effective? Did other major denim companies miss such strategies? Why? Why not?

REFERENCES

Amed, I. (2008, October 16). Turkey: Counterfeit culture. Retrieved October 14, 2010, from http://www.businessoffashion.com/2008/10/turkey-counterfeit-culture.html

Ar, A. A. & Saydan, R. (2004). Marka olusturulmasinda konumlandirma strateji ve Mavi Jeans ornegi, *Mevzuat Dergisi,* 7(81), Retrieved December 06, 2009, from www.mevzuatdergisi.com/2004/09a/02.htm.

Articlebase (2009). The history of Mavi Jeans brand. *Articlebase.com,* Retrieved December 9, 2009, from http://www.articlesbase.com/clothing-articles/the-history-of-mavi-jeans-brand-1556413.html

Benetton (2005). Press Release. *Benetton,* Retrieved December 23, 2009, from http://press.benettongroup.com/ben_en/releases/2005-04-21

CIA, The World Factbook (2009a), Maps, Political World, *CIA,* Retrieved October 19, 2009, from https://www.cia.gov/library/publications/the-world-factbook/docs/refmaps.html

CIA, The World Factbook (2009b). Country Information. *CIA,* Retrieved December 17, 2009, from https://www.cia.gov/library/publications/the-world-factbook/index.html

Eraslan, H., Bakan, I. & Kuyucu, A. (2008). Turk tekstil ve hair giyim sektorunun uluslararasi rekabetcilik duzeyinin analizi. *Istanbul Ticaret Universitesi Sosyal Bilimler Dergisi,* 7(13), 265–300.

Euromonitor (2009). Clothing and footwear in Turkey: Market Report, *Euromonitor,* October 2009. Retrieved October 25, 2009, from www.euromonitor.com/Clothing_And_Footwear_in_Turkey

Haber Turk (2006). Kizlar Gece Dekolteli Gunduz Dusuk Belli: Genclik Arastirmasi, *Haber Turk,* Retrieved December 23, 2009, from http://www.haberturk.com/haber.asp?id=3867&cat=200&dt=2006/10/24

HTP Arastirma ve Danismanlik and Retailing Institute (2003). Turkiye Hazir Giyim Tuketim Endeksi. Retrieved November 4, 2009, from www.ampd.org/images/.../02_TurkiyeHazirGiyimTuketimEndeksi.ppt

Invest in Turkey (2009a). 10 Reasons to Invest in Turkey. *Republic of Turkey Prime Ministry, Investment Support and Promotion Agency.* Retrieved

January 4, 2008, from http://www.invest.gov.tr/en-US/investmentguide/ Pages/10Reasons.aspx

Invest in Turkey (2009b). Cisco, Success Stories, *Republic of Turkey Prime Ministry, Investment Support and Promotion Agency.* Retrieved January 15, 2008, from http://www.invest.gov.tr/SuccessStories.aspx?ID=15

Invest in Turkey (2009b). Nortel, Success Stories, *Republic of Turkey Prime Ministry, Investment Support and Promotion Agency.* Retrieved November 15, 2008, from http://www.invest.gov.tr/SuccessStories.aspx?ID=8

Kocak, A. (2006). Turkey in transition. Expectations in the textile and apparel industry for the next two decades, *The Woolmark Company,* Retrieved November 8, 2009, from http://www.remarkablesolutions.com/Turkey_ in_Transition.pdf

Konuk, C. (2008). Buyuyen perakende sektorunun insan kaynaklari ihtiyaci da artiyor. *Perakende.org,* Retrieved December 18, 2009, from http:// perakende.org/haber.php?hid=1200989474

Lambert, J. (2006). One step closer to a Pan-European Shopping Center Standard: Illustrating the new framework with examples, *Research Review,* 13(2), 35–40.

LC Waikiki (2009). Corporate History. LC Waikiki, Retrieved November 15, 2009, from www.lcwaikiki.com

Machnicka, M. (2009). Turkey attracting foreign retailers. Report: Retail in Turkey 2009. Market Analysis and Development Forecasts 2009–2010. *PMR Publications.* Retrieved November 12, 2009, from www.ceeretail. com/wp_705/Turkey_attracting_foreign_retailers_April_2009.shtml

Mavi Jeans (2009). Retrieved November 15, 2009, from www.mavi.com

Ministry of Labor and Social Security (2009). Types of Permissions, *Republic of Turkey, Ministry of Labor and Social Security Department of Work Permits for Foreigners,* Retrieved December 23, 2009, from www.yabancicalismaizni.gov.tr/eng/index.html

PWC and AMPD (2007). Turk Perakende Sektorunun Degisimi ve Ekonomi Uzerindeki Etkileri, *PriceWaterHouseCoopers and Turkish Council of Shopping Centers and Retailers.* Retrieved November 4, 2009, from www.pwc.com/tr/tr/publications/retail-sector.jhtml

PMR Publications (2009). Turkey attracting foreign retailers (April, 2009). Retrieved November 10, 2009, from http://www.pmrpublications.com

Savasci, I. (2003). The New Trends in Retailing: The Development of Private Labels and Applications in Turkey. *Yonetim ve Ekonomi.* 10(1), 85–102.

State Planning Organization (2004). Sector Profiles of Turkey: A General Outlook, *General Directorate for Economic Sectors and Coordination, Turkish Prime Ministry,* Retrieved November 14, 2009, from http://ekutup.dpt.gov.tr/imalatsa/2004.pdf

Suzer, H. (2005). The Most Powerful Foreigners, *Capital* (March 1, 2005), Retrieved November 17, 2009, from www.capital.com.tr/haber. aspx?HBR_KOD=2117

The Undersecretariat of Treasury (2009). Retrieved November 17, 2009, from http://www.treasury.gov.tr/irj/go/km/docs/documents/Treasury%20 Web/Legislation/Foreign%20Direct%20Investment%20Legislation/ FDI%20Law.pdf

Turkish Council of Shopping Centers and Retailers (2009). *Sektorel Bilgiler.* Retrieved November 15, 2009, from http://www.ampd.org/sektorel_ bilgiler/liste.aspx?SectionId=5

WowTURKEY (2009). Retrieved on November 15, 2009, from www.wowturkey.com

Yilmaz, N. (2007). Istanbul becomes management club. *Turkish Daily News.* Retrieved December 17, 2007, from http://www.turkishdailynews. tr/article.php?enewsid=91518

THAILAND 8

John Walsh

OBJECTIVES

After reading this chapter, you will

- ▶ Understand why Thailand is an important emerging market
- ▶ Grasp various aspects of retailing in the country
- ▶ Recognize the unique characteristics of a Thai consumer
- ▶ Know about foreign direct investment regulations for investing in Thailand

Thailand is a middle-income country located in the mainland of Southeast Asia with a per capita income of around $8,100 per annum and an economy in the largest 30 in the world (Asia Development Bank, 2008). It is about twice the size of Wyoming. Its capital, Bangkok, has a population of around 6.5 million urban residents and 12 million metropolitan residents from a national population of some 66 million. It has the reputation for being the hottest capital city in the world, with an average maximum daily temperature of around 90°F. Standards of living are much lower outside Bangkok, and there are sharp divisions between the cities and the countryside. Principal secondary cities include Khon Kaen (population 148,000), Chiang Mai (population 150,000), and Ubon Ratchathani (population 122,000), and over the past decade, modern retailing

TABLE 8.1 Fast Facts about Thailand

Capital	Bangkok
Population	66.7 million
Type of government	Constitutional monarchy
GDP: purchasing power parity: in US$	$540.1 billion
Age structure	0–14 yrs: 20.8%
	15–64 yrs: 70.5%
	65 yrs plus: 8.7%
Religion	Buddhist: 94.6%
	Muslim: 4.6%
	Christian: 0.7%
	Other: 0.1%
Ethnicity	Thai: 75%
	Chinese: 14%
	Other: 11%

Source: CIAfactbook.gov

driven by international investment has spread to these cities where before it had been limited to the capital city. Thailand has its own royal family and has been a constitutional monarchy since the 1932 Revolution, which overthrew the absolute monarchy system. It is a parliamentary democracy with a prime minister (Table 8.1). His Majesty the King is the head of state.

Thailand has become an important emerging market, especially since the beginning of the twenty-first century. With a cost structure that is reasonable, a stable economy, skilled workforce, a good regulatory system, and desirable incentives for investments, Thailand has become an attractive country for foreign investors (Thailand's investment, 2008). The country's government is trying to work toward improving the conditions further to simplify and attract foreign investment. It has identified fashion as a centerpiece of its campaign to move the economy away from low-cost manufacturing to more creative activities because fashion is a large part of Thai consumption and exercises a powerful hold on the imagination. Thailand also represents a complex marketplace in which Western and local goods compete against increasingly influential Korean and Japanese products. Due to the large size of the market, apparel producers need to look at local factors when designing the merchandise for Thai consumers.

THE RETAIL LANDSCAPE: MODERN FORMATS GAINING POPULARITY

Compared to traditional wet markets (open food market) and mom-and-pop grocery shops, supermarket chains and shopping centers are proving very popular and, for many Thai people, new retail opportunities are provoking something of a revolution in daily life, ranging from frozen food (which facilitates single rather than family eating) to buying in bulk because malls tend to be located outside of town or city centers and so are accessed primarily by car (Feeny et al., 1996). Increasingly, consumers prefer to shop from a single location and retailers are responding to this by ensuring a wide range of goods and services are available in every space. According to one elderly couple, "when the weather is hot, we go to the shopping center for free air-conditioning."

Apparel retail is an important part of this process. As a central part of the manufacturing industry that has helped pull Thailand out of poverty, textiles and apparel occupy a significant part of modern Thai history and continue to be a major strength of the economy. Apparel is a notable part of Thailand's crucially important export effort (it is one of the most open countries in the world in terms of international trade and, therefore, very vulnerable to changes in the international business environment) and accounted for 42 percent of the $7.27 billion textile export market. Exports of apparel in particular are increasing as the quality of fashion items increases, partly thanks to government-sponsored initiatives, while costs remain comparatively constant.

With increasing competition in all fields from China in particular, Thai manufacturers are striving to add value to their

▲ **FIGURE 8.1** A storefront display indicating "Thainess." Thainess is introduced in a store or a product to make it appear more exotic and, therefore, appealing to a customer. Photo by John Walsh.

products in all categories, through improving technology and design and increasing the unique qualities of "Thainess" to make distinctive and often exotic items. These factors are clearly evident in the domestic retailing sector, where foreign and homemade items compete directly against each other in all but the most high-end sectors (where foreign brands dominate) and the low-end sectors, which are dominated by locally made products or imports from neighboring countries (Jitpleecheep, 2009a).

CONSUMERS: MOVING TOWARD MODERNISM

As a developing, middle-income country that was economically depressed at the end of World War II, Thailand has changed rapidly over the past few decades. Whereas there has been an emergence of a new middle class with often considerable spending power and aspirations in terms of consumer goods, they preserve a number of cultural

▲ **FIGURE 8.2** Traditional Thai dress. © Idealink Photography/Alamy.

practices and superstitions concerning the type and variety of apparel that should be worn. Clothing has traditionally been subject to sumptuary laws in most of mainland Southeast Asia and this practice continued until the twentieth century, in which several of the despotic paternalists who led the government between the 1930s and 1960s sought to ensure that urban residents dressed in ways that were recognizably "modern" and based on Western modes. Historically, Thais have worn Indian cotton or Thai silk *phanung* or sarong-type clothes and very little else. In rural Thailand, many people, especially the poor, continue with this style, and this further restricts the penetration of modern retailing methods in the Kingdom.

Two other factors of Thai apparel wearing that are unusual from a Western perspective are also worth mentioning. The first is that there are approximately 700,000 or more ethnic minority people resident in Thailand, most of whom are hill tribes people living in different parts of the north of the country (in addition to unknown numbers of unregistered or undocumented ethnic minority people). In many cases, cultural traits, which may have been intensified by the desire to pander to the interests of tourists, extend to the clothing that the women of these ethnic minority people wear on a daily basis. Because these clothes are made within the community and are homemade where possible, the people wearing these clothes are outside the market system when it comes to most forms of apparel.

Second, all male Buddhist Thais are expected to be ordained and live as a monk at some period of their lives. Buddhist monks wear distinctive saffron-colored robes, and presenting new robes to monks on special occasions, as well as to boys and men about to be ordained, is a regularly recurring feature of apparel buying. These robes are now available in chain supermarkets, and there is no need for specialist buying.

The Buddhist religion (which is professed by more than 94 percent of the population according to most estimates) includes a superstitious component that often manifests in the use of apparel to protect the body, the family, and important physical items. This superstitious component is most commonly seen in the amulet industry. Amulets are worn on chains around the neck, either under the clothes or on the outside in more flamboyant cases. Amulets are usually made by or at least in conjunction with particular Buddhist monasteries and blessed by the monks; many believe they have supernatural powers. In other cases, this superstition is manifested by sacred or magical tattoos worn on the body or on white cloth worn as a singlet. Cosmetic tattooing has also become popular among younger people, and in some cases the traditional, sacred images are incorporated into new designs.

▲ **FIGURE 8.3** Picture of an amulet. This amulet depicts a superstitious component of Buddhist religion. Amulets are blessed by the monks and considered to have supernatural powers to protect the wearer. Getty Images.

Separate and specific marketing efforts toward men, women, and children are predominantly the preserve of the urban middle and upper classes. Outside of these classes, apparel purchasing is based primarily on need and convenience; that is, the need based on a hot and wet climate and the nature of work and daily life. In the case of footwear, for example, the flip-flop or thong-type sandal is generally the only type needed because it is the most practical in wet conditions (they dry much more quickly than other shoes) and are hardy enough to survive being drenched in mud or water. The following sections, therefore, relate primarily to the privileged and urban classes.

WOMEN

Apparel retailing remains dominated, nonetheless, by the size, shape, and coloring of Thai women, which differs from those of Western women. Western visitors to Thailand can shop only at high-end brand outlets because clothes sold at other places do not fit them well. Even those sized as XL or above are too small for the majority of European or American women. It is necessary, therefore, for designers and distributors to consider specifically tailored items for Thai consumers. This tailoring requires attention to detail with respect to size and shape for clothing, as well as coloring for cosmetics and product range for health products. The result is that the most commonly found high-end cosmetics and beauty products tend to feature those products that have a sufficient reputation for high-technology (for example, Clarins, Body Shop, and L'Occitane) or else that are aimed specifically at East Asian women (for example, Oriental Princess and Anna Sui). The same is, broadly speaking, true of clothing, in that the most prestigious brands are available along with those that are more tailored to the Thai consumer. Some hybrid brands cling on at the margins; for example, British India is a brand that is gaining some traction for quality and suitable application of the value-cost equation while catering to the larger Thai consumer or, of course, nonethnic Thai customers.

MEN

There tends to be a lack of role models for men who are fashion conscious and essentially acceptable to a modern audience. The traditional image of a Thai man consists of deference, diligence, and obedience, which is disliked by the young, with its more attractive obverse of the *nak leng* ("tough man"), a sharp-dressed (usually in neo-colonial style), hard-living individual whose wealth and success is demonstrated by the ostentatious display of material goods (for example, gold jewelry, prestigious foreign car, muscular servants, and numerous *mia noi* or "little wives," whose presence is widely tolerated in a supposedly monogamous culture). This is a normal image and is anti-modern, which in turn has a knock-on effect on modern marketing techniques. Whereas media personalities are permitted to display a more modern image, such an image is nearly always combined with an eventual display of obedience, combined with a return to traditional values (including, of course, appearance). All of this sets a limit to the extent to which Thai men will accept or be interested in having goods and services marketed to them, apart from the forms that are essentially traditional or conservative in nature. This is truer of older men than younger men, who are generally more comfortable and familiar with the internationalized Thai society and economy. There are also a larger number of younger male role models who appear in the media in a variety of different fashions. In addition, Thailand's tolerance for the "lady boys" (or *katoey*), means that some such flamboyant individuals have been able to push the envelope for what is considered acceptable in terms of apparel and fashion. Consequently, although it has been difficult to market to this traditional Thai consumer, as retail tastes have become internationalized, teenagers and younger men have shown more openness to clothes and items that would not be considered acceptable to older consumers. Some male undergraduate students have been known to observe, "Now I can wear what I like as long as my family cannot see me."

BEAUTY INDUSTRY IN THAILAND

Thailand has many beauty salons, hairdressers', spas, and clinics throughout that are primarily aimed at women. Even when service retail outlets are explicitly unisex in nature, customers as well as staff are overwhelmingly female. Although massage and good health are applicable to all ages, only women of younger ages are considered suitable people to use beauty products related to those activities. Older women certainly do use massage services but from a medically therapeutic basis mostly. Few older women use spas for cosmetic purposes rather than for health; however, as the extent of the middle classes in Thailand spreads and the number of older female role models increases, marketing to the older and less economically privileged has also increased. Beauty products, for example, broadly defined to include natural remedies and dietary supplements, are now available through the multiple convenience stores that are so prevalent throughout the Kingdom. In this way,

▲ **FIGURE 8.4** A consumer shops for cosmetics. AFP/Getty Images/
Saeed Khan.

the range of items that was previously reserved for younger, richer
women is now increasingly being diffused to the mass market.

Women's beauty products are extensive and increasing in
scope, not just in terms of the range and nature of products and
services provided but also in increasing the age range of women
who like to use them. In urban settings, the target market for
beauty products for women is increasing in age. In terms of range
of goods, women are offered the opportunities not just to appear

younger and to conform more closely to specific ideals of beauty as exhibited by professional models and celebrities but also to change their bodies so as to become more Westernized in nature. In Thai society, the most beautiful people are often considered to be those with mixed Thai-Western parents, and the beauty industry promotes the idea that appearance can be enhanced by whitening the skin, increasing bust size, and having cosmetic surgery to change the shape of the nose and eyes in particular. Thailand is considered a center for this kind of cosmetic surgery because of expertise in the particular physiognomy of Asian people and also the economy of scale available through providing gender reassignment surgery to local people and international visitors. In this industry, modern high-technology products can merge with longstanding traditional remedies to provide the supposed advantages that are possible.

Thai people have an interest in appearing both beautiful and fashionable if they can afford it. This interest is evident in the extensive network of beauty parlors, spas, massage centers, cosmetic beauty clinics, and, increasingly, weight loss clinics that are common throughout urban Thailand. It has been intensified in the twenty-first century by a new emphasis on healthy eating and living, which has led to the distribution of a variety of products that promote one or more of the qualities of aesthetic beauty and good health. A number of products combining these virtues are sourced from China or at least from ethnic Chinese communities because of the respect paid to traditional Asian medicines and methods. It is quite common, for example, to find Chinese shampoos that promise men they will reverse hair loss. Korean ginseng, meanwhile, is also growing in prevalence because of the belief in its health-promoting activities and because of the trendiness of Korean products and ideas of all kinds.

Men are more likely to have beauty products directly marketed to them by virtue of their health-promoting aspects rather than their ability to enhance aesthetic appeal. Where beauty products are promoted directly tends to be through point-of-sale activities in hairdressers' and similar locations. A variety of men's interest magazines now offer new ideas for male grooming: The majority of these magazines use licensed content from the Western countries where they originated, often with local additions and the use of local talent as models and role models. These magazines are more open to promoting beauty products than are mass media such as television, where male beauty products are still viewed by a large part of the audience as either excessive embrace of non-Thai globalization or effeminacy.

CHILDREN

Children outside of the urban, middle classes have few opportunities to choose apparel because of lack of resources (and, owing to the climate and conditions, lack of need for a choice), and those within those classes are most commonly enrolled in so many extra-curricular activities that they do not have the time to work in order to buy their own apparel. Inevitably, therefore, marketing to children involves extensive use of the "nag factor" and peer pressure.

In the case of younger children, advertising images are presented of happy and contented Asian children—that is, they portray traditional Asian values of family orientation and obedience. Older children and teenagers generally find themselves looking at the vaguely rebellious Western style that is known, somewhat inaccurately, as hip-hop or, more recently, Korean or Japanese pop or R&B styles. The rise of reality television shows such as *Academy Fantasia* (in which contestants are filmed night and day, with heavy censorship of any improper behavior, competing to be the year's best new singing and dancing star) has led to the merging of Asian and Western styles in this regard.

LUXURY RETAIL IN THAILAND

Although luxury retail opportunities are possible in Thailand, they are very much restricted to a few urban areas because of the unequal distribution of income in the country and in terms of

▲ **FIGURE 8.5** Child models backstage at the Children's Peanut Fashion Show on Children's Day in Bangkok, Thailand. Reality television has a major influence on clothing worn by Thai children. © Barry Lewis/Alamy.

access because most people cannot afford to buy those kinds of products. In spatial terms, luxury is available in a small number of central Bangkok shopping malls, high-end hotels, and mostly in the capital, but in a small number of locations in other parts of the Kingdom as well. This includes products such as luxury cars (there are special distributors for brands such as Lamborghini and Ferrari), speedboats, jewelry, and the usual range of consumer goods. Given the relatively low costs of labor, especially in the service sector, providers of goods and services may come to the customer rather than vice versa. Service standards also tend to be high because of the competition with Singapore and Hong Kong as a destination for international shoppers.

Historically, the ability to shop for luxury goods in Thailand was highly correlated with the ability to travel overseas. These days, despite the many ways in which such travel has been simplified through removal of visa requirements for most citizens of the Association of Southeast Asian Nations (ASEAN) and the rapidly increasing provision of budget air travel, that assumption that ability to shop for luxury goods is related to ability to travel overseas still remains. Those who enjoy luxury items are those, by and large, who can go overseas to shop for them. Preferred destinations in this context are Europe and North America. Because Thailand has never been formally colonized in the modern age, there is not one particular overseas country to which people immediately look for comparison and fashionable trends, although Europe is generally preferred to the United States because of previous historical connections. However, given what has been said about the nature of Thai consumers, other Asian countries are the critical locations for shopping trips. In particular, Hong Kong and Singapore are primary shopping destinations, due to their proximity and range of available brands and outlets, combined with suitable service, food, and accommodation.

In the first decade of the twenty-first century, the development of retail opportunities in central Bangkok has ensured that, in practical terms, travel overseas for shopping is not required anymore because the same products are available in Thailand, and tourists can travel to Bangkok to shop. In 2005, the Thai government introduced the Thailand Elite Card for foreign visitors to Thailand. Members pay up to $50,000 (1.5 million baht) to receive free first-class travel from Thai Airways, special VIP services, and an enhanced visa. The program has struggled due to lack of interest and various complaints. The lack of joined-up government among the relevant agencies and ministries has meant that projected benefits of membership, such as privileges in buying and owning land, have failed to be realized, and the project was considered to be a failure (Saengsawang, 2009). In 2010, lengthy pro-democracy demonstrations closed down much of the central luxury shopping region of Bangkok and, after the military launched a series of violent attacks that left more than 90 dead and thousands injured, one of the large shopping centers burned to the ground.

APPAREL RETAIL FORMATS: NEW IS IN, BUT OLD IS NOT OUT

Retailing in Thailand has changed significantly since the 1960s. From a situation of temporary markets selling low-cost goods, the country now offers a large number of high-end retail-based shopping malls offering fashion items from all around the world. However, this development is very limited spatially and in terms of population. The bulk of economic development takes place in the capital city Bangkok, which dominates the economic, political, cultural, and institutional spheres in Thailand. Although retail development has been spreading to other towns and cities since the turn of the century, these sites are also subject to strong segmentation within the population as most people, especially in rural areas, continue to rely on such traditional formats as temporary markets and street vendors for apparel purchases.

The most common traditional retail formats in Thailand are temporary markets, mom-and-pop stores (family-owned shops), and street vendors. Historically, Thai shops were part of businesses operated by small-scale entrepreneurs, often ethnic Chinese in origin who would frequently open a venture known as a Chinese-family business (CFB), which was characterized by family ownership and control, hierarchical management, unwillingness to expand beyond the limits of what one person could manage, and opportunistic diversification in new ventures that could be spun off to be managed by other family members. Even today, a large number of Thai firms are family owned rather than publicly owned through stocks and shares (and there are also combination ownership structures) even among the very largest firms.

Shops were usually opened in the rows of shop-houses, which are so characteristic of Southeast Asia, and for marketing relied primarily on word-of-mouth, passing foot traffic, and personal networks of connections. When larger stores did emerge, they usually acted as wholesalers as well as retailers, redistributing goods sourced from overseas or from domestic manufacturers to the neighborhood retailers in addition to direct sales. Overall, the retail and wholesale industry was fragmented, with no national or multinational chains in operation. This situation changed as a result of the presence of American and allied troops using Thailand as a base for fighting in Vietnam, Cambodia, and Laos. The troops provided a stimulus to the creation of a more modern retailing system in which larger, partly foreign-owned stores could provide economies of scope and scale to provide items for consumption primarily by foreigners and high-society Thai people with international tastes.

A feature of most shopping centers, especially those not located in central Bangkok, is that they are usually surrounded by street vending space. Vendors might draw lots on a daily basis to determine their particular location or else a more permanent system might be in place as vendors pay the center's owners a fee for opening their stalls outside. Shoppers can adjust their shopping preferences based on cost and other personal preferences. Shopping inside offers higher prices in an air-conditioned environment, with generally higher levels of quality and range of sizes; shopping outside is less comfortable and may require haggling. Street vendors have developed a reputation for tough bargaining and, in a low-trust society like Thailand's, shoppers are concerned that they will lose face if they pay more for an item than their friends and family members believe they should have done.

Items provided by street vendors need not be inferior to those available within the shopping center and not just because it is possible for some entrepreneurs to source the same items from the same factories where they are manufactured. Within the overall population of street vendors, there exists a subset of trained and enterprising entrepreneurs who have been adding value to their stalls by such measures as personal brand creation, batch manufacturing of personally designed items, international sourcing, and

▲ **FIGURE 8.6** Street vendor selling apparel. Apparel sold in these street stalls is similar to those sold in local stores. Photo by John Walsh.

franchising of stalls. These entrepreneurs are in contrast to the majority of vendors who operate stalls largely undifferentiated from each other, with items sourced by wholesalers or family members and relying on calling out to passing individuals as the principal means of marketing. These stalls are staffed by individual owners, family members, or hired staff who are mostly paid low wages (possibly below statutory minimum wage levels) but offered some measure of commission. Street vendors may occupy a permanent position in one market area or may rotate their business around a variety of different temporary or seasonal markets.

In Bangkok, wholesale markets and nearby factories represent important sources for products. Outside Bangkok and especially in rural areas, traveling merchants will supply and resupply a number of different stalls with the same range of goods, leading to repetition of product offerings and few opportunities for vendors to add value to their businesses.

MODERN FORMATS

The traditional retailing continued until the inauguration of the 1999 Foreign Business Act, after which major changes became evident. This act enabled foreign investors, for the first time, to create majority-owned retail outlets that were less than $3.3 million (100 million baht) in extent, and that did not deal in food and beverages or any agricultural products. Large-scale retailers felt obliged to use nominees (that is, Thai individuals or organizations guaranteed to act as sleeping partners) to circumvent the regulations. Using this approach, large companies such as the UK's Tesco Lotus and France's Carrefour established ownership of their chains by buying out local partners and then embarking on a period of rapid expansion that gave rise to local protests and environmental concerns (Kanchoochat, 2008), including demonstrations and boycotts. Tesco Lotus now employs 36,000 people in Thailand and has 8,400 franchisees in the country in a variety of formats, from hypermarkets to express services.

▶Hypermarkets

These formats devote ample space to various categories of apparel products, mostly in the low-cost sectors in which the chain specializes.

▶Specialty Stores

New ventures such as the Tesco Plus Shopping Mall at Srinakharin district in Bangkok offers specialty stores with more up-market brand names, including Body Glove (USA), Bossini (Hong Kong), and City Chain (Thai-Chinese). New entrants have also emerged in the large retail malls, including PC Land Co, which is planning to open a $50 million (1.5 billion baht) project at Bang Bua Thong district in Bangkok called The Square. In Chiang Mai, the Thai-owned

Renova Group will open Vian Panna on a piece of land measuring seven rai (one rai is 1,600 square meters or 17,200 square feet).

Retail sales increased by 4 to 5 percent in 2009, despite the economic crisis and ongoing political instability throughout the year, largely because of the opening of new stores that were supported by previous government development in Bangkok of the public transport system (including light rail and underground train services) and the metropolitan infrastructure. The government's version of economic stimulus programs created around the world is called Thai Khem Kaeng ("strong Thailand") and, although funds were disbursed throughout 2009 at a snail's pace, it is hoped that this spending will help sustain retail sales through 2010. Clearly, retail sales are supported more in the higher-end sectors rather than the lower end, where most suffering is felt and the great majority of jobs lost.

▶Department Stores

Within retail malls, apparel is available both within department stores (for which rent is payable and service costs are shared to various extents) and in specialty stores outside of the department store but within the mall. Most of the international brands found in the high-end stores retain their international ownership but may have an extensive presence at the board and management level; it is a generally held belief that Thai senior management is essential in business success, not just because of their local business knowledge but also because of their access to requisite connections in the public and private sectors.

STORE OWNERSHIP: REGULATED BY LAW

Thai investors ostensibly hold ownership of retail space, but it is clear that foreign investors ultimately hold control. Future government activity may force international investors to reveal their real level of ownership of retail companies and comply with the law, but given the fragility of investor confidence in the Kingdom and the

▲ **FIGURE 8.7** In the interest of proper operation of international brands, Thai professionals are hired for their connections in the public and private sectors. Photo by John Walsh.

fact it has persisted since at least the military coup of 2006, it is more likely that sleeping dogs will be allowed to lie.

Ownership of retail outlets is regulated by various laws, which are in turn based upon the developmental principles of the Thai state. These principles promote export-oriented economic growth with low labor cost competitiveness and are based on the desire to ensure that no land falls into foreign ownership. The need to strike a balance between these two impulses has been met in part by the 1999 Foreign Business Act and possible much-discussed but not yet seen future legislation, which may be countered by the investment incentives to foreign investors provided by the Board of Investment (BOI). In other words, more restrictions from one arm of government are usually balanced by concessions from another arm of government.

Thailand is very vulnerable to external economic shocks (such as recessions elsewhere in the world or sudden changes in commodity prices) because of its reliance on exporting, particularly the exporting of low-value-added agricultural products, as well as the importance of the tourism industry and the large proportion of GDP devoted to purchasing oil and gas from overseas. As a result of these various factors, the foreign business lobby has historically had an important role in influencing the legal framework and environment. The most important member of the lobby has been Japan, most of whose investment has been in manufacturing (and distribution of some of the automotive products made or assembled in Thailand) and whose requests have by and large been granted. More vociferous foreign investors, including Americans and Europeans, who have had more interest in retailing, have had less success in achieving their goals because of resistance to the concept of cultural hegemony in much of the state government and the desire to protect local jobs and lifestyles. There is also the need to protect vested Thai interests in the retail industry. Consequently, until 2008, all or nearly all of the retail outlets in Thailand were officially locally owned. It is not known, although there is much anecdotal evidence, to what extent retail outlets were in fact controlled by foreign investors who had placed official ownership in a local partner, perhaps a Thai spouse.

FDI REGULATIONS: A NOT-SO-OPEN MARKET

The industry was governed by regulations introduced in 1972, which permitted ownership of up to 49 percent of a business, by foreign interests—land was and is not available for sale to a foreigner at all. Foreign investors have, therefore, always been required to take a Thai partner or partners in order to go into business. The regulations also provided for various other ways in which business could be organized, including local partnerships and cooperatives.

In considering Thai law, it may be helpful to understand that Thai law generally provides for freedom in positive rather than restrictive ways: In most Western cultures, an individual is free to do anything unless restricted by a specific law; in Thai culture, people, organizations, and institutions can perform any act only if there is a valid law that specifically gives them the right to do so, for example, in opening new types of business operations currently unregulated. Consequently, adoption of innovations and exploitation of new forms of retailing are hindered by the need to create and implement the necessary law to permit these acts to take place legally. Lawmaking can be a lengthy business.

As Thailand enters into more types of economic integration, in the form of free trade agreements and other treaties, the ability of foreign investors to own and operate retail outlets or retail distribution businesses in the country will certainly increase. In some cases, increased opportunities are push-led (that is, the dynamic comes from an agreement making opportunities available and investors then taking advantage of them) and some are pull-led (that is, investors petition government to make opportunities available to them and, presumably, others). Foreign investors have become accustomed to working through semi-legal ownership structures when existing legislation prevents them from exercising the level of control they desire. Whereas liberalization of ownership progresses at a slow pace, it is unlikely that the restrictions on ownership of land in Thailand by foreigners will be lifted in the foreseeable future.

A barrier to entry that is maintained by the private rather than the public sector is the patronage system that, in Thailand, restricts access to resources and public goods to a limited group of well-connected people. Although it is possible to break into the required networks through the use of capital, it nevertheless makes it difficult for new arrivals to compete on a level playing field. In sectors such as property development and tourist resort management, access to patronage is manifested through extortion by organized criminal gangs. In apparel, new entrants have to operate with a restricted number of partners and at disadvantageous terms. For example, the supermarkets and hypermarkets of Thailand generally operate in the same way that those in many other Asian countries do by making shelf space and position available to intermediaries prepared to pay. The same is said to be true of attracting media attention to PR activities or just considering products and events. Product placement is also a significant part of Thai media, particularly on television.

INTERNATIONAL BRANDS: IN NEED OF THAI PARTNERS

The 1999 Act enabled an increase in the extent of ownership and control of shops in various categories, which encouraged an increase in international investment, from Britain, France, and the Netherlands in particular. Multiple retail chains and shopping malls operated by the British-Thai Tesco Lotus Group, the French Carrefour chain, and the Dutch-Thai Makro warehouses opened in Thailand. Smaller shops are almost entirely Thai owned, and franchising is often managed through contract with a local partner, such as Thai company CP (Charoen Pokphand) does for the 7-11 chain in Thailand (4,030 stores) and its Lotus franchises in China (79 supercenters) under the Chia Tai Group brand (Charoen Pokphand Group, 2010). Department stores routinely are operated and owned by Thai management companies, with the exception of Japanese investment in some department stores, which has witnessed only mixed levels of success.

INTERNATIONAL BRAND MARKET ENTRY STRATEGY

International brands entering Thailand generally do so through joining existing distribution chains leading to the large shopping centers and their networks. There are some alternatives to this, as for example the alternative distribution network created to support the successful Amway Multi-Level Marketing venture, in which members sell to their families and friends and recruit new people to join as members from whose sales they are able to claim a fee. However, particularly as a result of legal changes initiated by the Asian meltdown of 1997, powerful incentives have been put in place to encourage new entrants to join existing channels.

Having been one of the most open economies for inward investment for some decades, as well as having joined the World Trade Organization (WTO) in 1995, Thailand has few formal barriers to investment in the country. However, those few barriers can be significant in effect. For example, it is illegal for foreign individuals or corporations to own land in Thailand, with a few minor exceptions. Unable to buy land, foreign corporations must operate at a level of uncertainty that is uncomfortable for them. To reduce that uncertainty, investors will generally try to circumvent the regulations through a joint venture agreement with a local partner in which the international investor is the principal active partner. Such joint ventures give undue power to the local partner. By contrast, using what is called a "nominee" (i.e., the person whose name appears on forms as the official owner but who may not actually be the real owner) as the local partner means tarrying with illegality because an accusation can be made at any time, including an admission made by the nominee. The same problems affect any foreign national who marries a Thai person and then tries to buy a house. However, despite numerous representations at all levels of government, the Thai state has resolutely refused to concede any meaningful changes to the law.

A second informal barrier to entry is the occasional use of outbreaks of nationalism and xenophobia in the popular media, which may then be used to color public and political discourse. Generally, xenophobia is aimed at neighbors for political reasons—for example, at the end of the first decade of the new century, both Cambodia and Singapore were vilified for supposed transgressions. People at even the highest levels of government are known to repeat long-standing accusations about the perfidies of foreigners of all nations, which has the effect of keeping these ideas in the minds of the public. On the other hand, many Thai people continue to have the belief that overseas items are inherently superior to their locally produced counterparts.

CULTURAL INFLUENCES ON TEXTILE AND APPAREL RETAILING

Clothing plays a role in informal ritual moments in Thailand. For example, it is a practice among young people to use their first-ever month's salary to buy new clothes for their parents to show gratitude for raising them. It is also a practice to "clothe" Buddha images and statues by adding some golden decorations or adornments, depending on the size of the image concerned. On numerous occasions, on regular or seasonal bases, religious, cultural, or superstitious influences are influential in determining what people wear, as well as various aspects of behavior and language. These influences are one of the many factors that structure the wardrobe of Thai people and limit it in marketing terms, especially for foreign brands or innovative products.

In addition to cultural influences, physical and climatic influences also affect apparel retailing. Despite some changes brought about by urbanization and changing dietary and lifestyle patterns leading to emergent obesity (Escobar, 2009), Thai people as a generality are shorter and slighter than Westerners. This difference is especially noticeable among women, who find Western clothes as carried by, for example, Marks and Spencer to be unsuitable, as well as expensive in comparison with the quality. Marks and Spencer and others in both South Korea and Japan face a similar problem. Indeed, it is fashion from these two countries that are more trendsetting in Thailand, particularly among the young and among women. Since around 2005, Korean media products have increasingly influenced the cultural scene of the Kingdom, as manifested by the popularity of Korean food, soap opera, pop music, and fashion. Hairdressers advertising specialism in Korean-style coiffeurs have begun to open, and the Korean film star Kim Jeong Hoon has been named an ambassador for Thai tourism (*The Nation*, 2007).

INFLUENCES ON APPAREL RETAILING: FADDISHNESS AMONG CONSUMERS

Thailand uses a similar retailing environment to other East Asian countries: That is, shops tend to be staffed by many workers who

▲ **FIGURE 8.8** A magazine stand showing fashion magazines with international celebrities as well as magazines with local celebrities on the cover. © David Crausby/Alamy.

approach and attend customers as soon as they come near their products. Consumers expect this level of service and may express dissatisfaction if the attendant is insufficiently knowledgeable, impolite, or does not show interest in the customer. Thai consumers are often characterized by faddishness and by a desire for personal aesthetic appeal that is also reflected in the large number of beauty salons, hair salons, spas, and massage outlets that may be found and is typical of many East Asian societies. In some cases, faddishness becomes controversial when it leads people, generally but not exclusively young women, into cosmetic surgery on the one hand and, on the other, the use of decorated teeth braces and spectacles that have no medical purpose or value. Some other features of apparel retailing are discussed in the following sections.

CUSTOMER SERVICE EXPECTATIONS

Customers can expect not just retail assistance but additional services at low cost. For example, trousers for both men and women are usually produced in a range of waist sizes but at the same length. It is understood that, after the purchase has been made, shop assistants will hem the pants within 45 minutes to an hour (outside of peak shopping hours) and for a low cost—less than US$1 per item. Where this service is not available, many tailors operate street businesses or small shops in which adjustments of various types can be made. Individuals will often use a regular tailor who is known to them and who can, therefore, be trusted to make the adjustments correctly (perhaps after two or three attempts). This work supplements the principal work of tailors or, for some, it may represent the main line of business. Shoe and boot repairs, for example, as well as watch repairs, may be conducted both by inside and outside shops. Especially for the latter, using the service tends to be a case of caveat emptor, and it is considered important to know who the service provider is.

COLOR-CODING OF CLOTHING

Thai society has, especially since the political events of 2006, become increasingly color coded in terms of clothing. There has traditionally been a custom of wearing different colored clothes on specific days of the week, as well as to mark certain ritual or celebratory occasions. For example, attending a funeral requires wearing black clothes and attending a wedding, New Year's, or other celebration requires wearing red, especially among the very large ethnically Chinese population. Additionally, certain days of the week were marked down for special remembrance of His Majesty (HM) the King, when people wear yellow, and HM the Queen, whose color is blue. For some years, this was an occasionally remembered custom but it became intensified in 2006, when street protests led by the fascist "People's alliance for democracy" (PAD) movement made a big play of wearing yellow on most days, with the implication that anyone who did not wear yellow was in some ways disloyal to the throne, which is very nearly the most damaging thing that can be said against any Thai person. Street protests were followed by a military coup and, despite the martial law and cancellation of the Constitution that followed this disaster, pro-democracy demonstrations began to emerge and the protestors chose to wear red as their own color. Political disputes, which continued into 2010, remain characterized by the use of rival colors, which has had a considerable impact on the clothes that people wear and buy. Generally, most people now avoid wearing a color that would mark them as politically active for fear of negative consequences—for example, people were encouraged to avoid wearing the traditional red for the 2010 Chinese New Year and wear pink instead (Wancharoen, 2010).

GOVERNMENT INFLUENCES

The Thai establishment has been enforcing nationalism upon the country for a number of decades and, as part of this, the clothes that people wear have become politicized. In the years leading up to World War II, Western attire was promoted as a form of modernization of the country and, although this is no longer necessary as policy, uniforms of various kinds are still widely used throughout the country. Civil servants and government officials wear uniforms on a daily basis or for special occasions, and university students are expected to wear a standardized uniform when at the university (although private universities have a little more latitude, if they choose to take it). Corporate uniforms are also prevalent

▲ **FIGURE 8.9** Protesters wearing red clothing. Street protestors wear a particular color to show affiliation with a particular political party. This influences the choice of color among clothing worn by regular people. Photo by John Walsh.

throughout the private sector, in part because so many people are poor and cannot afford many suitable changes of clothing, especially in workplaces where the clothes might be damaged or dirtied. One consequence of this situation is that most working people have a more limited range of clothes than do people in comparable positions in many Western countries. Further, the hot climate means that fewer types of clothes are necessary: even in winter, people rarely wear more than an extra sweater or a light jacket. Shawls have become fashionable among office workers in air-conditioned spaces but, in general, most people in their nonworking hours content themselves with T-shirts and shorts.

THE FOREIGN RETAIL BILL

The Foreign Retail Bill divides new stores into four categories based on size—120 to 299 square meters, or 1,292 to 3,218 square feet; 300 to 999 square meters, or 3,229 to 10,753 square feet; 1,000 to 2,999 square meters, or 10,764 to 32,281 square feet; and 3,000+ square meters, or 32,292+ square feet—and establishes location and opening hours' guidelines for each (Theparat & Phusadee, 2009). It also specifies the nature of committees to be established to determine whether individual projects can be given permission to proceed. Given the nature of Thai committees, this step will certainly lead to a lengthening of the process by which permission may be received. Representatives of local retailers and wholesalers are concerned that the proportion of the total retail market controlled by large retail chains has been estimated at up to 60 percent of the 1.4 trillion baht ($47.7 billion) annual market.

INFRASTRUCTURE DEMANDS

There appears to be a trend for consumers to try to find all their shopping needs within one center, which affects the marketing of goods within such a center. Shopping tends to be a family-oriented or at least social experience in Thailand, much more so than in most Western countries, and routinely includes at least one meal. Transportation, in Bangkok in particular, is such that the majority of people will travel by car and, consequently, there is a need for extensive (and comparatively cheap) parking. The air conditioning in shopping malls is also a big draw, and a number of people will visit malls simply or at least partly as a means of staying cool while passing the time. Unlike India, for example, where guards ensure that "undesirable" persons are not permitted to enter shopping malls, the power of peer pressure and social exclusion tend to ensure that malls are filled with people who are of the class or status at which goods are marketed.

INTERNET RETAILING

Internet retailing in Thailand remains a small and niche segment, but it is growing. Internet access is largely restricted to urban cores and to the middle classes, although there are now large numbers of low-cost Internet cafes that are principally used by young people wanting to play online games. Because Thailand is a low-trust society, people are reluctant to use credit cards to buy items sight unseen. The widespread use of credit cards is in any case comparatively recent and although penetration of the market is quite strong, use of individual cards is comparatively slight. The Internet infrastructure itself is limited in capacity and irregular even in the center of Bangkok, and provision of wireless access is very scarce. There is, therefore, scope for increase in this market (Sukasame, 2008).

GETTING TO KNOW DOMESTIC COMPETITORS: RACE TO ACQUIRE PRIME RETAIL LOCATIONS

Mostly foreign-owned chains, such as Tesco Lotus, followed by Carrefour, Big C (Thailand), and Tops (Thailand), have become the leading retail chains in Thailand. For department stores, the most common is Robinson's but probably the most influential player is the Central Pattana Group (both are Thai organizations). Owing to

Thailand's restrictions on land ownership and control of retail businesses, local property developers (such as Central) remain very influential. They are generally responsible (in whole or in part) for developing the large shopping centers that are now opening beyond the major cities of the country for modern retail methods, as well as operating many of the more important centers in Bangkok itself. Foreign brand managers customarily look for some sort of partnership with a local developer both to gain access to location-specific knowledge but also for legal requirements and the need to navigate complex zoning and administrative requirements. It is only when the foreign investor has gained extensive experience of the Thai market that it is able to move ahead independently. This has been the case for Tesco Lotus and also for the Minor Group, whose American founder Bill Heinecke has lived in Thailand for many years and which provides cluster marketing for a range of food and beverage brands (e.g., Sizzler [US-Australian] and American brands Swensen's, Dairy Queen, and the Pizza Company).

Besides Robinson, the principal department stores include Central and The Mall, with smaller numbers of Japanese stores Zen, Tokyu, and Isetan. Robinson is operated by Central Retail Chain, which has become a leading retailer in the country. Founded in 1956, it opened Thailand's first department store through the expansion of an existing general merchandise operation. It then opened the first lifestyle department store in 1990, incorporating apparel, furnishings, and various other categories of consumer goods, and the first hypermarket in 1994. There are 22 Robinson department stores in Thailand, of which 9 are in Bangkok and the remainder in the provinces.

There are more than 100 shopping centers in Bangkok, including the figurehead Siam Paragon Center at peak-retail center Siam Square and the enormous Seacon Square in Srinakarin, which was the fifth-largest shopping center in the world at the time of its opening. Well-known international brands are represented in nearly all shopping centers in one form or another, although there is segmentation into higher- and lower-end markets. For example, the recently opened Union Mall center on the eternally busy Ladprao Road is positioned as a lower-end mall for local residents (Bangkok residents customarily drive everywhere) and people using the attached subway. Most outlets are aimed at lower-middle-class customers on the ground floor, with low-cost originals and accessories for young shoppers on the upper floors and an extensive food court area and supermarket in the basement, which has a few bulk staple goods available. High-end goods are not available in this center, but most malls will segment customers according to location within the mall overall.

In terms of business strategy, there is little to differentiate among rival department stores and retail chains from the perspective of consumers. Key competitive advantages lie in the ability to acquire land in attractive areas and the right to develop it, especially when the land is set to increase in value in line with anticipated improvements in physical infrastructure (e.g., new public transport facilities are built). Critical competencies involve the ability to move in the right circles, to have deep pockets for future investments, and the willingness to subcontract other functions to specialists. This tends to make the large retail spaces rather homogenous places to go shopping.

Other than retail stores and malls, there are alternative selling formats that are creating competition in the retail market. Bangkok has some very important, large, wholesale and retail market complexes such as Pratunam, Bobae, and Chatuchak. Each of these consists of numerous outlets offering smaller or larger ranges of products, be they permanent or temporary in nature, and inside or outside. A wide range of customers may be found, and some specialization of retail space is evident to deal with the different segments of the market. Customers range from teenagers shopping for accessories and fashion items to export agents.

At the brand level, the market divides into three distinct strategic groups of products competing against each other:

▶ At the top level are products sold in department stores and specialty shops within shopping centers, which are often foreign branded goods marketed through reputation and placed within the retail space, supplemented by point-of-sale activities. Loyalty schemes are popular, with multistore cards made available for use in a broad range of outlets and points schemes linked to cash discounts and other benefits. These loyalty schemes are in addition to store-based credit or debit cards. Additionally, both Western and Asian festivals are used as the basis for sales and other promotions. Christmas is followed by Chinese New Year and then Valentine's Day. Some sales are themed, and sales staff is expected to participate by wearing appropriate costumes. In other cases, the sale is simply an excuse for additional discounts.

► The second level of products is contained within shopping centers or retail districts but is separate from the high-level brands. This level includes individual shops on different levels from the department store within the shopping center or removed from it; because Thai consumers are, by and large, not willing to walk very far, the spatial location of an outlet within a larger mall indicates the quality and price of the products likely to be sold there. In some cases, the more (relatively) remote locations shade into illegality as pirated goods are made available. Periodic sweeps of shopping centers aimed at confiscating pirated goods and arresting those involved in their distribution and sale are often made public beforehand so that little difference is made in the long term after the immediate sweep. Goods at this level are generally marketed through availability and perhaps individual sales abilities. It is common for all products in a similar category to be sold in a specific area, which has the effect of reducing price as a means of determining sales: Just as in a traditional wet market selling fresh meat, fish, and vegetables, market vendors must live and work cheek by jowl with each other on a long-term basis, and the antipathy that might be caused by aggressive price reductions is deterred for that reason.

► The third level of goods is sold outside or in low-quality shop-houses, as they are perceived (although the location within a city or town of the shop-house might lend it additional cachet). Haggling over the price is common, and customers will need to have a good idea already of what is fashionable in order to find something that they like because vendors will try to sell all of their stock as if it were of equal trendiness.

HOW MATURE IS THE RETAIL INDUSTRY? MARKETS STILL OPEN FOR DEVELOPMENT

There is considerable scope for apparel retailing to grow in Thailand. Although Bangkok appears to have reached a saturation phase for new retail developments, further schemes continue to be built. Shopping centers have been opened in the coastal resort Pattaya and in the northern capital of Chiang Mai (e.g., Central Airport Plaza) and are planned or opening in Khon Kaen (Central Plaza) and elsewhere. Shopping centers tend to have clustered within them the same group of brands: Central malls offer the Tops supermarket, B2S (stationery and books), Office Depot, Power Buy (consumer electronics), and Robinson department store. Similarly, the Minor International Group clusters leading restaurant outlets (Sizzler, Burger King, Swensen's, Dairy Queen, and others), which may then be attached to a shopping complex managed by a retail chain. So the shopping experience is becoming homogenized across the country.

BUYING AND SOURCING FOR APPAREL RETAIL STORES: EXTENSIVE LOCAL MANUFACTURING

In most retail chains, professionalization of local staff has meant that Thai employees have been inducted into internationalized best practices. In the Body Shop chain, for example, newly hired employees are expected to work at every level of retail activity before being permitted to enter into management training. Training of staff is generally considered to be an important component part of assimilating new employees into corporate culture. In few areas of retail management is this more true than in buying, which in Thailand has traditionally been an activity founded on the creation and re-creation of existing network connections. The attempt to professionalize the buying function is assisted by the presence of extensive manufacturing capacity throughout the Kingdom, both Thai and internationally owned. It might also be pointed out that the continuing weakness of the labor movement in the country enables the buyers, like all managers, to minimize any mistakes by requiring workers to rework any items at what is effectively their own expense. In recent times, the professionalization of Thai retail staff has been so successful that some are now being recruited internationally (Sruthijith & Chakravarty, 2010).

At the individual entrepreneurial level, buying can be quite sophisticated, although for the majority of street vendors or small shops, the buying function extends no further than a convenient nearby wholesale market—indeed, in many provincial markets, stall owners are tied to wholesalers who oblige them to stock whatever goods they might make available. However, on a more sophisticated level, there is a subset of street vendors and small shop owners in Bangkok who, as white-collar victims of the 1997 financial crisis, decided to remain in the city and put to use their business skills rather than return to rural, agricultural underemployment. Accordingly, they have established in some cases international supply chains, importing in one case clothes from Korea (in crates marked for charitable causes) and, in others, establishing their own brands that could be serviced through contract manufacturing in the Rayong region of southern Thailand, which enabled small-scale batch production in a variety of different configurations. In the event that goods are not sold on a timely basis, they may be passed on first to secondary-value locations (marked up because further from the center of fashion) and then to non-urban locations.

In Bangkok in particular, rental costs for retail spaces are very expensive, and entrepreneurs cannot afford to keep unsold products on the premises. Vendors revealed that, in the case of fashion-conscious Bangkok-based university female students (hence, mostly middle- or upper-class individuals), items are bought and worn no more than two or three times before being discarded. As a result, if products are not sold more or less immediately, it is unlikely that they will be sold in the location concerned and so they are at once pushed on to the next place in the selling chain.

As in many other developing countries, local authorities have for some years maintained a fairly lax attitude toward intellectual property rights (IPR). This attitude stems from a lack of capacity to police the issue properly, a lack of political will to do so, and the strong incentives that exist for entrepreneurs to reduce costs and risks in producing new items through copying existing intellectual property. IPR piracy manifests itself in Thailand in several ways: direct replication of existing products with inferior materials for sale as a fake through outdoor markets; passing off inferior products for protected branded items (which can be dangerous for customers when it involves medication or some kinds of cosmetics); copying of protected designs or elements of trade dress (e.g., patented or copyrighted elements) and using them in products under other brands; or obtaining samples from factories contracted to produce branded goods under license and using these for sale or as production prototypes. Some of these manifestations are clearly examples of theft and may be punished by the courts, when the police are able and willing to identify miscreants. In other cases, however, a general tolerance toward copying the work of others throughout society may be witnessed at all levels. That high-quality products are so far beyond the ability of most people to own tends to promote the idea that it is perfectly rational to accept a fake good, even when most, if not all, people know it is a fake.

The degree of IPR piracy has reduced the willingness of international investors to invest in Thailand and has reduced the reputation of certain branded products (when consumers do not realize that they are fakes), while allowing some entrepreneurs to benefit from the work of others. However, following the example of South Korea, the Thai government has been inspired to take action against pirated goods in the main markets and malls of Bangkok and, to some extent, in the other urban centers. Thai manufacturers themselves have gained sufficient experience as to be able to eschew piracy and can instead develop their own brands, with the assistance of CAD technology and flexible manufacturing systems. As more free trade agreements are signed and membership of the World Trade Organization intensifies, internationally accepted norms concerning IPR are becoming more embedded in Thai society. Most developed Western countries had similarly lax attitudes toward IPR during their own periods of development and have only changed their tunes in comparatively recent years now that they have the power to protect their own products.

RETAIL CAREERS: DEFICIENT IN CERTAIN SKILLS

Thailand was a poor country at the conclusion of World War II but has since become a middle-income country. It has managed this transformation through export-oriented manufacturing with competitiveness based on low labor costs. As wages have slowly risen over the years, combined with the emergence of China and Vietnam as alternative targets for investment in manufacturing, Thailand's factory-based economy has become less and less sustainable. In response, the government made plans to identify suitable alternative sunrise industries and industrial clusters in which it could invest and develop. It identified the fashion industry as a suitable future industrial cluster, owing to the size of the domestic market and sources of supply, existing manufacturing capacity, and the possibility of training skilled designers. The 2006 military coup significantly decelerated these plans because emphasis was placed on social conservatism and promoting the role of the military in the country. However, led to a considerable extent by the private sector, the fashion industry is being developed at every stage of the value chain. This development has meant that career opportunities are emerging in the retailing of apparel in Thailand.

There still remain certain skill deficiencies that are not being met by local staff. For example, the head of one very prominent international cosmetic chain complained that he had to go to Hong Kong to find competent visual merchandising staff. The government responded by promoting a series of industrial clusters in which it was hoped a long-term competitive advantage could be established and sustained. Clearly, providing the conditions for new jobs was an important part of that process, and the flagship Bangkok Fashion City event showcased the talents of young designers, as well as numerous models and, less visibly, support staff, technicians, manufacturing agents, and the like. Inevitably, policies such as this are difficult to evaluate accurately and do not produce results in predictable time frames.

Further, the legacy of the 3Ls (low-skilled, low-wages, and long-hours) labor market strategy makes new jobs in retailing less attractive. Thai workers have one of the longest work weeks in the world, but their productivity at work remains disappointingly low and careers in retailing have tended to follow this pattern. Although many Thai executives have benefited from international education and exposure to international best practices, innovations have yet to spread to the retail or personal service sectors of the economy, by and large.

A non-Thai person wanting to work in Thailand must be in possession of a valid work permit. These are available in various categories and, for professional or management positions for people from Western countries in particular, the process of obtaining a permit has become much less onerous than it was even a few years ago. The employer is responsible for collecting the paperwork required and the representative, together with the prospective employee, is required to visit a specific office, depending on where the head office of the business concerned is located. This office is not the same as the immigration office because the functions belong to different ministries. For management positions, the employer will routinely meet all fees, which are comparatively minor in any case. For brief assignments in Thailand not involving payment by an organization incorporated in the country, a work permit is not generally required, and visas are also not usually required for most

▲ **FIGURE 8.10** Bangkok fashion week. AFP/Getty Images/Christophe Archambaul.

residents of developed countries; however, it is always wise to check requirements beforehand because these might change.

The number of college-level courses available has increased notably, and more are expected to open (*The Nation,* 2006). Educational institutions now offering courses in fashion design or related subjects include Chulalongkorn University, Kasetsart University, Srinakharinwirot University, Academia Italiana, and the Raffles Design Institute.

The government has made efforts to promote the role of entrepreneurs in the economy, together with all kinds of small and medium-sized enterprises (SMEs). It has established the SME Bank, the Department of Industrial Promotion, and the Office of SME Promotion. Managers can obtain some training from governmental agencies and support for production and, in particular, exporting. Of course, these schemes suffer from the usual problems of lack of supply and the difficulties entrepreneurs face in finding time for the right kind of training.

THE FUTURE OF APPAREL RETAIL: DOMINATED BY INTERNATIONAL RETAILERS

The future of retailing as a whole is at something of a crossroads in Thailand as a result of the reversion to a conservative, nationalist approach first by the junta from 2006 to 2008 and then its successor, the military-installed Abhisit regime. This government is at best ambivalent toward the business sector in general and international investment in particular. Retailing has been a very visible part of its policy approach because the extension of modern retailing through Thailand has been very closely associated with the spread of international investment and capitalism in the country.

Initially, international investors started retail investment as part of joint ventures with locally owned companies, but the government slackened the requirement to do so in the early years of the twenty-first century. Upon this slackening, international companies began buying out their local partners and assuming more control over operations and growth. The most rapid and extensive growth has been undertaken by supermarket-based chains like Tesco Lotus (nearly 400 stores of different sizes nationwide), Carrefour (39 branches nationwide), Tops (114 branches nationwide), and Big C (67 branches nationwide) (MacKinnon 2008; Carrefour 2009; Tops Supermarket, 2008; Big C Supercenter 2010). These chains are also important centers for apparel marketing, both as centers for sale themselves and as part of shopping center complexes, which have external space open for street vending (Maneepong & Walsh, 2009).

As of the end of 2010, the administration was still delaying implementation of the Foreign Retail and Wholesale Bill, which is intended to regulate further the ways in which international investment projects might be approved (or not) and where such projects could be located. Zoning regulations in Thailand have for many years been widely considered to be subject to compromise through corruption, and those charged with protecting local interests have vociferously complained that irregularities have taken place between international investors and colluding politicians.

Whether or not these irregularities actually took place was secondary to local advocates' ability to gather local support among communities and individuals who felt threatened by the spread of retail chains. The announcement of any new branch of Tesco Lotus was, for example, for a while met by a campaign of opposition by local people and pressure on local planning authorities.

To summarize the previous points, when investing in Thailand, it is important to remember that:

▶ Thailand is undergoing a retail revolution not just in terms of the types of products available but the types of retail opportunities provided and the extent of locations at which consumers can access items.

▶ Thai consumers require adaptations to many products in terms of size, shape, color, and with respect to some cultural factors.

▶ Despite evolving regulations concerning foreign investment, it is almost certain that investors will require a local partner to assist with ownership of land, navigation of regulations, and providing location-specific information.

▶ The marketplace is becoming a battleground in which emergent local brands are competing with Western brands on the one hand and increasingly popular Korean and East Asian styles on the other hand.

Another aspect of Thailand that foreign investors need to know about is the labor laws in the country. Although the principles of freedom of association and collective bargaining are recognized in Thailand, in practice the nature of labor law means that labor unions have relatively little power and few rights compared to Western countries. Although this attitude seems unlikely to change much in the 2010s, the pressure applied by newly signed free trade agreements may have an impact.

Case Study 1

GAP IN THAILAND

A number of foreign ventures in Thailand have ended in failure or at least only partial success for a variety of reasons. Burger King, for example, drastically reduced its scope after the enormous increase in popularity of the goddess Kuan Yin and the attendant voluntary abstinence from beef led a spokesperson to observe that "Thailand is a chicken country." The Sogo department store ran into trouble due to financial problems in its home country of Japan. Others have been victims of the 1997 or the 2008 financial crises, or have held off investment because of political instability, pandemics, or natural disasters. Achieving success has required not just vision and understanding of the marketplace but, in many cases, the patience to wait until sufficient consumers exist who might be attracted to the products and who will be willing to resist counterfeited goods. An example of such a firm is Gap, which did not open its first dedicated shop in Thailand until 2010 (through Minor International PLC), partly because of the presence of so many fake goods and the lack of maturity in the market. However, having determined that 2010 is the correct moment to enter the market, having opened the first store in 2010, the company will open three new stores in the short term and plans a total of eight by 2014. This late-market entry means that the company has more choice in terms of appropriately qualified and skilled senior and middle-ranking staff, while also being able to take advantage of best practices from rival brands. It also means that Thai consumers have had a chance to become accustomed to Western styles, colors, and prices, and so should be more willing to accept the products. The downside, of course, is that rivals have had time to build customer loyalty and familiarity. However, because Thai consumers are characterized by desire for the new, brand loyalty is not generally seen as a powerful barrier to entry in consumer goods markets.

Source: Jitpleecheep, Pitsinee, "MINT Expects Food Response to Gap in Thailand," *Bangkok Post* (March 6, 2010). Retrieved on December 15, 2010, from http://www.bangkokpost.com/business/marketing/33991/mint-expects-good-response-to-gap-in-thailand

Discussion Questions

1. In a country in which intellectual property rights are only loosely respected, to what extent is it worthwhile for an international investor to try to suppress pirated versions of its products?

2. How can brand loyalty be developed in consumers who, through rapid globalization, seem to have become addicted to whatever is new?

3. The Gap plans to open numerous shops to provide a variety of locations for shoppers to access its products. For what market segments is this strategy appropriate?

Case Study 2

TESCO-LOTUS: TESCO FOR THAIS

Tesco Lotus is a British retail chain that sells apparel, household items, electronics, and furniture, and operates in both supermarket and hypermarket formats. Tesco bought a 92 percent stake in Lotus retail stores by signing an agreement with Charoen Pokphand (CP). Tesco stores have now spread throughout Thailand (Tesco Lotus, 2010).

When Tesco opened in Thailand, although consumers were delighted, there were many sectors that were not happy about international retailers entering the market. Local retailers and distributors had difficulty competing with Tesco and hence joined the protestors. These protestors spread the belief that international retailers were a threat to traditional Buddhist Thai beliefs.

Tesco claims to serve about 29 million customers each month and has invested more than 84 billion baht (USD 2.74 billion) in Thailand since 1998. They provide employment to more than 15,000 Thais in their stores. The company also exports a large amount of Thai products to Tesco UK. Tesco purchases more than 300,000 tons of vegetables and fruits from local farmers. Tesco has also been participating in many charitable activities. The company supported tsunami victims in 2004 by donating 12.75 million baht (USD 416,000). The company formed a charitable organization called Tesco for Thais that donates money for various charities across Thailand. Tesco has committed 155 million baht (USD 5,047,216) to planting 9 million trees in Thailand's national forest reserves. They have a research center, which was created in 2002 as a Product Demonstration Center. Tesco promotes itself as a price-competitive retailer. The majority of its customers are from the working class and middle class (Tesco Lotus, 2010).

Although Tesco has tried to become a part of the local economy, it has often been involved in controversies. It has been a symbol of globalization and commercialization of Thailand and its consumers. This is not necessarily a good thing because it is in contrast with a happier past where people were interested more in their country rather than in personal gain. Consumer behavior in Thailand has changed since Tesco entered the market. Availability of ready-made frozen food has resulted in changes in family life. Use of foreign food has resulted in obesity among urban office workers. But, Thai people do enjoy shopping at the air-conditioned stores and like the fact that the store does not offer expensive products, hence is less intimidating than the high-end malls.

Discussion Questions

1. What should Tesco do to avoid problems in Thailand?
2. What should a new entrant into Thailand be careful of? How can a retailer interested in investing in Thailand be better prepared?
3. Should Tesco be doing something more to change the mind-set of the local population that protests against it?

REFERENCES

Asia Development Bank (ADB) (2008). Key Indicators for Asia and the Pacific
      2008 (Manila: ADB, 2008). Retrieved March 10, 2010, from http://www.
      adb.org/Documents/Books/Key_Indicators/2008/pdf/Key-
      Indicators-2008.pdf

Big C Stores (2010). Big C Supercenter. Retrieved March 10, 2010, from http://
      www.bigc.co.th/en/stores/

Carrefour, Thailand—Opening of the 37th Carrefour Hypermarket (2009).
      Retrieved March 1, 2010, from http://www.carrefour.com/cdc/group/
      current-news/thailand-opening-of-the-37th-carrefour-hypermarket.html

Charoen Pokphand Group (2010). *Marketing and Distribution Business.*
      Retrieved March 1, 2010, from http://www.cpthailand.com/Default.
      aspx?tabid=242

Dressed for Success (2006, March 27). *The Nation.* Retrieved March 10, 2010,
      from http://www.nationmultimedia.com/smartlife/20060327/

Escobar, P. (2009, July 2). Superfat Hits Asia, *Asia Times Online.* Retrieved
      March 1, 2010, from http://www.atimes.com/atimes/Southeast_Asia/
      KG02Ae01.html

Feeny, A., Vongpatanasin, T. & Soonsatham, A. (1996). Retailing in Thailand.
      International Journal of Retail and Distribution Management, 24, 38–44.

Jitleecheep, P. (2009). Improvement in Store. *Bangkok Post Economic Review,
      Year-End 2009* (2009a), p. 16.

Kanchoochat, V. (2008). Services, Servility, and Survival: The Accommodation
      of Big Retail, in P. Phongpaichit & C. Baker, eds., *Thai Capital after the
      1997 Crisis,* Chiang Mai: Silkworm Books, 85–104.

Maneepong, C. & Walsh, J. (2009, March). A New Generation of Bangkok Street
      Vendors: New Businesses, Old Policies. *Paper presented at the 8th
      International Symposium of the International Urban Planning and
      Environment Association (IUPEA),* March 23–26, 2009, at the University
      of Kaiserslautern, Germany.

Saengsawang, W. (2009, December 22). Special Report: Thailand Elite Card on
      Bumpy Road," *National News Bureau of Thailand Public Relations*

Department (December 22, 2009), available at: http://thainews.prd.
go.th/en/news.php?id=255212220007

Songkran Fun Gets Under Way in Earnest (2007, April 14). *The Nation*
Retrieved March 10, 2010, from http://www.nationmultimedia.com/
search/read.php?newsid=30031869

Sruthijith K. K. & Chakravarty, C. (2010, January 19). Reliance Retail Hiring
Professionals from Thailand. *The Economic Times of India*. Retrieved
February 10, 2010, from http://economictimes.indiatimes.com/news/
news-by-industry/services/retailing/Reliance-Retail-hiring-
professionals-from-Thailand/articleshow/5474885.cms

Sukasame, N. (2008). The Essence of Online Retailing: A Case Study of
Thailand. *Journal of International Business and Economics, 8*(2), 117–21.

Thailand's investment market retains its attractiveness (2008, May 9). *The
Nation*. Retrieved March 15, 2010, from http://www.nationmultimedia.
com/2008/05/09/business/business_30072622.php

Tesco Lotus (2010). Retrieved October 25, 2010, from http://www.tescolotus.
com/left.php?lang=en&menu=corporate_th&data=profile

Tops Supermarket (2008). Company Profile. Retrieved January 15, 2010, from
http://www.tops.co.th/companyprofile/index.html

Wancharoen, S. (2010, February 10). New Year Revelers Will Be Pretty in Pink.
Bangkok Post. Retrieved February 15, 2010, from http://www.
bangkokpost.com/news/local/32614/new-year-revellers-will-be-pretty-
in-pink

MEXICO

9

Mohammad Ayub Khan

Diana Bank

Jaya Halepete

OBJECTIVES

After reading this chapter, you will

- ▶ Understand the evolution of the Mexican retail market from the 1980s onwards
- ▶ Grasp the role of foreign direct investment policies in the Mexican retail market
- ▶ Determine the effects of the Mexican consumer's preferences on buying decisions
- ▶ Understand cultural factors influencing the retail market in Mexico

Mexico's location at the crossroads of North and Latin America and the Pacific and Atlantic Oceans is a compelling factor for many international investors. They see Mexico as a logical place to invest in to spring into the North and South American markets. Its two coastlines provide easy access to ports for international businesses. Mexico is a regional power in economic development and international business, and the only Latin American member of the Organization for Economic Cooperation and Development (OECD), which it joined in 1994.

TABLE 9.1 Fast Facts about Mexico

Capital	Mexico City
Population	113.7 million
Type of government	Federal Republic
GDP: purchasing power parity: in US$	$1.465 trillion
Age structure	0-14 yrs: 29.1%
	15-64 yrs: 64.6%
	65 yrs plus: 6.2%
Religion	Roman Catholic: 76.5%
	Protestant: 6.3%
	Pentecostal: 1.4%
	Jehovah's Witnesses: 1.1%
	Other: 4.1%
	Unspecified: 13.8%
	None: 3.1%
Ethnicity	Mestizo (Amerindian-Spanish): 60%
	Amerindian: 30%
	White: 9%
	Other: 1%

Source: CIAfactbook.gov

As the "rich men's club," the OECD has been very careful whom to accept. As Mexico started with entry negotiations, it had to open its economy and submit to deep economic changes, which it did. Because Mexico has always managed to recover well from its economic woes and is considered an upper-middle-income country, economic ups and downs have reinforced government intentions to develop new policies, restructure the economic system, and participate in international business. In the 1970s, during what was coined the "Mexican Miracle" by historians, Mexico advanced relatively quickly in terms of economic development. However, in the 1980s, the lack of economic competitiveness threw Mexico into a deep financial crisis, and the economy stagnated to the point that the country defaulted on its payments. In 1986, Mexico joined the World Trade Organization's (WTO) precursor, the General Agreement on Tariffs and Trade (GATT), which resulted in the reduction of taxes imposed on imports and exports. Furthermore, Mexico started to liberalize foreign trade by reducing tariffs on most imported goods accompanied by industry deregulations, such as opening many sectors, including the retail sector, to foreign ownership (Marinov, 2006). Since then, and due to OECD and WTO membership, the country has made steady progress, except for the 1994 devaluation of the peso due to bad internal macroeconomic decisions and the global financial crisis in 2008.

Mexico's economy has a couple of perennial weak spots. It is highly dependent on the U.S. economy, which receives 80 percent of Mexico's exports. The country also contends with environmental challenges, including massive earthquakes such as the 1985 event that destroyed Mexico City and left many thousands homeless, and hurricanes mainly in the Gulf of Mexico and the Caribbean. In spite of all this, Mexico remains one of Latin America's leading emerging economies.

Mexico's is the 11th-largest economy in the world. The creation of the North American Free Trade Agreement (NAFTA), a 1994 trade agreement between Mexico, Canada, and the United States, has significantly and positively influenced Mexico's image for investors both foreign and domestic. Mexico's trade figures with the United States and Canada—including textile and apparel products—have tripled since NAFTA was established (Market Latin America, 2005).

Mexico has one of the highest percentages of young consumers in the world (Table 9.1). Of its estimated 103 million people, 59 million are 30 years old or younger (INEGI, 2010). That is more than 50 percent. The percentage of potential consumers between the ages of 20 and 44 is substantially high in Mexico (41 percent). This portion of the population is crucial for retail markets, including apparel products. Other tendencies, such as increasing urbanization in Mexico (over 29 cities have reached the half-million inhabitant mark) are positive indicators for national and international retail businesses. Furthermore, government institutions are introducing checks and balances to eradicate malpractices related to industrial policies and standards. By improving quality, price, and service, Mexico continues to improve its business practices in a highly competitive world.

THE RETAIL LANDSCAPE:
AN EMERGING MARKET ALL THE WAY

Mexico's retail market dates back to the 1930s and 1940s in Mexico City. By the early 1960s, retail stores started expanding into other cities; they found potential markets in Monterrey and Guadalajara, the biggest urban areas after Mexico City. Though the retail business saw periodic ups and downs throughout the last century, with uncooperative government business policies, an unstable political environment, and increasing poverty and financial crises, the retail business continued to evolve and gained momentum in the late 1980s and early 1990s. There was a slight break in the momentum in 1994–1995 because of the sharp peso devaluation. Since 2008, Mexico has been the second-largest retail market in Latin America after Brazil, with a value of USD $310 billion (Economist Intelligence Unit, 2009).

Traditionally, retail businesses have concentrated their business efforts in urban areas with a large population of economically powerful consumers. They provide one job in five outside agriculture (Tilly & Alvarez Galván, 2006). About 44 percent of the Mexican population lives in one of 25 big cities, and retail businesses have focused on these cities. Of the dominant apparel products (women's wear, menswear, and childrenswear), the women's wear market in 2008/09 represented 57 percent of the overall market value, followed by menswear at 40 percent.

Research analysts expect the Mexican apparel retail industry, which did not show attractive growth indicators from 2004 to 2009, to have slow retail sales growth in 2010–12 and price competition among Mexican retailers to intensify (The Economist Intelligence Unit, 2009).

Large retail outlets have existed in Mexico since the 1940s, but the growth of super- and hypermarkets accelerated only after 1994, with NAFTA. For instance, the number of supermarkets in Mexico nearly doubled from 544 in 1990 to 1,026 in 2000 (Reardon & Berdegué, 2002). Furthermore, in 2001–2002 the share of top five supermarket chains was 80 percent of the food sales, and the share of foreign multinational chains in supermarket sales was over 70 percent (Reardon & Berdegué, 2002). Despite this dominance by large retailers, in areas with low population densities or low income, consumers prefer to buy produce, dairy products, and meat from traditional retailers (Euromonitor, 2005). Such consumer attitudes and buying behavior may prove to be an impediment for further concentration of retail trade.

CONSUMERS: FROM "MALINCHISTA" TO MAINSTREAM CONSUMER

Mexican consumers are culturally similar across the country, as they derive from a common ancestry, mainly a mixture of Mexican Indian and Spanish descent (Marinow, 2006). Mexican consumers shop once or twice a week for themselves but several times a week for their children. Most consumers are price sensitive, but those with purchasing power tend to buy products with popular brand names. Socio-demographic factors also define the purchasing behavior of Mexican consumers. Around 20 percent of the population belongs to the high-middle class and high class (INEGI, 2010), so the preferences of these consumers will differ from those with lower annual earnings. Older consumers traditionally shop in small local shops. Younger consumers, especially those employed who do not have time to shop on a daily basis, shop once a week in large outlets (Marinov, 2006). Also, working women and women with children who are in charge of everyday household purchases are the targets of super- and hypermarket commercials and promotions.

Consumers in Mexico, coming from a traditional collectivist society, tend to be group-oriented (Hofstede, 2001) and are attentive to the wishes and feelings of others (Albert, 1996). In addition, Mexican consumers are status-oriented and exhibit their social standing through their possessions. For a Mexican, "*él que dirán* (what will people say)" is a very important consideration when shopping. In addition, Mexicans are known as "**malinchistas**." The word is derived from the name of a woman nicknamed "La Malinche." She was kidnapped by Spaniards and used as a translator after she had learned Spanish. For many Mexicans, she helped Spain in its Mexican conquest, and was hence considered a traitor to her people. Today someone who chooses a foreign product over a Mexican product is called a "*malinchista*," which shows that Mexicans have preference for foreign products as they consider them to be of better quality. For foreign retailers, this "malinchismo" part of the Mexican culture can be used in their sales and retail endeavors.

Mexican consumers like to buy high-fashion apparel. Lack of fashionable merchandise in the market has led consumers to buy fakes of American brands such as Gap, American Eagle, and Abercrombie & Fitch. "Mexican manufacturers can't bring the same design, color, fashion, durability, and excitement of the U.S. brands, so unless they work to change this, consumers will continue to buy U.S. brands in the illegal markets," said Miguel Angel Andreu of the industry think tank Instituto Textil Nacional (Freeman, 2010). Mexican flea markets sell these fake products to middle- and low-class consumers.

Although the buying habits of the upper and middle classes may not be the same as those in poorer classes, mainly due to income differences, factors such as group influence, affiliation, interpersonal relationships, social distinction, brand reputation, and individual aspiration also influence their buying decisions. Therefore, international retail businesses trying to penetrate the Mexican market should focus on marketing strategies that reflect emotional appeal, brand quality, and reference group.

Characteristics that distinguish Mexican consumers from others include:

- Mexicans like to buy products imported from other countries like the United States, Europe, and Canada, and many Mexicans go to U.S.-Mexican border supermarkets for shopping.
- They are highly quality-conscious but will sacrifice quality for a lower price.
- Store name and location are highly important to Mexican consumers.
- Consumers in Mexico like personal attention from providers and distributors of products or services. Customer service is very important.
- Whereas low-income consumers purchase generic products because of their lower price, higher-income groups buy branded products for their perceived quality.
- They perceive that foreign products in Mexico are better in quality than Mexican products, are competitively priced, and are available in multiple variations, in addition to giving the potential buyer a feeling of belonging to a higher society. For instance, the brand "Gap" is highly valued by the higher classes as a status symbol to show everyone that they have enough money to go to the United States and shop.
- The middle-aged, urban, educated upper class prefer to buy foreign products and world-recognized brands.
- Mexican consumers are looking for the hottest fashions, the biggest brands, and the best quality they can find.
- Mexico is considered to be a collectivist society, and Mexicans tend to be group-oriented and concerned about feelings of other people.

► Affluent Mexican consumers tend to purchase brands that convey status and power, and even poor Mexican consumers display a tendency toward conspicuous consumption (Vaezi, 2005).

WOMEN

Mexican women tend to be the primary shoppers and, therefore, the main decision makers. In Mexican society, men have tended to be the breadwinners, and women are those who control household finances, raise the children, and take care of their husbands. Because women tend to be more sensitive to their surrounding environment, the buying behavior of their peers affects their shopping habits (Galindo, n.d.).

Status is important for Mexican women, and their homes, cars, and other material possessions reflect who they are, or who they aspire to be. They spend a large part of their income (or their husband's) in providing clues to their social class. Mexican women take particular pride in a clean and orderly home. Similarly, Mexican women also tend very carefully to their looks. On Saturday mornings many Mexican women can be found at the hairdresser's, chatting with their friends and reading the latest gossip columns, on which they will freely comment to the woman sitting under the next hair dryer.

Therefore, regardless of the social class to which they belong, women are the main providers of a nice, clean home (although they themselves will not do the cleaning) and are impeccably dressed. Their shopping habits largely depend on those of the social class to which they belong.

MEN

Some studies (Rausch, 2002) have shown, against reasonable expectations, that Mexican men tend to be more brand conscious than women, especially those under the age of 22. This is especially true for certain beauty products, as well as branded clothing and home goods. Nevertheless, these purchases will be mainly made by the woman of the house (Galindo, no year), which could be a wife, mother, or even grandmother, because many Mexicans continue to live with extended family. Because men of working age provide the family income, they want to be taken care of and appreciated. This includes having a nice, clean, and orderly home, food on the table, and the respect and gratitude of their children.

Therefore, although males seem to have a strong preference for brands that confer status, they leave those decisions to the women in their households. Cars or computers, for instance, are considered bastions of men's knowledge for which they will shop personally.

BEAUTY INDUSTRY IN MEXICO

Mexico's cosmetics and toiletries market is ranked 11th in the world and second to Brazil in Latin America. The high-end cosmetics market is estimated to be between $330 and $400 million. The top brands in Mexico are Lancôme, Estee Lauder, and Chanel. Although television is the primary influence for choice of beauty products, particular influences vary by region. For example, Mexicans near the U.S. border use more hair colors, and color cosmetics are most popular in Guadalajara, the second-largest city in Mexico. Hair products are the most consumed cosmetic products in Mexico. Almost 98 percent of women wash their hair daily, plus they tend to have long hair; they require high quantities of hair products. Mexican women generally do not use conditioner due to a myth that it weakens hair (Joynes-Burgess, 2008).

The changing role of Mexican women, with 33 percent at work as executives, is increasing the demand for anti-aging products. A new market for natural products is also growing in Mexico. Makeup brands with minerals are expanding in the country. The beauty industry in Mexico is expected to grow to $7.7 billion by 2012 (Joynes-Burgess, 2008).

▲ FIGURE 9.1 Actress Paulina Gaytan attends the *Esquire Mexico Magazine* 2nd Anniversary Masquerade Party. Mexican consumers are influenced by international fashion and like to buy high-end apparel. WireImage/Victor Chavez/Getty Images.

Mexican men were not interested in beauty products until the media brought news of beauty product trends in Europe and the United States after Mexico started opening its economy in 1986. Until 2005, hardly any information was available about facial and body treatments. Brands such as Carlo Corinto Skin Essentials (France) have now started producing their products for the male Mexican market. Mexico has over 30 million men between the ages of 20 and 75, with 40 percent spending an average of $50 a month on personal care products, making it a very attractive market for beauty retailers (Canseco, 2007).

LUXURY RETAIL IN MEXICO

In the upper echelons of Mexican society, "cosmetics trends come from Europe and the United States," says Silvia Tapia, who heads the fragrance department at El Palacio's swank Santa Fé store. As the economy improves, even with their limited purchasing power, Mexican consumers look for luxury items (Magana, 2007). As their spending power increases, they are becoming more interested in luxury brands such as Louis Vuitton, Zegna, and Hermès, among others. They look for exclusive brands that make them feel special. Mexico has boutiques as well as shopping malls such as Perisur mall in Mexico City that sell luxury products. The successful entry of Saks, Inc. in 2006 proves that the Mexican market is ready for more luxury brands. The luxury market may be a worthwhile sector for foreign retailers interested in the Mexican market to consider.

APPAREL RETAIL FORMATS: HISTORY IN THE MAKING

The retail market in Mexico is divided into different segments: grocery retailing (hypermarket, supermarket, discounters, small grocery retailer, food/drink/tobacco specialists, open-air markets or **tianguis**); non-grocery store-based retailing; and nonstore

▲ **FIGURE 9.2** Fashion Week, Takasami, Maria Rosario Mendoza, Fashion Show, Guadalajara, Jalisco, Mexico. Fashion shows are popular in Mexico because consumers like to wear the latest fashion. © Douglas Peebles Photography/Alamy.

retailing (health and beauty specialists, clothing and footwear specialists, electronics, and appliance specialists). Although large modern outlets account for around 40 percent of formal retail sales, around 60 percent of the population is likely to make frequent small purchases at street stalls or independent outlets (The Economist Intelligence Unit, 2009).

TRADITIONAL FORMATS

These are made up of street vendors, who sell at stoplights and door-to-door, and open-air markets, where sellers congregate.

▸Street Vendors

Mexico's street market is estimated to be worth about 2 billion pesos market ($163 million) with about 200,000 street vendors across the country. Street vendors in Mexico belong to a union that protects them against agencies that try to shut them down. They often sell fake brand-name products, do not provide any guarantee, do not pay taxes, and offer much lower prices than modern retail formats. Subway stations and street locations are common places where one can find these street vendors. These vendors pay union fees and also pay rent. Street vendors contribute to the nation's economy by means of self-employment and generating wealth, so the government is not inclined to take strong steps to remove them from the market (Petche, 1992).

According to a report of the U.S. Department of Commerce, a substantial percentage of U.S.-made apparel products of all prices and quality levels are illegally imported to Mexico and sold in informal, open-air markets, sometimes *tianguis* or "market on wheels." They may be located in a city center, near subway stations, in front of formal stores, inside the malls, at beaches, or anywhere with pedestrian traffic. They are family-owned and sell cheap products, including vegetables, clothes, food, toys, and furniture, among other things (Zimmerman, 1997).

▲ **FIGURE 9.3** Street vendor in Mexico City. Street vendors are members of unions and form a large percentage of retail income in Mexico. © DC Premiumstock/Alamy.

FLEA MARKETS OR PULGAS

Flea markets and **pulgas** are temporary markets that sell knock-offs of American brands to Mexican consumers in search of fashionable products. They also sell handmade local products. Almost 60 percent of all the apparel sold in Mexico is from counterfeit trade that takes place in these markets. These markets are set up on certain days of the week.

MODERN FORMATS

Mexico has formats that are similar to the modern formats in other countries, such as warehouse clubs, hypermarkets, savings clubs, supermarkets, and department stores. The Internet has the lowest penetration in Mexico of all OECD countries (OECD, 2010), so Internet shopping has not been a form of shopping widely adopted.

▲ **FIGURE 9.4** Flea market, Puerto Vallarta, Jalisco State, Mexico. These types of flea markets may be located in any area and sell inexpensive and a wide range of products. Some also sell knock-offs of American brands. © Robert Harding Picture Library Ltd/Alamy.

Nonetheless, direct or home shopping does exist (Tupperware or Mary Kay are good examples) and is counted as part of the informal economy.

▶Department Stores

These include stores such as Sanborns, Sears, Liverpool, Palacio de Hierro, and Suburbia, as the most important ones in Mexico. These are not found on a stand-alone format, but as part of indoor or outdoor malls. The store format and product range are similar to those in American department stores.

▶Specialty Stores

These are high-end, niche-market stores that sell apparel products at high prices in exclusive retail stores and boutiques featuring the

▲ **FIGURE 9.5** Customers enter and exit a Chedraui grocery store in Mexico City, Mexico, on Friday, April 30, 2010. Mexican retailer Grupo Comercial Chedraui SAB gained on its first day of trading after selling an estimated 4.57 billion pesos ($375 million) of shares in an initial public offering. The sale ended a 22-month drought in Mexican IPOs. Bloomberg via Getty Images.

▲ **FIGURE 9.6** Customers shop at a Walmart store in Mexico City, Mexico. Walmart is highly successful in Mexico and operates in seven different formats in the country. Bloomberg via Getty Images.

likes of Armani, Calvin Klein, Hugo Boss, Versace, Zara, Dolce & Gabbana, and Gianfranco Ferre. For the most part, these too are part of indoor or outdoor malls.

►Hypermarkets and Warehouse Clubs

Large American chains, such as Walmart, Costco, and Sam's Club, have all expanded aggressively into Mexico and have penetrated the Mexican shopper's pockets, mainly via store credit cards.

STORE OWNERSHIP: MULTIPLE FORMATS

Mexico's retail industry has many different ownership formats. Many retail giants, such as Gigante, own many stores in different formats (warehouse clubs, savings clubs, and so on). There are some joint ventures between American and Mexican retailers, such as Radio Shack, that have performed very well. Franchise stores have been a very popular format in Mexico since the early 1980s. Gap Inc. is present in Mexico as a franchise store.

FDI REGULATIONS: MEXICO OPENS UP

Foreign investments started flowing into Mexico in the early 1980s as a result of unilateral moves to liberalize the country's economy. Mexican entry into the General Agreement on Tariffs and Trade (GATT) in 1986, followed by the establishment of NAFTA in 1994, accelerated the process of creating an open economy, which increased foreign direct investment (FDI) into the country. This influx stimulated the national government to design new laws to provide legal certainties for foreign investment in Mexico, to guide investments into productive activities, and to promote competitiveness. Political events further enhanced the credibility of the country as a solid investment hub when the first free presidential elections were held in 2000.

Since 1994, Mexico has signed free trade agreements with the European Union, the European Free Trade Association (EFTA) countries, Honduras, El Salvador, Guatemala, Costa Rica, Colombia,

Chile, Bolivia, Nicaragua, Israel, and Japan. It has also signed agreements of economic cooperation with Argentina, Brazil, Peru, Paraguay, and Cuba. Additionally, Mexico has signed 27 agreements for the promotion and reciprocal investment protection, which protect foreign capital flows by law inside the country. Several double taxation treaties have been signed so that companies in certain countries are protected against being taxed in both home and host countries; are not tempted to evade taxes; reduce taxes on dividends; and decrease taxes due to income consolidation.

According to Mexican laws, foreigners may:

▶ Hold equity in Mexican corporations or partnerships
▶ Acquire fixed assets, such as factories, via FDI
▶ Enter new fields of economic activity or manufacture new lines of products, such as biofuels
▶ Open and operate establishments (branch offices, agencies, stores)
▶ Expand or relocate existing establishments via joint ventures for industries considered strategic by the Mexican government (petroleum being the most sensitive of all)

After Mexico's entry into the OECD in 1986, the country had to change its investment laws so that in certain sectors, such as the retail industry, foreign investors could now own 100 percent of the companies of this sector. For example, Walmart entered the Mexican market in 1981 through a joint venture with Grupo Cifra, the largest retail group in Mexico. In a 50 percent equal equity stake, both companies established Sam's Club in Mexico. By 2000, Walmart had acquired a 100 percent stake in Grupo Cifra. Table 9.2 shows the changes in amounts of FDI in the Mexican retail sector from the early 1980s on.

The NAFTA negotiations brought about a substantial lowering of trade tariffs (from an average of 27 to 10 percent). NAFTA members follow domestic regulations in each other's countries. Imports of U.S. apparel products in particular increased significantly with

TABLE 9.2 Foreign retailers' entry modes and formats in Mexico

Name	Date and Model of Entry	Type of Store
Walmart (USA)	*1981*: Buys 49% of Futurama *1991* and *1992*: 50/50 JV with CIFRA for different formats *1997*: Acquisition of majority ownership stake in CIFRA *2000*: Increases its share to 60%	All big formats and specialized stores (clothes) and restaurants
Carrefour (France)	*1994*: JV with Gigante to develop hypermarket chain *1998*: Acquisition of Gigante stake in JV *2005*: Announces the end of its activities in Mexico	Hypermarkets
Auchan (France)	*1995*: 50/50 JV with Comercial Mexicana to open hypermarkets *1997*: End of JV with Comercial Mexicana *2002*: Sells its five hypermarkets to Comercial Mexicana	Hypermarkets
Safeway (USA)	*1981*: Enters a 49% JV in Casa Ley	Supermarkets
HEB (USA)	*1997*: Opens five stores in northern Mexico *1991*: JV of price club with Comercial Mexicana	Supermarkets
Costco (USA)	*1995*: Costco buys the Price Club share one year after the merger between Costco and Price Club	Discount Club
Pricesmart (USA)	*2002*: JV with to open membership club discount stores	Discount Club
FLEMING (USA)	*1992*: JV with Gigante to open supermarkets *1998*: sells stake in JV	Supermarkets
Kmart (USA)	*1993*: JV with Puerto de Liverpool *1997*: KMART and Liverpool sell their four stores to Comercial Mexicana	Supermarkets

Source: Cédric Durand, Externalities from Foreign Direct Investment in the Mexican Retailing Sector, Cambridge Journal of Economics, 31, p. 397

NAFTA, a welcome development for the well-off Mexican consumer. The acceptance of American-made products, an increasing ease in establishing direct operations in Mexico, and cheap labor costs motivated many U.S. apparel companies to move production into Mexico as Mexico was starting to open its economy in the early 1980s (Wade, 1997).

INTERNATIONAL BRANDS: TRANSFORMATION TO MIDDLE CLASS

Globalization and the emergence of newly industrialized economies such as Mexico have made the mobility of brands internationally a common phenomenon. Mexico's northern neighbor is a huge market where most international brands can be found. Brands such as Zara, Kenneth Cole, Dockers, and Julio, among many others, are popular in Mexico. Mexican demand for imported brand names is increasingly high, especially among the well-off and consumers who perceive that owning an imported brand puts them in a high class. Because the apparel retail market is fragmented and growing, the likelihood of new competitors entering the market is substantial. Data Monitor 2008 (a worldwide independent business information and market analysis company) data suggest that in five years time, the apparel retail market in Mexico will increase by over 5 percent. Although it is not an amazing growth rate, it is enough to absorb the in-flow of new competitors. International brand owners see the Mexican market as an attractive supplement to their national markets. Benetton Group, the Italian clothing company, has signed an agreement with Sears Mexico to expand the United Colors of Benetton brand in Mexico. Under the terms of the deal, the Italian clothing manufacturer will open 250 points of sale by 2010, of which 200 will be located in Sears stores across the country (Zargani, 2008). A Mexican consulting group, Grupo AXO, is advising Tommy Hilfiger, Guess, DKNY, Coach, and Thomas Pink on the best strategies to enter the Mexican market (Clark, 2008). Slim's Grupo Sanborns (Mexico) will acquire the license of Saks Fifth Avenue in Santa Fe Mall, one of the most luxurious malls in Mexico City (Jones, 2006).

Mexican consumers continue to show an interest in foreign products, ranging from electronics, upscale consumer goods, and novelty items. Furthermore, Mexican consumers view U.S.-made apparel products as being of high quality, in addition to projecting a good fashion image (Frastaci, 1999). As they tend to have a high brand loyalty, Mexicans are ready to pay for product features (mainly ease of use) that come with owning foreign-owned brands. Women in particular are more loyal to a particular designer than a retailer (Data Monitor, 2009).

Product attributes including brand name, price, design, and service are important criteria of a purchase decision in Mexico. Although Mexicans have a preference for U.S.-made products (which they consider of good quality and innovative), Mexican products are also in great demand because they are cheaper and attractive to price-sensitive consumers.

FACTORS INFLUENCING APPAREL RETAILING

Retailers interested in investing in Mexico's retail market will feel the impact of these factors on their businesses: free trade agreements, cost of doing business, history, culture, social classes, brand names and brand loyalty, and market segmentation.

FREE TRADE AGREEMENTS

Among the most important factors influencing apparel retailing in Mexico are the myriad free trade agreements Mexico has negotiated with the United States, Canada, Japan, and the European Union. NAFTA's provision of unilateral access to Mexican and U. S. textile markets has increased the potential and profitability of the textile sector. Mexican exports increased, which led to the growth of the industry and an increase in investment, both foreign and domestic, in the sector. The textile sector saw a downturn after

China's entry to the WTO in 2001, an event that brought a flood of cheap textile products into Mexico. And trade pacts with Caribbean, African, and Andean countries have increased the competitive environment in Mexico. The recession that hit in 2008 also hampered the steady growth of textiles in the country.

BUSINESS COST

Mexico traditionally held competitive advantages in its abundance of raw materials, low taxes, and cheap labor. But in recent years, due to increasing Chinese competition, Mexico has lost some of its competitive advantages. Production costs have risen because of modernization of infrastructure and industrial reforms, and the costs of labor, energy, and water have gone up enough to have substantial impact on the apparel retail market. The industry is furthermore challenged by smuggling, theft, and other illegal activities; poor faculty in developing new products; low-quality products; and decreasing quality of service (Ochoa, 2005).

HISTORY AND CULTURAL ASPECTS

Mexico shares a number of cultural and historic milestones with many Hispanic countries of Central and South America: European colonization, wars of independence, struggles for democracy, rigid class structures, and a wide rich/poor divide. But there is a marked distinction between Mexico and other Hispanic countries when it comes to buying behavior. Research shows that Mexicans appear to have a strong affinity with typical American values, such as a strong inclination for consumerism. Mexico forms an emotional as well as physical bridge between the United States and the rest of the continent. The unique relationship with the United States partly explains Mexican consumerism. At the same time, most Mexicans feel a degree of antipathy for their northern neighbor. They feel that Americans do not understand them and reject the idea that they share similar values. For most Mexicans, the loss of almost half their country to the United States in 1848 is still fresh. They deplore the populist view that regards them as aliens in the southwestern U.S. states in which they live and work in large numbers, while rich Americans party in Mexico's resorts, which only a few privileged local people can afford to visit. The population of Mexicans living and working in the United States is growing, and the flow of human and cultural traffic across the border is constant. Sixty-seven percent of approximately 42 million U.S. Hispanics are Mexicans. Twenty-eight million Mexicans or people of Mexican descent (roughly one third of Mexico's total population) now live in the United States.

SOCIAL CLASSES

Mexicans are a proud people, passionate about their own identity, and yet envious of the wealth they perceive comes with living in the United States. They aspire to American wealth and power but do not necessarily envy the United States. When Latin American consumers are asked about generosity and wealth in a social context, they talk about sharing knowledge and giving time and advice as well as money.

Mexican consumers almost exaggerate the use of brands to display status. The Mexican drive to display success can take the most unexpected forms. For example, working-class households keep oversized American refrigerators in the living room rather than the kitchen because they represent financial success. Working class and elite are affected alike by the drive to display status. Fake and counterfeit products span the drink, fashion, and accessory categories. If you order a bottle of premium spirit at a reputable bar, it is customary for the seal to be broken at your table to ensure it is not just a genuine bottle filled with imitation liquid.

ROLE OF BRAND NAMES

Upper- and upper-middle-class Mexicans tend to demonstrate status and economic power by ownership of branded products, especially foreign ones. These Mexicans can pay a high price for a premium branded product. Brand names such as BMW, Chivas Regal, Rolex, and Gucci are popular among this group. Hence, the tendency among high-end, educated consumers is toward buying products based on fashion, function, and service.

BRAND LOYALTY AND MARKET SEGMENTATION

The relationship between brand loyalty and market segmentation based on age is obvious in Mexico. Teens and young adults tend to buy the same products or brands as their peers. Additionally, this market segment responds to marketing efforts more than other segments, and they will change brands and products. In contrast, mature customers over 40 years old are more loyal to brands and less likely to change brands. However, the availability of choices has moderated such behavior, leading customers to compare purchase options and shop across sectors. A traditional department-store shopper of the past now shops in different formats, looking for choices, convenience, and availability. Consumers also shop frequently and visit retail stores in the hope of finding new products or brands that offer good design, leading fashion, and a competitive price.

GETTING TO KNOW DOMESTIC COMPETITORS: DIFFERENT PLACES FOR DIFFERENT PEOPLE

The biggest competition for a foreign retailer interested in investing in Mexico comes from Walmart, Soriana, Comercial Mexicana, Chedraui, and S-mart. These five companies are corporate entities that own stores in various formats such as supermarket, hypermarket, warehouse clubs, and so on. As the foreign company of the group, Walmart faces price wars against a purchasing **cooperative** formed by the four domestic companies, which gives them greater bargaining power. Walmart operates 1,104 units in Mexico through seven retail formats: Bodega Aurerra (discount stores that carry food and clothing), Sam's Club (for bulk purchases, same as in the United States), Walmart Super-center (grocery and general merchandise), Superama (general stores located in residential areas), Suburbia (aimed toward middle-income families), Vips (restaurants serving international cuisine), and Banco Walmart (banking). Another chain called El Palacio de Hierro, a luxury department store, is expanding quickly and may offer competition for luxury retailers interested in entering the market.

COMERCIAL MEXICANA

Established in 1930, Comercial Mexicana acquired retailers such as Sumesa Kmart and Auchan, among others, to establish stores in many different formats in Mexico. They have 214 retail stores in various formats. It is known in the market as a "very Mexican store" because it carries many typically Mexican products such as candy with hot spices, hot salsa, and so on that have been displaced by imports in other chains. It is also known for its low pricing to cater to various socioeconomic segments of the market. It sells food, perishable products, and clothing.

SORIANA

One of the oldest retail businesses in Mexico, Soriana began developing in the 1930s. In 1998, the company became more customer-service oriented. It is a public limited company that has recently expanded into almost every state of Mexico with 471 stores. Soriana is the second-largest retailer in Mexico. This retail chain focuses on local markets to bring the right regional product to the right location. The store sells food, toys, clothes, health and beauty products, and basic services for home. They also offer the lowest price for 100 goods every day.

CHEDRAUI

Chedraui is the fourth-largest Mexican retailer. It is a convenience store that sells groceries, apparel, and other nonperishable items. It

▲ **FIGURE 9.7** Soriana retail chain home page. It is the second-largest retail chain in Mexico with a store in almost every state and is known for its customer service. Courtesy of Soriana.

was founded in 1927. In 2005 it bought 29 supermarkets from the French chain store Carrefour. Carrefour left the Mexican market as their stores were underperforming due to intense competition from Walmart. Walmart is its main competitor.

S-MART

S-Mart is a Mexican grocery store chain that competes with Walmart and Soriana. S-Mart is an associate of Topco, which is a cooperative owned by other retailers' cooperatives and independent grocery stores and chains. It provides services such as procurement, quality assurance, and packaging for retailers. The store sells frozen and fresh food, health and beauty products, and so on. There are 46 branches of S-Mart in the north region of the country.

▲ **FIGURE 9.8** Chedraui convenience store logo. This is the logo of the fourth-largest retail chain in Mexico. Bloomberg via Getty Images.

GIGANTE

Gigante opened its first store in Mexico City in 1962. The company went public in 1991. They bought an existing Mexican supermarket, Blanco, and converted it into warehouse formats called Bodega Gigante. They brought the American companies Radio Shack and Office Depot into Mexico through joint ventures. The company then expanded internationally by opening a store in California. The company also has a savings club format in a joint venture with American company Price Smart. The company does not compete with Walmart in the lowest price field, but it does have promotional deals on an everyday basis.

EL PALACIO DE HIERRO

El Palacio de Hierro (The Iron Palace) is a chain of prestigious high-end department stores in Mexico. It is a part of the Mexican conglomerate Grupo Bal. It offers both national and international brands at competitive prices. The store sells high-end clothing, beauty products, furniture, electronics, entertainment products (such as video games), and so on. This group has 13 stores in Mexico.

HOW MATURE IS THE RETAIL INDUSTRY?
NOT QUITE THERE

Mexico has over 105 million consumers. Consumer expenditures are increasing with greater opportunities for employment and an increase in the per capita gross domestic product (Marinov, 2006). According to the Asociación Nacional de Tiendas de Autoservicio y Departamentales, A.C. (National Association of Retail and Department Stores, ANTAD), in 2010 there were approximately 18,890 retail stores in Mexico, including grocery, apparel, pharmacy, toy, and pet stores. After they have covered major cities, large- and medium-sized retailers fan out from metropolitan areas to smaller cities with small stores in the country as a market penetration strategy (Euromonitor, 2008).

The market for apparel products seems to have matured in large cities due to urbanization and the emergence of new regional markets. Real estate newcomers to the market, such as the American Kimco Realty Corporation, have increased choices for consumers and brought better-quality products to market because they have expanded the physical space used for retail stores and allowed for increased infrastructure (Journal of Property Management, 2008). Mexican apparel retail businesses are in search of new market options because the local market is saturated with large-format foreign competitors (Díaz, 2009). A highly fragmented Mexican market has room for many small players, making it a very attractive one for international expansion.

BUYING FOR APPAREL RETAIL STORES:
SHOP TILL YOU DROP

In the international textile industry, Mexico ranks fourth—behind the United States, China, and Hong Kong—in terms of market share (Portos, 2008). In the 1990s, production shifted from Asia to the Americas, and North American supply shifted from assembly to full production (which includes manufacturing fabric, cutting, and sewing the product). This dynamic lowered the share that Hong Kong, Taiwan, South Korea, and China held in the U.S. market. In Mexico, the production chain from fiber to textile to clothing is a leading production activity.

The textile and apparel industry is a top manufacturing sector in Mexico, second only to manufacturing since the 1990s (Rodriguez, 2006). Local industry supplies knit and woven woolen fabrics, but woven cotton and man-made fiber need to be imported. Most woven cloth for shirts, blouses, dresses, and summer skirts are imported without duty or restriction (according to NAFTA rules), and come primarily from the United States, which supplies over 75 percent of them. The remainder comes from Korea, Taiwan, and China, even though they have tariffs of over 500 percent.

How does a foreign apparel-product manufacturer establish a relationship with retailers in Mexico? A broad range of activities are required:

- ▶ Understand the Mexican market and consumer.
- ▶ Commit to local partners over the long term.
- ▶ Offer innovative products.
- ▶ Reflect up-to-date fashion with your products.
- ▶ Keep prices affordable.
- ▶ Provide personalized service.

Foreign manufacturers should provide value-added products, which should include better-quality products as well as innovation in fashion. Additionally, Mexican retailers demand high margins, on-time deliveries, and point-of-sale help. The Mexican market is competitive and sophisticated and demands a good amount of service. Other strategies involve offering flexible payment arrangements and wholesale prices or discounts because tariffs on imported goods are high, which makes them very expensive for local customers. For instance, Chinese textiles enter Mexico with a 500 percent tariff.

Foreign manufacturers who are interested in the Mexican market must be aware that women make up more than half of the population and represent the most important customer segment of the Mexican market. Women do (or guide) most of the shopping, for themselves as well as for their families.

As for distribution strategy, most international companies hire local distributors, but some open direct sales offices and subsidiaries in Mexico. Around 400 franchisers operate in Mexico, 40 percent of which are of foreign origin. It can take time to identify a suitable geographic location, understand the local distribution network, establish your own network, and build the necessary infrastructure. Furthermore, it is critical to conduct market research in order to understand the nature and degree of competition among the existing retailers, including the unofficial or informal retail market in Mexico, which trades products at throw-away prices.

RETAIL CAREERS:
IN LINE WITH ECONOMIC GROWTH

Because the retail market in general and apparel retailing in particular are growing sectors in Mexico, opportunities for employment in the sector are growing. The apparel industry is attractive to entrepreneurs because ownership does not demand much seed capital, technology, or sophisticated skill. Small investors either in groups or individually can enter the market and position themselves with new brands.

In general, salary structure varies among states or regions in Mexico. Salaries are relatively high in Mexico City, DF (Federal District), Nuevo Leon, Guadalajara, and Quintana Roo. Foreign companies in Mexico offer better compensation programs than their local counterparts. And a company's size can be a decisive factor in defining a salary structure for its employees. For example, a big company in Mexico City with 100 to 500 employees may pay its CEO a base salary of $10,000 per month, whereas in Monterrey, the capital city of Nuevo Leon, the base salary may be $20,000 per month. But in the city of Hermosillo (a relatively less-developed region of the country), the base salary may be only $5,000 per month. Other factors that influence pay include the university from which the employee graduated, whether they have a foreign degree, and their level of education. Connections and references can also play an important role in salary negotiation in Mexico.

Students coming from abroad to study in Mexican universities can find internship opportunities in local companies in different sectors, including retail; universities run internship programs in collaboration with neighboring businesses. For example, the Monterrey campus of Tecnológico de Monterrey (ITESM) in Nuevo Leon runs an internship program in which students who spend a semester or two in the company receive academic credit. Such programs are available for both undergraduates and graduate-level students.

International Business Strategies is a website that provides interesting and updated reports on the retail industry in different countries, including Mexico (http://www.international businessstrategies.com/market-research-reports). Fibre2fashion.com is another website that provides countrywide information on different industrial sectors, including job opportunities (http://jobs. fibre2fashion.com/). The website http://www.jobofmine.com/job/ search/country/Mexico/ also provides job information.

THE FUTURE OF APPAREL RETAIL: MORE ROOM TO GROW

The contribution of the textile and apparel industry to the national economy is significant. Mexico is a world-class producer and exporter of textile and apparel products. In this sector, Mexico has several competitive advantages, such as the infrastructure for textiles, that have been around the country since the early twentieth century, have the ability to supply to the U.S. market as well as the domestic market, and offer a wealth of export experience (Portos, 2008). Despite Mexico's competitive edge in this sector, it remains vulnerable to certain economic situations. According to a 2008 survey (Rodriguez and Ulises 2008), in economic and financial crises, consumers tend to spend less money on apparel products and even less on more expensive imported brands.

The young population ensures a steadily growing customer base for retailers (Latin America Monitor, 2005) and presages a potentially large market as the Mexican economy continues to grow (Frastaci, 1999).

Since the early 1990s, Mexico has made itself an attractive destination for foreign direct investment, become an open market, and carried out extensive privatization in different industries. Some useful things a foreign investor should know about Mexico include the following.

- ▶ Although informal-retail formats take away some market share, modern-format stores can compete with them by providing variety, convenience, good pricing, quality, and personal service.
- ▶ Mexicans visit malls for entertainment as well as shopping. Successful malls include entertainment venues, such as movie theaters or ice-skating rinks.
- ▶ Convenience matters to Mexican consumers. Ample parking space is a big draw at the mall.
- ▶ About 45 percent of Mexicans have a monthly income of less than $500, making this a worthwhile segment on which to focus.

▲ FIGURE 9.9 Sears fashion show. LatinContent/Getty Images.

Case Study 1

GRUPO SANBORNS: ON THE ACQUISITION TRAIL

Grupo Sanborns is the retail sector of the holding company Grupo Carso, one of Mexico's largest conglomerates, with stakes in many different industries, ranging from retail to technology. Its initial acquisitions included Mexican companies such as Sanborns, Fábricas de Papel Loreto y Peña Pobre, Empresas Frisco, Industrias Nacobre, and Porcelanite. Its owner, Carlos Slim Helú, is considered the wealthiest man on earth. In 1997, Grupo Carso acquired 70 percent of the American retailer Sears Roebuck Inc., with 66 stores in Mexico. This first entry into the retail sector proved profitable and augured well. By 2004, the group owned almost 85 percent of the company. In 2010, Sears represented 48.5 percent of the consolidated sales of the Grupo Sanborns. Although most of Sears' providers are Mexican, good-quality goods from Asia and other countries can also be found in the store (Grupo Carso, 2010). In 2008 the Italian retailer Benetton went into partnership with Sears. Carlos Slim Domit, son of Carlos Slim Helú and chairman of

Sears Roebuck Inc. in Mexico, said that: "Benetton is a highly prestigious international brand, and this partnership will allow us to continue offering fashion and high-quality products to our clients" (Zargani, 2008).

In 1994, Grupo Carso acquired Dorian's, a Mexican retail company founded in 1959 in Tijuana and serving the north of Mexico. Dorian's has around 71 selling points in most northern states and targets different Mexican markets. It has around 394 thousand square feet in sales areas. With this inroad the conglomerate increased its competitive advantage in the Mexican market and consolidated its position as one of the most important and successful Mexican conglomerates. In 2010, Dorian's constituted three percent of the total sales of Grupo Sanborns (Grupo Carso, 2010).

By 2003, after eight years of operating in the Mexican market with great success, Grupo Carso acquired JC Penney's six stores in Mexico, thus expanding the retail company's coverage into a wide range of national, private, and exclusive brands with style, quality, and competitive pricing. By merging JC Penney with Dorian's, it has further consolidated its position in the Mexican retail market.

Discussion Questions

1. Would you say that Grupo Carso implemented the right acquisition and consolidation strategy?

2. Carlos Slim Domit, son of Carlos Slim Helú and chairman of Sears Roebuck Inc. in Mexico, said that: "Benetton is a highly prestigious international brand, and this partnership will allow us to continue offering fashion and high-quality products to our clients." In the United States, Benetton and Sears don't necessarily cater to the same customers. Why do you think this partnership works in Mexico?

3. The Mexican retail market seems to be saturated by companies both foreign and domestic. And yet, more and more international retailers keep entering the Mexican market. How do you think Grupo Sanborns can continue to compete in an increasingly globalized industry?

Case Study 2

WALMART'S SUCCESS IN MEXICO

Walmart first stuck its toe into Mexico in 1991 through a joint venture with Cifra, Mexico's leading retail company, to develop Sam's Club warehouse stores in Mexico. The tremendous success of the first Sam's Club stores and the impending passage of the North American Free Trade Agreement encouraged further collaboration, and Walmart and Cifra expanded their joint venture through the 1990s. Walmart purchased a majority stake in Cifra in 1997. Prior to the joint venture, Cifra's lineup included Aurrera *autoservicios* (superstores selling food, clothing, and a variety of other items), Superama supermarkets, Suburbia department stores, and Vips restaurants. To this roster, Walmart added Walmart superstores (shifting Aurrera to a budget niche and relabeling its stores Bodega) and Sam's Club warehouse stores, as well as two new restaurant formats. As of 1993, Walmart–Cifra had fewer *grocery* stores (though more stores of all formats) than its competitors Gigante and Comercial Mexicana, but it had overtaken them by 2000.

Walmart has an impressive track record in Mexico. The conventional explanation for this success is that it has brought a set of superior management techniques and technologies. Press accounts have emphasized Walmart's low-price strategy, high-technology distribution network, and intense pressure on suppliers for discounts—"the same formula" as in the United States, according to *New York Times* reporter Tim Weiner.

Walmart rolled out its "everyday low prices" (EDLP) policy in Mexico in 1999 after inflation had diminished to the point where meaningful price comparisons were possible. The chain marked tens of thousands of items down as much as 14 percent, and has also passed on further savings, for example, when currency shifts decrease an item's cost to the company. Walmart also began to post price comparisons with other chains, a practice that got the retailer expelled from ANTAD, Mexico's National Association of

Supermarket and Department Stores, in 2002, because it is forbidden by Mexican law.

As in the United States, Walmart uses its buying power to drive down prices. According to an unhappy executive of a small clothing manufacturer in Mexico, "Walmart has driven many suppliers out of business. Walmart maintains its profit margin. . . . They never reduce *their* margin. They *do* pass on savings in price, but at the expense of the manufacturer. You can increase efficiency a certain amount, but. . . . For example, they may tell you, 'We're going to sell shirts at a discount of 40 percent—you, the manufacturer, have to cut your price 40 percent.' So the consumer benefits, but they're driving out of business the manufacturers that provide *jobs*."

Observers argue that another contributor to Walmart's success is its use of a wide range of formats to appeal to varied classes of consumers, particularly lower-income consumers. Executives of competing Mexican companies also take note of Walmart's minutely prescribed systems and procedures. "There's a sign on the Walmart headquarters saying 'Ordinary people coming into a company to do extraordinary things,'" commented an executive of another chain. He acknowledged that, "With the right systems, training, and tools, ordinary people *can* do extraordinary things."

Source: Tilly, Chris, "Wal-Mart in Mexico: The Limits of Growth," University of Massachusetts, Lowell. *Also appeared in* Lichenstein, Nelson, ed., *Wal-Mart: Template for 21st Century Capitalism?* New York: New Press, 2005. Retrieved December 15, 2010, from http://www.docstoc.com/docs/28797144/Wal-Mart-in-Mexico

Discussion Questions

1. What do you think Walmart did right in Mexico?
2. What does this case tell you about Mexican retailers?
3. What recommendations would you offer to retailers interested in entering the Mexican market?

REFERENCES

Anderson, J. (2010). Effects of increased trade and investment on human development in the US and Mexican border communities. *The Journal of Developing Areas, 43*(2), 341–362.

Apparel Retail Industry Profile: Mexico (2008, September). Datamonitor, p. 1, p. 24.

Bailey, W. & Gutierrez de Pineres, S. A. (1997). Country of origin attitudes in Mexico: The malinchismo effect. *Journal of International Consumer Marketing, 9*(3), 25–41.

Baker, Stacy. (2007, June 1). Global market review of discount apparel retailing —forecasts to 2012: 2007 edition: The global market for discount apparel. *Just - Style: Global market review of discount apparel retailing,* 5–36.

Bissell, B. (2003). Practical advice for investing in tourism and lodging projects in Mexico. *Journal of Retail & Leisure Property, 3*(1), 93–103.

Canseco, O. C. (2007, May). Latin male cosmetics sales grow. Retrieved March 1, 2010, from http://www.latinbusinesschronicle.com/app/article. aspx?id=1186

Clark, E. (2008, February 25), Mexico-based firm looks to steer retailers South for growth, *Women's Wear Daily, 195*(41), p. 28.

Di Gregorio, D., Thomas, D. & de Castilla, F. (2008). Competition between Emerging Market and Multinational Firms: Wal-Mart and Mexican Retailers. *International Journal of Management, 25*(3), 532–545.

Díaz, U. (2009, July 10). Visten con éxito su negocio. [Source: Reforma].

Durand, C. (2007). Externalities from foreign direct investment in the Mexican retailing sector. *Cambridge Journal of Economics,* 31, 393–411.

Frastaci, M. (1999, May). Approaching Mexican retailers. *Apparel Industry, 60*(5), p. 26–31.

Freeman, I. C. (2010, September 15). Mexico: Apparel investment needed to counter contraband. Retrieved October 18, 2010, from http://www.just-style.com/news/apparel-investment-needed-to-counter-contraband_id108921.aspx

Galindo, Azucena (n.d.). Psicología del Consumidor Mexicano. IDM Group (www.idm.com.mx).

Gereffi, G. (1997, November 1). Global shifts, regional response: Can North America Meet the Full-Package Challenge? *Bobbin,* p. 16–31.

Gereffi, G. (2009). Development Models and Industrial Upgrading in China and Mexico. *European Sociological Review, 25*(1), 37–51.

Gregorio, D. D., Thomas, D. E. & Castilla, F. G. (2008, September). Competitive dynamics between emerging market firms and dominant multinational rivals: Wal-Mart and the Mexican retail industry *International Journal of Management, 25*(3), 532–547.

Grupo Carso (2010). Retrieved March 9, 2010, from wwwgcarso.com.mx

Growing Opportunity (2007, March). *Chain Store Age, 83*(3), 24–24, 1/2p.

INEGI (2010). Edad mediana, población, comparación internacional, www.inegi.gov

Jones, F. (2006). Upscale Retail. *Latin Trade,* p. 13.

Joynes-Burgess, K. (2008, December). Mexico: Courage in challenging times. Retrieved March 1, 2010, http://www.katejb.com/work/ CourageinChallengingTimes.pdf

La Industria Textil y del Vestido en México (2008). *Instituto Nacional de Estadística y Geografía.*

León O., S. M. (2005, September). Corrupción y contrabando en el sector textil en México. *Cámara de Diputados* Reporte Temático N. 5.

Major Mexican Soft Goods Retailers (2007) Retrieved February, 2010, from http://www.trendexmexico.com/retinfo/msgret.html

Magana, M. (2007, November). The road to Eldorado. Retrieved March 4, 2010, from http://www.landor.com/index.cfm?do=thinking. article&storyid=558&

Marinov, M. (2006, January). *Marketing in the Emerging Markets of Latin America.* UK: Palgrave Macmillan.

Marketing to Mexican consumers (2005, March). *Brand Strategy,* 43–45.

Mexico Company: JC Penney pulls out (2003, November) *EIU ViewsWire.*

Mexico: Just the facts (2007, February 19). *Journal of Commerce,* p. 1.

Mexico may be on the rebound (1996, January). *Apparel Industry, 57*(1), p. 16.

Mexico Monitor. Retrieved March 5, 2010, from http://www. latinamericamonitor.com

Mexico Retail Report (2008). Bharat Book Bureau. Retrieved February 10, 2010, from http://www.bharatbook.com/Market-Research-Reports/Mexico-Retail-Report.html

Min-Young, L., Youn-Kyung, K., Lou, P., Dee, K. & Forney, J. (2008). Factors affecting Mexican college students' purchase intention toward a US apparel brand. *Journal of Fashion Marketing and Management, 12* (3), 294–307.

Olaf, C. (2002, March). Salary survey: Part II. *Business México,* 12(3), 19–20.

Olvera, S. & Violeta, M. (2009, March 24). "Pega el dólar caro a idas de 'shopping'." [Source: El Norte.]

Petche, N. (1992, September 1). Street-Wise Marketing. *Business Mexico.*

Portos, I. (2008). La industria textil en México y Brasil: dos vías nacionales de desarrollo. *Universidad Nacional Autónoma de México.*

Rausch, L. (2002). Cross-cultural Analysis of Brand Consciousness. Unpublished.

Shopping centers head down to Mexico (2008, July) *Journal of Property Management,* Vol. 73 Issue 4, p. 6–6, 1/3p.

Tilly, C. & José L. A. G. (2006). Lousy Jobs, Invisible Unions: The Mexican retail sector in the age of globalization. *International Labor and Working-Class History, 70,* 61–85.

Wade, D. (1997, February 12). Guess' Again: Not All Apparel Jobs Flee US. *The Christian Science Monitor, 12.*

Zacarias, R. T. (2005, February 25). Grupo Sanborn's adquiere tiendas de cadena JC Penney; [Source: El Universal].

Zargani, L. (2008, May 28). Benetton Inks Deal with Sears Mexico. *Women's Wear Daily, 195*(113), 1–7.

Zimmerman, S. (1997, September). Shopping in Mexico: the tianguis. Retrieved March 3, 2010, from http://www.mexconnect.com/articles/152-shopping-in-mexico-the-tianguis

FUTURE OF EMERGING MARKETS

10

Jaya Halepete

OBJECTIVES

After reading this chapter, you will

- ▶ Understand the cycle of emerging markets
- ▶ Be able to compare various emerging markets
- ▶ Understand the pros and cons of investing in various emerging markets

Emerging markets remain attractive for an average of five to ten years, after which they get saturated or the level of competition increases tremendously. During this period, foreign retailers enter the market, and the government of the country works at making the market investment friendly. Some investors succeed and some fail based on the mode of entry, time of entry, and level of understanding of the market.

Of all the emerging markets discussed in the preceding chapters, some countries are closer to being saturated, such as Romania and Thailand, than others such as India. Increasing competition and growing real estate prices make the market less attractive to foreign investors. Being close to maturity does not necessarily mean that there is no opportunity in the market. But it means that one has to be well prepared when entering that market. Retailers face major investing challenges in countries such as Russia; other countries such as Turkey have friendly investment environments

TABLE 10.1 Investing in Brazil

Pros	Cons
• World's fifth-largest country	• Bureaucracy
• Fashion oriented	• Corruption levels still high
• Flourishing middle class	• High taxes
• Public policies focusing on low-income families' revenue improvement	• Complex tax system
	• High taxes for imported goods
	• Informal and gray markets
• Relatively young population	• Infrastructure bottleneck: airports, roads, ports, etc.
• Democratic system	
• Economic stability	• Competition, both domestic and foreign, is fierce in some industries (banks, retail, etc.)
• Institutional stability	
• No major geopolitical issues	
• Steady economic growth	• Extremely high interest rates
• Positive attitude toward imported goods	• Still a very unequal country, measured by HDI (human development index)
• Regional (Latin America) leadership	

and encourage foreign direct investment. Although there is always a chance of success for innovative concepts, most retailers selling a basic mix of merchandise will need to look for newer countries to invest in. The following sections look at the pros and cons of investing in each country discussed in this book (Tables 10.1–10.8).

COMPARISON OF EMERGING MARKETS

The emerging markets included in this book share some factors that make them attractive to foreign investors. Most of them have a large population with increasing income levels. The consumers of these countries also have a favorable outlook toward foreign brands and retailers. The countries are working to make it easy for foreign investors to invest in the country by relaxing foreign direct investment policies.

TABLE 10.2 Investing in Romania

Pros	Cons
• The sixth-largest market in the European Union	• High levels of corruption
• Increasing incomes of population	• In some areas, the prevalence of bureaucracy in some administrative procedures
• Harmonization with European legislation	• Insufficient development of infrastructure (roads, rail transport)
• Still low competition in some markets	• Insufficient legislation stability, especially in the fiscal sector
• Positive consumer attitude toward foreign products	
• Robust economic growth (although jeopardized by the 2008 financial crises)	
• Educated labor force	
• Strategic geographical position	
• Increasing levels of productivity	

TABLE 10.3 Investing in China

Pros	Cons
• Second-largest economy in the world	• Consumption power varies tremendously among cities, making it a very diverse market
• Trend of increasing consumer spending	• Intense competition
• Growing affluent middle class	• Need to customize products for Chinese market
• High level of interest of consumers in foreign brands	• Market saturation in premier cities
• Hub for sourcing apparel	
• Open market for foreign investors	

Some common drawbacks of investing in the emerging markets are lack of proper infrastructure and prevalence of corruption. These are common problems in a lot of emerging markets due to lack of availability of funds to keep up with infrastructure-

TABLE 10.4 Investing in India

Pros	Cons
• Second-largest population in the world and growing	• High level of corruption and bureaucracy
• Increasing disposable income among a very large middle class	• Lack of qualified retail talent
• Market dominated by unorganized traditional retailers	• Infrastructure problems
• Government relaxing regulations for foreign direct investment	• Complex market with tremendous cultural differences among the local population
	• Very few cities with upper-class population for luxury retailers
	• High cost of real estate
	• High importing duties

TABLE 10.5 Investing in Russia

Pros	Cons
• Huge market (9th country by population in the world)	• High level of corruption and bureaucracy
• Huge premium segment potential	• Obsolete legislation
• Considerable high amount of free-market niches	• Lack of qualified domestic managers for senior and top positions
• Positive attitude toward foreign products	• Probable problems with logistics
• Economic growth	

related issues. Because retail is not very well developed in most of these nations, there are problems with the supply chain not being streamlined like in the United States or some other European countries (such as the United Kingdom and France, for example).

TABLE 10.6 Investing in Turkey

Pros	Cons
• Large population (75 million)	• Slight political instability
• Favorable investment laws	• High local competition
• Brand-focused consumers	• Differences among Turkish consumers in various segments
• Large segment of young and brand-conscious consumers	• Regional differences
• Positive attitude toward foreign products	
• Economic growth and increasing purchasing income	
• Key location as potential regional headquarters	
• Qualified and relatively cheap labor	
• Raw material availability and quality	

Emerging countries such as China and India have a lot of diversity in their population. Due to the complex nature of consumer makeup, it is difficult to customize products to satisfy the needs of all the consumers. These emerging markets are varied with very low levels of brand loyalty. Many companies are tweaking their products to suit the local tastes, such as Unilever making foamier soaps and shampoos for these markets as compared to their Western counterparts (Easier said than done, 2010). Foreign investors need to spend extra time to understand these diverse groups of consumers and research their needs to be successful in these markets.

FUTURE EMERGING MARKETS

Over the past three years, Brazil, Russia, India, and China have outperformed many developed European markets as well as the U.S. market. Investors in these markets have profited from being

TABLE 10.7 Investing in Thailand

Pros	Cons
• Government trying to attract foreign investors	• Culturally different consumers
• Opening up of the market for foreign direct investment	• Lack of skilled retail professionals
• Large market size	• Corruption
• Room for growth	• Products require adaptation in terms of shape, color, and size
• Good regulatory system	• Need to have a local partner to assist with ownership of land, navigate through regulations
	• Intense competition

TABLE 10.8 Investing in Mexico

Pros	Cons
• Large, free-market economy (110 million people; 14th-largest economy in the world)	• High level of corruption, cronyism, and bureaucracy, which favor large established Mexican monopolies
• Wealthy minority who demands high-quality brands	• Growing violence and insecurity due to the war on drugs
• Growing middle class who is changing buying and consumption patterns due to increasing purchasing power	• Brain drain of college-educated managers due to low salaries and lack of incentives
• "Malinchista" attitude toward foreign products	• Probable problems with logistics in the south of the country due to a lack of infrastructure
• Proximity to the U.S. market (largest border between a developed and a developing nation)	
• Country with the most free trade agreements in the world, including the wealthiest economies	

the first movers (Turner, 2010). In the 1990s only Asia was considered to be the most attractive market in which to invest due to a large population and a growing middle class in countries like China and India. But many oil-rich Middle Eastern countries with urban populations and lack of organized retail markets will soon become attractive investment markets. Latin America has also been quick to recover from the latest economic downturn, making it attractive to foreign retailers.

A.T. Kearney has conducted research to find the most attractive emerging markets, taking into consideration market attractiveness, country risk, market saturation, and time pressure. Based on this research, some countries such as Kuwait, Saudi Arabia, United Arab Emirates, Uruguay, and Peru have been included in the top ten most attractive emerging markets. The research also includes countries such as Tunisia, Albania, Egypt, Vietnam, and Morocco to watch out for in the future. These countries will be the next set of emerging countries to study to understand the market for investment.

Countries such as Kuwait, Albania, Macedonia, the Dominican Republic, Bosnia, and Herzegovina will soon be considered as the most important emerging markets based on their current retail performance. The global recession has brought out these smaller markets that have been insulated from foreign competition for a long time. Although both old and new emerging markets are attractive investment sites for various companies, it is important to follow certain steps to minimize the risks involved with investing in emerging markets. It is important to use a less risky channel of entry such as wholesale format or e-commerce. It is also very important to study the market well before investing in the market. A foreign investor should try to use local partners whenever possible and also employ local talent for their business (Ben-Shabat, Moriarty, and Neary, 2010). By following these steps, the risks of investing in an unknown market are reduced considerably.

THE EMERGING EMERGING MARKET: BUSINESSES WILL LEARN TO LOOK BEYOND THE BRICS

During the runup to the Iraq war Donald Rumsfeld, then America's defense secretary, famously distinguished between "old" Europe and "new" Europe. In 2011 a growing number of businesspeople will distinguish between the "old" emerging markets and "new" emerging markets.

The rich world will continue to suffer from anemic growth for years to come. The emerging world, by contrast, will be a whirling hub of dynamism and creativity. Over the next decade it will account for more than 50 percent of global growth. It will see 700 million people enter the middle class. And it will also account for a disproportionate share of business innovations.

But in 2011 businesspeople will increasingly ask themselves, "Which emerging markets?" The "old" ones, the group that Goldman Sachs dubbed the BRICs (stands for Brazil, Russia, India, and China), are suffering from the law of diminishing returns.

Three of them—Brazil, India, and China—are rather like the most popular girls at the school prom: a little too full of themselves. India and Brazil can be haughty. China has taken to bullying and even swindling its suitors. The Chinese courts imprisoned four Rio Tinto executives for receiving bribes while taking no action against the Chinese officials who offered the bribes. The Chinese government engaged in a vicious fight with Google over the search giant's attempt to prevent it from spying on its customers. As for Russia, it should never have been admitted to the foursome in the first place. The government is corrupt and capricious; the population is shrinking; the country's wealth owes more to an accident of geology—those oil and gas deposits—than to creativity or innovation.

So why not look elsewhere, to "new" emerging markets? These come in two varieties: "overlooked" countries that can rival the BRICs in terms of prosperity, and "frontier" countries that are only just beginning to emerge from their chrysalises.

The biggest concentration of overlooked markets is in Africa (which is in many ways an overlooked continent). Africa's star performers are South Africa, Egypt, Algeria, Botswana, Libya, Mauritius, Morocco, and Tunisia. Collectively these countries match the average GDP per head of the BRICs.

But there are also huge overlooked emerging giants in every corner of the world. In the Middle East, Turkey and Saudi Arabia will attract a lot of attention. Turkey is one of the world's most dynamic economies (and certainly more dynamic than its ancient sparring partner, Greece). Saudi Arabia has been liberalizing its business environment rapidly, according to the World Bank's annual "Doing Business" survey. In Latin America people will take another look at Mexico for its successful companies and thriving middle class. But the biggest praise will be for Indonesia: it will be the emerging-market star of 2011, with analysts lauding its innovative companies, growing middle class, and relative political stability.

The frontier markets are poorer and riskier than the overlooked ones. They include Sri Lanka, Bangladesh, and Pakistan in Asia, as well as Kenya, Nigeria, and Rwanda in sub-Saharan Africa. You will hear a great deal about the unexpected merits of frontier economies in 2011. Nigeria, home to the tenth-largest oil reserves in the world, has stabilized its politics. The World Bank listed Rwanda as its champion pro-business reformer in 2010. Analysts will develop a special enthusiasm for Vietnam, which is well placed to steal outsourcing jobs from China: It is adding 1 million people a year to its workforce and has a literacy rate of more than 90 percent. Mobile phone companies have already discovered Vietnam's consumers: mobile phone penetration has gone from one of the lowest in the emerging world to one of the highest. Other consumer companies will be hot on their heels.

NEVER MIND THE VOLATILITY, FEEL THE VITALITY

These are hardly easy markets: There are good reasons why they are underexplored. Mexico is wracked by a drug war. Saudi Arabia is a closed society. Frontier markets are by their very nature unpredictable—prey to the wiles of dictators and the whims of nature. But they present numerous things that are irresistible to the West's growth-starved companies. They offer huge opportunities for investment in infrastructure. General Electric wants to provide Africa with the machinery that it needs to grow: any young GE-er who wants a chance to rise to the top has to spend some time working in Africa. IBM wants to provide the computing power.

Africa contains a disproportionate share of the world's mineral wealth at a time when mineral prices are soaring. It also contains a disproportionate share of the world's young people at a time when the West faces a demographic squeeze; by 2040 it will be home to one in five of them. Many local stock markets are booming: Egypt's market produced annual returns of 39 percent between 2000 and 2008, in a period when the average return was 2 percent. True, this growth is volatile; but in 2011 an increasing number of companies, looking at the West's flat markets, will decide that volatility is at least a sign of life.

Above all, the overlooked and frontier markets offer businesses a chance to get in on the ground floor. Companies that move first will enjoy lots of advantages. They will be able to forge deals with aggressive young companies: companies such as Angola's Banco Africano de Investimentos, which is expanding in Europe and Brazil, and Egypt's Orascom Telecom, which is expanding across the Middle East and beyond. They will be able to strike infrastructure deals with local governments. And they can shape the tastes of future consumers.

Companies that succeed in these neglected emerging markets are not only putting down roots in the world's most fertile soil. They are giving themselves a chance to establish business habits for years to come.

Source: Wooldridge, Adrian, "The emerging emerging markets: Businesses will learn to look beyond the BRICs," *The Economist,* Nov 22, 2010. Retrieved on December 10, 2010, from http://www.economist.com/node/17493411?story_id=17493411]

Discussion Questions

1. Why do you think that some emerging markets have been overlooked by foreign investors?
2. Why are Brazil, China, and India compared to the "most popular school girls at the prom"? Do you think it's justified?
3. What do you think makes the current emerging markets riskier?

REFERENCES

Ben-Shabat, H., Moriarty, M. & Neary, D. (2010). Expanding opportunities
for global retailers. Retrieved December 7, 2010, from
http://www.atkearney.com/images/global/pdf/2010_Global_Retail_
Development_Index.pdf

Easier said than done (2010). Retrieved December 7, 2010, from
http://www.economist.com/node/15879299

Turner (2010). Retail investors move into emerging markets. Retrieved
December 7, 2010, from http://www.efinancialnews.com/story/
2010-12-03/ima-shows-emerging-markets-at-record-high

GLOSSARY

38 STORE (ROMANIA): Store that sells every product for a euro, similar to an American dollar store.

A
ACQUISITION: An existing company purchased by another.

APPAREL WHOLESALE MARKET (CHINA): A retail format that acts as a manufacturer's showroom, wholesale store, and retail store.

ATACAREJO (BRAZIL): A Brazilian retailing format that combines retailing and wholesaling under one roof with almost no expectations of customer service.

C
CAMELÓDROMOS (BRAZIL): Small-sized and popular street shopping centers that sell low-quality and inexpensive Chinese-made products.

CAMELÔS (BRAZIL): Unregistered street traders that sell in neighborhoods.

CASH-AND-CARRY STORES: A wholesaler that sells to member retailers and other businesses at discounted prices on condition that they pay in cash, collect the goods themselves, and buy in bulk.

CATALOG RETAILING (RUSSIA): Sale of products through the catalog supplied by a retailer or a brand.

CONSUMER AFFLUENCE: The ability of consumers to spend on clothing, calculated based on per capita clothing sales.

CO-OPERATIVE STORE (CONSUMER CO-OPERATIVE STORE): A store that is owned and controlled by members of the co-operative who use the products. In this retail outlet format, members enjoy not only the benefits of good-quality products at fair prices but also a share of the profits (a dividend) based on the amount of each member's purchases.

COLLECTIVIST SOCIETY: A group of individuals who conform to the goals of a collective, such as the family, tribe, or religious group.

COLOR-CODING OF CLOTHING (THAILAND): Association of colors with political groups; very common in Thailand.

CONSIGNMENT SALE: Sale in which the owner transfers possession of goods, but not title of the goods, to a third party. The third party then sells the goods and returns the proceeds to the owner.

COOPERATIVE (MEXICO): A group of small retailers/producers that get together to run a single store so as to reduce cost.

D

DESIGNER STORES (CHINA): Single-branded stores that carry merchandise of any one luxury designer label such as Louis Vuitton or Chanel.

DIRECT INVESTMENT: A method of entry in which the foreign company owns 100 percent of the company.

DIRECT SALE: The sale of any consumer product or service by way of personal explanation and demonstrations, done mostly in homes.

DISTRIBUTOR (INDIA): Foreign retailer that sells through local retail chains.

E

EXCLUSIVE MULTIPLE BRAND/NONBRANDED STORES (INDIA): Privately owned single stores that carry branded as well as nonbranded traditional and Western clothing based on the needs of the local consumers. Some beauty stores could be large chain formats, too.

F

FACTORY STORES (RUSSIA): Manufacturer-owned stores that are located near the factory and sell new as well as last season's merchandise.

FASHION BOUTIQUES (CHINA): Privately owned shops on major commercial streets in big cities that sell high-priced items in limited quantities.

FIRST MOVER'S ADVANTAGE: A sometimes insurmountable advantage gained by the first significant company to move into a new market, or the edge that any company/retailer gains by entering a particular market before any competitors.

FRANCHISING: A license given to a manufacturer, distributor, or trader that enables them to manufacture or sell a named product or service in a particular area for a stated period.

G

GLOBAL TIER: The first of four distinct groups in emerging economies, the global tier consists of consumers who want products and goods to have the same attributes and quality as products in developed countries.

GLOCAL TIER: The second of four distinct groups in emerging economies, the glocal tier consists of consumers who demand customized products of near-global standard and are willing to pay a shade less than global consumers do.

GREENFIELD INVESTMENT: When a foreign company invests in a country by starting the construction from ground up.

GROSS DOMESTIC PRODUCT (GDP): An indicator to measure the economic prosperity of a country that represents the total dollar value of all goods and services produced over a specific time period.

H

HYPERMARKET: Supermarkets and department stores combined together, such as Walmart.

I

INDO-WESTERN CLOTHING (INDIA): Basic Western clothing (like T-shirt or shirts) with an Indian element such as embroidery or traditional print added to it.

INFORMAL ECONOMY: System of trade or economic exchange used outside state-controlled or money-based transactions, practiced by most of the world's population. It includes barter of goods and services, mutual self-help, odd jobs, street trading, and other such direct-sale activities. Income generated by the informal economy is usually not recorded for taxation purposes, and is often unavailable for inclusion in gross domestic product (GDP) computations.

J

JOINT VENTURE: A contract between two companies to conduct business for an agreed-upon duration of time.

L

LICENSING: An agreement by which a company (the licensor) permits a foreign company (the licensee) to set up a business in a foreign market using the licensor's manufacturing processes, patents, trademarks, and trade secrets in exchange for payment of a fee or royalty.

LOCAL BAZAAR (TURKEY): Cash-only stores set up by individuals alongside streets, with permission from local authorities, that sell food products, clothing, furniture, jewelry, and antiques.

LOCAL TIER: The set of consumers that follows the glocal tier of consumers in an emerging market economy. These consumers are happy with products of local quality at local prices.

M

MAIN STREET: The primary street of a town, where most of its shops, banks, and other businesses are located.

MALINCHISTAS (MEXICO): Mexican consumers who prefer foreign products over Mexican products.

MANUFACTURER OUTLET (CHINA): An outlet store owned by the manufacturer of a brand that sells off-season products.

MOM-AND-POP STORE: A small retail business, as a grocery store, owned and operated by members of a family.

N

NAK LENG (THAILAND): A typical Thai tough man who is well dressed and shows off wealth through expensive possessions such as jewelry, cars, and many servants.

NEIGHBORHOOD STORES (BRAZIL): Mom-and-pop stores converted to neighborhood stores to include grocery, cleaning products, and health and beauty products.

O

OFF-PRICE STORES (BRAZIL): Stores that sell previous-season merchandise at substantial discounts.

ONLINE RETAILING (RUSSIA): A nonstore format where consumers buy products through the Internet.

P

PRIVATE LIMITED COMPANY: Type of incorporated firm that (like a public firm) offers limited liability to its shareholders but (unlike a public firm) places certain restrictions on its ownership.

PUBLIC LIMITED COMPANY (PUBLICLY HELD COMPANY): Incorporated, limited liability firm whose securities are traded on a stock exchange and can be bought and sold by anyone. Public companies are strictly regulated, and are required by law to publish their complete and true financial position so that investors can determine the true worth of its stock (shares).

PULGAS (FLEA MARKET) (MEXICO): Market in Mexico that sells knock-offs of American brands.

R

RETAIL-APPAREL INDEX: An indicator of the rank of a country as an emerging market attractive to foreign investors based on all the important drivers that make a market attractive to foreign investors.

S

SALVAR (TURKEY): Baggy pants worn by Turkish men in villages and the eastern part of Turkey.

SECONDHAND STORE (ROMANIA): Stores sell inexpensive, branded or non-branded clothing from Western Europe on weight basis or at a fixed flat price.

SECONDHAND LUXURY BRAND BOUTIQUE (CHINA): Stores that sell used luxury products.

SPECIALIZED RETAIL NETWORK (BRAZIL): Similar to franchising, a network of stores controlled by a central office that decides the pricing and promotions policies in the stores.

SPECIALIZED SMALL STORES (BRAZIL): Family-owned businesses mainly located on city streets and in shopping centers.

STANDS (IN MARKET AND STREETS) (ROMANIA): Informal retail formats that sell inexpensive products of inferior quality mainly sourced from China. Located near high-consumer-traffic areas.

SUPERMARKET: A large, self-service store that carries a wide variety of food, household products, and other goods, which it sells in high volumes at relatively low prices.

THE STORAGES (ROMANIA): Suburban wholesale stores where stands source their merchandise.

T

TIANGUIS (MEXICO): Market on wheels, informal stores located in city centers, near subway stations, inside the malls, at beaches, or anywhere with high consumer traffic.

V

VENDING MACHINE (RUSSIA): A self-service retail format where products are stocked in a vending machine and people insert cash or a credit card to make a purchase.

W

WAREHOUSE CLUB (WHOLESALE CLUB; MEMBERSHIP WAREHOUSE): A cut-price retailer that sells a limited selection of brand-name grocery items, appliances, clothing, and other goods at substantial discounts to members, who pay an annual membership fee.

WHOLESALE CLUBS (RUSSIA): Stores that offer limited merchandise for members, like Sam's Club or Costco in the United States.

WHOLLY OWNED SUBSIDIARY: A subsidiary in which the parent holding company owns virtually 100 percent of the common stock.

ABOUT THE EDITOR

Jaya Halepete served as assistant professor of fashion merchandising at Marymount University during the writing of this book. She has published papers in various journals such as *Clothing and Textiles Research Journal, Journal of Fashion Marketing and Management,* and *International Journal of Retail Distribution and Management.* Her research interests are in the area of international retailing, international consumer behavior, and fair trade. She is a member of the Academy of International Business, International Textile and Apparel Association, National Retail Federation, and American Collegiate Retailing Association. She has a PhD in textiles and clothing from Iowa State University.

ABOUT THE CONTRIBUTORS

Andrada Busuioc is a researcher within the Group of Applied Economics, a think tank that provides an independent research capacity for all aspects of applied economics in Romania. She has been involved in various projects, ranging from macroeconomic analyses to market studies, and various aspects of applied economics. Prior to that, Andrada was an economic journalist, covering business, macroeconomics, and banking. Andrada is also an assistant teacher at the Academy for Economic Studies Bucharest where she is also pursuing a PhD.

Flavia Silveira Cardoso is a member of the marketing faculty, as well as academic coordinator for the Professional Masters in Marketing and Communications program at Universidad de San Andrés in Argentina. She has over 15 years of experience in marketing, focusing on brand management and consumer behavior, with business and academic exposure in Europe, the U.S., and Latin America, where she was brand manager for top multinationals such as General Motors, Prudential, and Chubb

Insurance. She has an MBA from Purdue University, a specialization in marketing positioning from UC Berkeley, and a BA in communication from ESPM in São Paulo, Brazil. Her research interests are retailing and consumer behavior, and she is working on her PhD dissertation at ESCP Europe in Paris.

Andrey Gabisov coordinates international projects for an advertising agency in Russia. A PhD student at the Graduate School of Management at St. Petersburg State University, Gabisov is actively involved in research projects for the university's Research Center for Marketing and Innovations, with a focus on retailing and private labels. He has worked for several big FMCG and B2B companies.

Luciana de Araujo Gil is a lecturer at the Nanyang Business School/NTU/Singapore. She has served as a reviewer for Brazil's Congresso Brasileiro de Iniciação Científica. Gil has been the recipient of awards from Brazil-CAPES/US-Fulbright & CAPES Association through IIE, MSU, Tinker Foundation Incorporated–TFI. She received her PhD from Michigan State University.

Xin Liang Gu is a professor of textile marketing at Glorious-Sun School of Business and Management at Shanghai's Donghua University.

Diana Bank Guzman teaches international business and marketing at the Campus Puebla of Tecnológico de Monterrey and at the University of the Americas in Puebla, Mexico. Her main research interests include business diplomacy and DFI in emerging economies. She has worked for the House Subcommittee on Western Hemispheric Affairs and the Mexican Embassy´s North American Free Trade Agreement (NAFTA) Office, concentrating on lobbying activities for the passage of the NAFTA. From 1996 to 2000, Diana worked in the Israeli office of the marketing communications department at BMC, a U.S.-based software company. She has an MBA from Columbia University's Graduate School of Business and a PhD from Israel's Bar Ilan University.

Mohammad Ayub Khan teaches international business and serves as a University Honors Program Director at the Campus Monterrey of Tecnológico de Monterrey in Nuevo León, Mexico. He has occupied several other academic positions at the university including chairmanship of the international business department, coordination of international business academia, coordination of the internationalization programs of the Academic Division of Administration and Finance. He has been a visiting faculty at universities such as Superior School of Commerce in Paris, France; University of the Incarnate Word and Trinity University in San Antonio, Texas; and University of Applied Sciences in Bocholt, Germany. He holds an MBA degree from Pakistan (Peshawar University), an IMBA from the UK (Glasgow University), a PhD in business administration from the U.S. (TUI University). He has obtained academic certificates in international management, business leadership and education from Denmark (Aarhus Business School), the U.S. (Monterey Institute of International Studies), and Mexico (Tecnológico de Monterrey).

Laubie Li is associate head of school and executive director, MBA Programs, as well as associate professor of business at the International Graduate School of Business (IGSB) at University of South Australia. He does consulting for clients such as Mars International, AUSAID, and Uncle Bens of Australia. Li's teaching, research, and consulting activities focus mainly on internationalization, organizational restructuring, international joint ventures, and strategic management. His current research interests are Chinese relationship management, learning organization, and strategic congruence in the internationalization process. He serves on the editorial boards of the Academy of Management Learning and Education and Career Development International.

Chuanlan Liu is an assistant professor of apparel merchandising at Louisiana State University. She has been doing research and teaching in areas of merchandising, retail market and strategies, international retailing, and global entrepreneurship in retail. She is also the director for the Public Livelihood Economy Research Center at Central University of Finance and Economics in Beijing, China. Liu has authored several articles and publications in these subject areas. She earned her PhD from the Department of Consumer Affairs at Auburn University.

Silvio Abrahao Laban Neto teaches marketing and is the associate dean for MBA programs at Insper in São Paulo, Brazil. He is a former executive of such consulting and retailing companies as Accenture, Carrefour, Walmart and Pão de Açúcar Group. He has served as the co-chair of ECR (Efficient Consumer Response) Brazil and Latin America and served in the board of GCI (Global Commerce Initiative). His research interests lie in the areas of marketing, marketing and technology alignment, social networks, retail management and strategy, as well as relationship marketing. He holds a PhD in marketing from FGV-EAESP.

Mansi Patney has a PhD from Iowa State University with research interests in areas such as international retailing, retailer strategies, cross-cultural consumer behavior issues, and classroom teaching strategies.

Liviu Voinea is the executive director of the Group of Applied Economics, a Romania-based think tank. He is also a senior lecturer at the Academy of Economic Studies Bucharest and at the National School of Political Studies and Public Administration Bucharest. He has coordinated various projects in areas such as macroeconomics, market research, European integration, and public policy. As an academic, he has specialized in areas like policy planning and evaluation, statistical analysis, and project management, and he has published numerous articles and books on topics such as macroeconomics, international trade, and European integration.

John Walsh is assistant professor at Shinawatra University in Bangkok, Thailand. His books include works on entrepreneurialism and management communications in the Thai context. He received his doctorate from Oxford University in the area of international management, and he has subsequently published widely in the area of social and economic development in Thailand and the Mekong region and related subjects.

Wlamir Xavier is a PhD candidate at UNIVALI University in Brazil and a research assistant at Lauder Institute of International Studies at the Wharton School at the University of Pennsylvania. He has been a lecturer in marketing and business strategy in both Brazilian and international markets since 1990. His research interests include performance drivers in MNC from emerging economies and internationalization strategies. He also performs consulting activities in the Brazilian retail industry, focusing on sales force automation and strategy.

Serkan Yalcin is a senior doctoral candidate in the PhD program in marketing and international business at the John Cook School of Business at Saint Louis University in Missouri. His academic experience has included positions in Turkey, the Republic of Georgia, Kyrgyzstan, and the U.S. His research has appeared in such academic journals as *Journal of International Entrepreneurship, Multinational Business Review, Journal of Promotion Management, Journal of Developmental Entrepreneurship, Personnel Review,* and *Central Eurasian Studies Review.* Additionally, his work has appeared in the *Handbook of Research on Asian Entrepreneurship and Proliferation of the Internet Economy: E-commerce for the Global Adoption, Resistance, and Cultural Evolution.* Focusing on emerging markets such as Turkey, Russia, and the CIS region, Mr. Yalcin's research expertise are in cross-cultural consumer research and international marketing strategy.

Youssef Ahmad Youssef is associate professor at Unisul Business School in Brazil, visitor professor at Sprott School of Business at Carleton University in Canada, and the president of the Federation of Canadian Brazilian Businesses (FCBB). His research interests are international business, international knowledge management, and international entrepreneurship. Youssef is a member of the American Academy of Management and has long term experience in the Brazilian Market as marketing vice president at Web Intelligent Systems S.A. and marketing director at Digitro Technologia ltd. His PhD is from Federal University of Santa Catarina in Brazil.

Jun Ying Yu is a lecturer at Glorious-Sun School of Business and Management at Donghua University in Shanghai, China.

Irina Zgreaban is a researcher within the Group of Applied Economics, an independent nonprofit organization that provides research in applied economics in Romania. She has been involved in research and consultancy projects in different areas such as labor market discrimination, European funds implementation monitorization and evaluation, and competitiveness. She is an assistant teacher at the Academy for Economic Studies of Bucharest and is currently enrolled in a PhD program at the same university in the field of the economics of education.

Ai Tian Zhang is a PhD candidate at Glorious-Sun School of Business and Management at Donghua University in Shanghai, China.

INDEX

Page numbers in italics refer to figure or tables.

CHAPTER OPENER CREDITS

TITLE PAGE: Laoshi/Getty Images

CHAPTER 1 An interior shot of the Carlos Miele flagship store in São Paolo, Brazil. Courtesy of WWD

CHAPTER 2 Street scene and fashion boutiques in Ipanema, Rio de Janeiro, Brazil; Woman trying on sweater. © Y.Levy/Alamy; © GoGo Images Corporation/Alamy

CHAPTER 3 Bucuresti, Bucuresti Mall; Models wearing orange and black dresses in the Liliana Turoiu Udrea show in Romania. © allOver photography/Alamy; Courtesy of WWD

CHAPTER 4 Woman shopping in retail store; Shopping in Causeway Bay. Sky View/Getty Images; Greg Elms/Getty Images

CHAPTER 5 Two men look in the window of an expensive clothes shop in the DLF Emporio Mall in Vasant Kiunj, New Delhi, India; Brigade Road in Bangalore, India. © Ruby/Alamy; © David Pearson / Alamy

CHAPTER 6 Exterior view of a city in Russia; Window-shopping in Russia. Courtesy of WWD; AP Photo/Sergei Pashchenko

CHAPTER 7 Indoor bazaar, Marmaris, Datca Peninsula, Mulga Province, Turkey. © Greg Balfour Evans/Alamy

CHAPTER 8 Exterior view of the Siam Paragon store in Bangkok, Thailand; The outdoor fountain and plaza at Siam Paragon shopping complex alongside BTS Skytrain's Siam Station is illuminated after twilight in central Bangkok, Thailand. Courtesy of WWD/Joyce Barrett; © B.S.P.I./Corbis

CHAPTER 9 El Salvador, San Salvador city, Shopping Center Mall Multiplaza of the Mexican architect Ricardo Legorreta; Couple shopping in store in Merida, Yucatán, Mexico. © Age Fotostock/Superstock; Tony Anderson/ Getty Images

CHAPTER 10 Shopping mall in Leblon, Rio de Janeiro, Brazil. © Lonely Planet Images/Alamy